Anger Management Core Concepts Series

Proven Techniques for Managing Conflict, Reducing Stress, and Restoring Balance

Julian Smith

Preface

A man slams his fist on the table during a family dinner. A driver leans on the horn for twenty seconds, face red, while traffic crawls. A teenager storms out of the classroom after a minor comment from the teacher. Anger appears in so many places, and while the scenes differ, the pattern is familiar: a sharp rush of energy, words or actions that feel unstoppable in the moment, and consequences that linger long after the episode ends. Anger is one of the most recognizable human emotions, yet it remains one of the least understood.

For centuries, people have tried to figure out how to handle anger. Philosophers warned against it, religious traditions debated whether it could ever be righteous, and modern science has dissected its biology. Despite all that study, many still struggle with the same questions.

Why does it come so fast? Why does it feel so strong? And why does it often lead to regret? The truth is that anger isn't just a problem of the modern world. It's a deeply ingrained part of human nature.

This book is written for anyone who has felt anger disrupt health, relationships, or work. It's also written for those who want to understand it before it becomes destructive. The goal isn't to banish anger completely, because that would be impossible and even harmful. The goal is to understand it, regulate it, and redirect it in ways that reduce harm and build clarity.

The chapters are structured to guide you step by step. They start with the foundations of anger itself, then move into practical methods, then into broader applications. Each chapter builds on the last so that by the end, you'll have a clear map for managing anger across all areas of life.

Chapter 1 begins by looking directly at **anger at its core**. You'll see why it exists in the first place and how psychologists explain its role in human survival. You'll learn the different forms it takes, from the quiet but corrosive patterns of passive anger to the explosive force of aggressive anger, as well as the healthier alternative of assertive anger. Common myths will be addressed, such as the idea that venting gets anger out of the system, or that some people never feel it at all. The chapter also examines the biology, including how hormones and neurotransmitters fuel anger and why brain regions sometimes make it feel uncontrollable. Social and environmental triggers are discussed, from traffic to cultural expectations, followed by an exploration of short-term versus long-term anger patterns. The chapter ends with a clear picture of the costs of leaving anger unmanaged: the effects on the body, on close relationships, and on career trajectories.

Once those foundations are clear, Chapter 2 shifts to **recognizing triggers and early warning signs**. The chapter explains how to identify your personal triggers, the small physical cues that warn of rising anger, and the thinking patterns that intensify it. You'll also see how situational factors amplify reactions and how journaling or tracking patterns can make triggers more visible. This chapter is practical because it teaches awareness. Without awareness, no strategy can succeed. With it, anger becomes something that can be anticipated and guided rather than denied or ignored.

Chapter 3 explores **the science of emotional regulation**. Here the focus is on how the brain's systems either escalate or calm anger. The role of the prefrontal cortex is explained, showing how it allows self-control when engaged properly. The stress response is unpacked, clarifying the fight-or-flight system and why anger feels so energizing. The chapter also contrasts emotional awareness with suppression, emphasizing why suppression seems helpful in the moment but is damaging over time. Breathing and other physiological regulation techniques are introduced, alongside strategies for building frustration tolerance and understanding personal thresholds.

From there, Chapter 4 offers **practical techniques for calming down**. It goes through methods like progressive muscle relaxation, mindful breathing, visualization, and mental reframing. You'll read about why counting and time-outs work, and why physical activity can dissipate anger when nothing else seems to help. Distraction and redirection are also covered as useful tactics for short-term management. This chapter turns the science of regulation into tools you can apply in everyday life.

Chapter 5 moves into **communication and conflict resolution skills**. Anger often shows up in interactions, so knowing how to speak and listen makes the difference between escalation and resolution. You'll learn the difference between assertive and aggressive communication, as well as techniques for active listening. The chapter explores how to use "I" statements to express needs without blame, and how to de-escalate tense conversations before they spiral. Negotiation and compromise strategies are outlined, and the role of tone and body language in either fueling or calming anger is explained.

In Chapter 6 the attention turns to **cognitive and behavioral strategies**. These strategies are designed to rewire patterns that feed anger. Cognitive restructuring teaches how to challenge angry thoughts. Habit loops are explained, showing how anger can become a cycle and how to break it. The chapter covers exposure and response prevention, frameworks for problem-solving, reinforcement systems that encourage self-control, and the use of self-talk to replace destructive thought patterns with constructive ones.

Chapter 7 broadens the focus to **long-term lifestyle approaches**. Here you'll see how sleep, diet, exercise, time management, and social support influence emotional stability. Sleep deprivation lowers tolerance for frustration. Caffeine and alcohol can both intensify irritability. Regular exercise regulates mood and provides a release valve for tension. Time management reduces daily stress that often acts as kindling for anger. Building supportive relationships provides a buffer, while strategies for preventing burnout keep emotional regulation intact over the long run.

The next step, in Chapter 8, looks at **special contexts and situations**. Anger doesn't show up the same way in every domain of life. At work, it's often tied to deadlines, unfair treatment, or power struggles. In romantic relationships, it appears in patterns of communication, expectations, and disappointments. Parenting introduces another layer, as children test boundaries and parents face stress. Road rage is discussed as a modern phenomenon where anonymity and stress combine.

Cultural differences in anger expression are also explained, showing why what provokes anger in one culture may be tolerated in another. Finally, the chapter looks at anger in competitive environments such as sports, where intensity is high and tempers run short.

Chapter 9 addresses **professional help and advanced strategies**. While many people can manage anger through self-awareness and daily strategies, some require additional support. This chapter describes when therapy is necessary and how cognitive-behavioral therapy has become one of the most effective treatments. It explores group programs and workshops, medication when biological imbalances are present, and technologies like biofeedback and neurofeedback. Digital tools and apps are also discussed as modern aids for tracking and regulating anger.

The book closes with Chapter 10, which includes a **historical timeline and glossary**. The timeline traces the evolution of ideas about anger, from early philosophical debates to modern neuroscience and psychology. The glossary provides definitions of key terms, so that concepts introduced in the book are easy to revisit and remember.

The structure of the book is intentional. It starts with explanation, moves into recognition, then into science, practical strategies, communication, deeper strategies, lifestyle, contexts, professional supports, and finally the historical and definitional wrap-up. This approach makes it easier to absorb the material without being overwhelmed.

It's important to remember that anger itself isn't the enemy. Without it, people would tolerate unfairness, ignore injustice, and fail to protect themselves. The challenge isn't eliminating anger but guiding it.

When anger is understood and managed, it can actually serve growth, clarity, and fairness. When unmanaged, it corrodes health, isolates people, and blocks progress.

The book is written in a simple, direct style so that the science is clear but not overwhelming, and so that strategies feel accessible rather than distant. The examples come from everyday life because that's where anger is most often felt and where it most often causes harm. You don't need advanced knowledge to understand this material. You need curiosity and willingness to reflect.

One final note before beginning. Many people feel shame about their anger. They believe it marks them as weak, unstable, or flawed. Shame only deepens the problem. The reality is that anger is universal. Every person feels it, and every person has struggled at some point to manage it.

The difference isn't whether anger exists but how it's handled. By reading carefully, practicing consistently, and reflecting honestly, anyone can improve their relationship with this emotion.

Overview

Chapter 1: Understanding Anger at Its Core

- The psychology of anger: why it exists
- Types of anger: passive, aggressive, assertive
- Common myths and misconceptions about anger
- The biology of anger: hormones, neurotransmitters, and the brain
- Environmental and social triggers of anger
- Short-term vs. long-term anger patterns
- The costs of unmanaged anger: health, relationships, career

Chapter 2: Recognizing Triggers and Early Warning Signs

- Identifying personal triggers
- Physical cues that signal rising anger
- Cognitive distortions that fuel anger
- Situational factors that intensify reactions
- Journaling and tracking patterns

Chapter 3: The Science of Emotional Regulation

- The role of the prefrontal cortex in self-control
- Stress response and anger: fight-or-flight explained
- Emotional awareness vs. emotional suppression
- Breathing and physiological regulation techniques
- Building tolerance to frustration
- Understanding emotional thresholds

Chapter 4: Practical Techniques for Calming Down

- Progressive muscle relaxation
- Mindful breathing and meditation practices
- Visualization and mental reframing
- Counting and time-out strategies
- Using physical activity to dissipate anger
- Distraction and redirecting focus

Chapter 5: Communication and Conflict Resolution Skills

- Assertive vs. aggressive communication
- Active listening techniques
- "I" statements and expressing needs clearly
- De-escalating tense conversations
- Negotiation and compromise strategies

- Managing tone and body language

Chapter 6: Cognitive and Behavioral Strategies
- Cognitive restructuring to challenge angry thoughts
- Habit loops and breaking anger cycles
- Exposure and response prevention for triggers
- Using problem-solving frameworks instead of venting
- Reinforcement and reward systems for self-control
- Self-talk and thought substitution

Chapter 7: Long-Term Lifestyle Approaches
- The role of sleep in emotional stability
- Diet, caffeine, and alcohol's effect on anger
- Regular exercise as a regulator of emotions
- Time management and reducing daily stress
- Building supportive relationships
- Preventing burnout and overload

Chapter 8: Special Contexts and Situations
- Anger in the workplace
- Anger in romantic relationships
- Parenting and anger management at home
- Road rage and public encounters
- Cultural differences in anger expression
- Anger in competitive sports and performance settings

Chapter 9: Professional Help and Advanced Strategies
- When to seek therapy
- Cognitive-behavioral therapy (CBT) for anger
- Anger management groups and workshops
- Role of medication in anger control
- Biofeedback and neurofeedback approaches
- Digital methods and apps for tracking progress

Appendix: Historical Timeline and Key Terms
- Timeline of anger management research and approaches
- Glossary of key terms and definitions

Conclusion

References & Recommended Readings

Table of Contents

Chapter 1: Understanding Anger at Its Core ... 9

Chapter 2: Recognizing Triggers and Early Warning Signs ... 31

Chapter 3: The Science of Emotional Regulation ... 48

Chapter 4: Practical Techniques for Calming Down ... 66

Chapter 5: Communication and Conflict Resolution Skills ... 84

Chapter 6: Cognitive and Behavioral Strategies ... 101

Chapter 7: Long-Term Lifestyle Approaches ... 120

Chapter 8: Special Contexts and Situations ... 136

Chapter 9: Professional Help and Advanced Strategies ... 156

Appendix: Historical Timeline and Key Terms ... 169

Conclusion ... 176

References & Recommended Readings ... 177

Chapter 1: Understanding Anger at Its Core

The Psychology of Anger: Why It Exists

Anger often feels explosive, but its origins are structured and adaptive. It exists because it served an evolutionary purpose long before modern society gave us laws, therapy, and conflict-resolution workshops. In the simplest sense, anger is the body's way of preparing for action when something blocks a need or threatens a boundary. Without it, humans would've been far less equipped to survive in hostile environments.

Early humans lived in small groups where resources were scarce and threats constant. Food, territory, and social standing determined survival. When a rival tried to steal food or invade territory, anger surged. That surge did two things: it primed the body for confrontation and it signaled to the rival that further intrusion would be met with resistance.

In this way, anger evolved as both an **internal energizer** and an **external communicator**. Even today, anger sharpens attention, raises confidence in one's ability to act, and creates the physiological conditions necessary for defense or challenge.

From a psychological perspective, anger operates as part of the **approach system**, which is distinct from the withdrawal system associated with fear. Fear urges retreat to avoid harm. Anger, in contrast, pushes forward toward confrontation. This difference is why people sometimes feel "stronger" when angry than when afraid. The anger response encourages risk-taking and diminishes hesitation, which may help in battles for dominance or fairness but can also produce reckless choices.

Researchers often describe anger as a **secondary emotion**, meaning it emerges in response to more fundamental feelings like hurt, shame, or frustration. When someone feels disrespected, the underlying sensation may be vulnerability, but anger quickly rises to cover that vulnerability and demand recognition. This transformation makes anger highly adaptive socially. By showing anger instead of sadness or humiliation, an individual can protect their image in a group and deter further mistreatment.

Anger also serves a **moral function**. People often feel it not because of personal harm but because of violations of fairness, justice, or loyalty. Think about how someone reacts when seeing a stranger bullied. They may intervene out of anger, even though they're not the direct victim. This moral anger helps uphold social norms. It signals disapproval, reinforces rules, and motivates punishment of those who violate group standards. Societies actually depend on this kind of anger to maintain cohesion, though it must be balanced to avoid cycles of revenge.

The psychological presence of anger is tightly connected to **perceived control**. If a person believes they can influence the source of their frustration, anger is the likely reaction. If they believe the situation is beyond their influence, sadness or resignation is more common.

For example, if someone cuts you off in traffic, anger arises because honking, glaring, or accelerating feels like possible actions that can restore fairness. But if a hurricane destroys property, many people feel grief rather than anger, because the event is beyond control. This distinction highlights anger's motivational quality: it pushes action when the mind perceives change is still possible.

Another important psychological layer is the link between anger and **goal obstruction**. The "frustration-aggression hypothesis," developed in the 1930s, suggested that frustration inevitably leads to aggression. While later refinements showed that frustration doesn't always cause aggression, the link between blocked goals and anger remains strong.

When efforts feel thwarted, anger is often the first emotional spark. Athletes who face unfair refereeing decisions, employees denied promotions, or students hindered by bureaucratic obstacles often feel anger before anything else. This isn't irrational; it's the brain recognizing blocked investment and urging action.

Modern research also shows that anger can **enhance persistence**. In experiments, participants experiencing mild anger worked longer on difficult tasks than those in neutral states. Anger seems to tell the brain, "Don't give up, push harder." This adaptive side of anger contradicts the common view that it's purely destructive. When harnessed carefully, anger can fuel determination, energize protest movements, and give individuals the courage to confront systemic injustices.

Anger's existence also ties into its **social signaling value**. Even subtle signs of anger, such as a frown, narrowed eyes, or a sharper tone of voice, alert others that boundaries are being tested. These signals can prevent conflicts from escalating because they warn others early. If everyone suppressed anger completely, others might never know when they were overstepping until damage had already occurred. Thus, anger as expression is functional, but its usefulness depends on timing, intensity, and context.

Psychologists also distinguish between **state anger** and **trait anger**. State anger refers to the temporary emotion in response to a specific trigger. Trait anger refers to a personality characteristic where a person is prone to frequent, intense episodes.

While state anger serves adaptive purposes, trait anger often leads to chronic stress, health problems, and social conflict. This difference shows why anger exists at one level as a healthy mechanism but becomes destructive when it shifts into enduring personality tendencies.

Anger's existence is also deeply tied to **identity and values**. People become angry when something they value is attacked or disregarded. A person who values punctuality grows angry at lateness. Someone who values honesty erupts when lied to. Because values differ, anger responses differ. This explains why one person shrugs off an insult while another reacts intensely. The underlying psychological truth is that anger points directly to what matters most to an individual. If you know what makes someone consistently angry, you know what they care about most.

Interestingly, anger isn't always destructive for relationships. In couples, controlled expression of anger often strengthens bonds. When one partner calmly but firmly shows anger about neglect or unfairness, it brings issues into the open. Bottled-up anger often corrodes relationships silently. This paradox—anger harming when uncontrolled but helping when expressed constructively—reflects its adaptive foundation. It evolved to highlight boundaries, not to destroy them.

Finally, psychologists note the role of **appraisal**. Anger isn't produced by the event itself but by the interpretation of that event. If someone bumps into you in a crowded subway, you may feel irritated if you interpret it as intentional, but you might feel nothing if you assume it was accidental. This appraisal mechanism shows that anger exists not just as a reflex but as part of **cognitive evaluation**. Humans constantly judge intent, fairness, and respect, and anger is the body's way of registering perceived violations of these judgments.

In sum, anger exists because it motivates defense, communicates disapproval, upholds values, and signals when important needs are under threat. It is an **adaptive emotion** shaped by evolution, psychology, and social dynamics. Without it, survival, justice, and goal pursuit would be weaker. The challenge isn't eliminating anger, but understanding its roots so it can be guided rather than left uncontrolled.

Types of Anger: Passive, Aggressive, Assertive

Anger rarely appears in a single form. It doesn't always arrive in shouting matches or physical violence. Sometimes it hides behind sarcasm or silence. Other times it's expressed clearly, without hostility, and leads to resolution instead of conflict. To understand how anger influences people's lives, psychologists often divide it into three expression styles: **passive anger**, **aggressive anger**, and **assertive anger**. These forms differ in visibility, impact, and long-term consequences.

Passive anger can be hard to recognize at first glance. The person experiencing it often avoids direct confrontation. Instead of admitting they're upset, they delay, withhold cooperation, or deliver indirect criticism. Imagine a coworker who's angry about extra work but doesn't say anything. Instead, they respond with late emails, a sarcastic tone, or quiet resistance. The anger is present, but it leaks out sideways. Passive anger usually arises when people fear open conflict or believe direct expression will make matters worse. It offers short-term protection but creates confusion in relationships because the message isn't clear. Over time, it damages trust since others sense hostility but can't pinpoint its cause.

Aggressive anger is the most visible and often the most damaging. It involves direct expression aimed at overpowering or punishing someone else. Raised voices, insults, intimidation, and sometimes physical acts fall into this category. People resort to aggressive anger when they feel a strong need to assert dominance, when they lack skills for calmer communication, or when the surge of adrenaline overwhelms rational restraint. Aggressive anger can secure immediate compliance. A boss yelling at staff might get them moving faster, but at the cost of morale and long-term cooperation. Families fractured by aggressive anger often struggle for years with the aftereffects of fear and resentment. Although it satisfies the short-term urge for control, it erodes bonds and leads to cycles of escalating hostility.

Assertive anger differs sharply. It's direct, but not destructive. A person expressing assertive anger acknowledges their feelings, explains them clearly, and addresses the issue without belittling or attacking others. For example, instead of snapping at a partner for being late, someone using assertive anger might say, "I feel disrespected when you keep me waiting. I'd like us to plan our timing more carefully." The emotion is present and visible, but it's channeled toward problem solving. Assertive anger requires awareness, restraint, and practice, which is why it's considered the healthiest style. It builds clarity rather than confusion and strengthens relationships instead of breaking them down.

Understanding these styles helps uncover why some people find anger destructive while others can use it to improve situations. Anger in itself isn't the deciding factor. The difference lies in how it's expressed.

Some cultures even teach children that anger should be silent, leading to passive patterns, while others normalize shouting as a way to release emotion, leading to aggressive patterns. Assertive anger often requires deliberate teaching since it doesn't always come naturally.

The three forms can be compared more concretely through their traits and outcomes.

Expression Style	Common Behaviors	Psychological Motives	Short-Term Effects	Long-Term Outcomes
Passive Anger	Sarcasm, avoidance, procrastination, withholding effort	Fear of conflict, desire to protect self-image, low confidence	Temporary avoidance of confrontation	Confusion in relationships, simmering resentment, erosion of trust
Aggressive Anger	Yelling, insults, intimidation, physical force	Need for dominance, impulse discharge, lack of regulation skills	Immediate compliance, temporary relief	Broken relationships, fear, retaliation, health issues
Assertive Anger	Calm but firm language, "I" statements, direct requests	Desire for fairness, respect for self and others, self-awareness	Clear communication, de-escalation, constructive action	Stronger relationships, improved self-control, reduced stress

Passive anger often leaves both parties dissatisfied. The angry person feels unheard, while the recipient senses something is wrong but doesn't know what to address. This gap fosters ongoing tension. For example, in marriages, passive anger may appear as silent treatment. The partner receiving silence feels isolated and frustrated, while the one delivering it may believe they're avoiding conflict. In reality, both suffer from the lack of clarity.

Aggressive anger tends to escalate situations. Once one party raises their voice, the other often responds in kind, leading to a spiral. Even if the aggressor "wins" the confrontation, the underlying issues remain unresolved. Repeated exposure to aggressive anger increases cortisol levels, strains the cardiovascular system, and creates chronic stress responses in everyone involved. Children raised in households where aggressive anger dominates often develop heightened sensitivity to conflict, carrying those patterns into adulthood.

Assertive anger, on the other hand, can transform conflict into collaboration. It validates the emotion without letting it dictate destructive action. It signals respect for both self and others. Assertive anger can still sound intense, but the intensity is directed toward clarity rather than punishment. It allows people to stand firm without creating unnecessary harm.

A workplace manager who calmly explains their frustration with missed deadlines, while also proposing a solution, shows assertive anger. The employees understand the seriousness but don't feel attacked, so they're more likely to adjust behavior willingly.

Psychological studies show that people who practice assertive anger consistently experience lower levels of chronic stress. This makes sense: rather than bottling up irritation or exploding unpredictably, they process it in real time with constructive outcomes. Their relationships are more stable because others trust their communication style.

Importantly, assertive anger doesn't mean avoiding strong emotion. It means integrating emotion with rational communication so the message is both honest and manageable.

These categories aren't fixed traits. People often shift between them depending on context. Someone may be passive at work because they fear consequences, aggressive at home where they feel safer to unload, and occasionally assertive when they're calm enough to think clearly. Recognizing this flexibility is critical for growth. The goal isn't to erase anger or suppress it entirely, but to move more interactions into the assertive category.

Learning to identify which form of anger is present requires observation. Passive anger often feels like tension without explanation. Aggressive anger feels overwhelming and leaves regret afterward. Assertive anger feels uncomfortable but productive, because the issue is discussed openly and directly. Building awareness of these distinctions gives individuals a framework for change.

The roots of these styles can be traced back to childhood. Children raised in households where anger was punished often learn to express it passively. Those raised in environments where yelling was the norm learn aggressive styles. Few children receive training in assertive anger because it requires adults to model controlled expression. As a result, many adults arrive in therapy unable to distinguish between being assertive and being aggressive. They may believe that any direct expression is harmful. Relearning how to show anger constructively becomes one of the key tasks of anger management programs.

Passive anger has subtle costs beyond relationships. People who habitually suppress direct expression often experience higher rates of depression and anxiety. Their internal stress accumulates without release. Aggressive anger has costs that show up both socially and legally. Assault charges, broken partnerships, and workplace terminations often follow patterns of repeated aggressive expression. Assertive anger, while healthiest, still requires balance. If overused or poorly timed, even assertive statements can sound like demands. The key lies in calibration: acknowledging anger without letting it dominate the exchange.

Research on anger regulation emphasizes that these categories align with levels of **emotional intelligence**. Low awareness and poor control correlate with aggressive anger. Low awareness combined with fear correlates with passive anger. High awareness and deliberate regulation align with assertive anger.

Emotional intelligence training often shifts people gradually from passive or aggressive tendencies toward assertive expression, showing that this isn't an innate skill but a learnable one.

Cultural norms shape which form is more common. In some collectivist cultures, harmony is prized, and anger expression is discouraged, so passive forms become more prevalent. In more individualistic cultures, open expression is normalized, which increases the frequency of aggressive forms. Assertive anger cuts across both contexts, but its acceptance depends on whether the culture values direct confrontation or indirect preservation of social ties. This means strategies for teaching assertive anger must adapt to cultural expectations.

The three types also differ in their neurological patterns. Aggressive anger strongly activates the amygdala and reduces activity in the prefrontal cortex, leading to impulse-driven outbursts. Passive anger shows more sustained physiological arousal without outward discharge, producing internal stress. Assertive anger balances amygdala activation with prefrontal regulation, resulting in controlled expression. This neurological evidence supports the idea that assertive anger is healthier both emotionally and physically, since it avoids the extremes of repression and explosion.

Examples help bring the distinctions into focus. Consider a workplace scenario where an employee is asked to stay late again after already working extra hours. With passive anger, they might quietly agree but then delay tasks intentionally. With aggressive anger, they might snap at their manager or refuse rudely. With assertive anger, they could say, "I've already worked late twice this week, and I need rest. Can we find a fairer schedule?" The difference in outcomes is dramatic. Passive anger leaves unresolved resentment, aggressive anger damages the relationship with the manager, and assertive anger opens the door to negotiation.

These types of anger show that expression matters more than the emotion itself. Anger is universal, but its consequences depend on whether it's hidden, unleashed, or guided. By categorizing anger in this way, people can start to recognize patterns in their own lives. Do they withhold and sulk? Do they lash out quickly? Or do they manage to communicate firmly without escalation? Each recognition is a step toward change.

In practical terms, training oneself toward assertive anger often involves small shifts. Replacing accusations with statements of personal impact. Pausing to breathe before responding. Choosing words that describe emotions rather than assign blame. These steps gradually build a habit of clear but respectful communication. They don't eliminate anger, but they transform it into a force that strengthens rather than weakens connections.

Common Myths and Misconceptions About Anger

Anger is one of the most misunderstood emotions. People often repeat ideas about it that sound plausible but collapse under closer examination. These myths not only distort how anger is viewed but also shape how people respond to it in themselves and others. Dispelling them is critical because misconceptions can reinforce destructive habits or prevent individuals from learning healthier ways of expression.

One of the most common myths is that **anger is always bad**. Because anger often shows up in shouting matches, fights, and regrettable decisions, many assume the emotion itself is harmful. The truth is different.

Anger is neither good nor bad on its own. It's a natural emotional response with evolutionary roots. It can protect boundaries, motivate action, and expose injustice. What makes it damaging isn't its existence but how it's expressed or suppressed. When directed constructively, anger can highlight problems that need resolution. When misdirected or left uncontrolled, it can certainly create chaos, but that's an issue of regulation, not inherent morality.

A second misconception is that **venting anger gets it out of your system**. Movies and popular advice have long suggested that punching a pillow or screaming into the air releases anger like steam from a kettle. The problem is that research consistently shows venting often intensifies the emotion rather than resolves it.

When people practice aggressive forms of release, the body's arousal system stays active, and the brain becomes primed for more aggression. Instead of calming down, individuals can become even angrier. Effective strategies involve calming physiological arousal, reframing thoughts, or expressing concerns assertively. Venting may feel satisfying in the moment, but it reinforces aggressive neural pathways and normalizes explosive responses.

A related myth is that **suppressing anger is healthy**. Since open aggression damages relationships, some people conclude the opposite must be better: push it down, ignore it, or pretend it isn't there. Suppression can reduce conflict in the short term, but it extracts a cost. The body remains in a state of heightened stress when anger is bottled up. Over time, this increases the risk of hypertension, cardiovascular disease, and immune dysfunction. Psychologically, suppressed anger often transforms into resentment, cynicism, or depression. Relationships suffer as well because suppressed anger leaks out indirectly, through sarcasm, avoidance, or emotional distance. The healthiest alternative isn't suppression but recognition and assertive communication.

Another myth claims that **anger makes you honest**. People sometimes excuse hurtful words spoken in fury by saying, "I was just being real." While it's true that anger lowers inhibition and makes people more likely to blurt out unfiltered thoughts, this doesn't mean what's said reflects core truths. Anger distorts perception, exaggerates grievances, and pulls attention toward threat. Words spoken in that state are shaped by heightened arousal and narrowed focus, not balanced reflection. Believing that anger automatically produces honesty gives people a pass to act recklessly and then dismiss responsibility afterward. Real honesty emerges when individuals express feelings with clarity and self-control, not when they lash out without filter.

There's also the widespread belief that **some people never feel anger**. Certain individuals claim they don't get angry, presenting themselves as calm and unshakable.

In reality, anger is universal. It may manifest differently, often in quieter forms that others don't recognize as anger. People who insist they never feel it may experience irritability, tension, or passive behaviors instead. Denial of anger doesn't mean absence; it usually indicates a lack of awareness or a cultural upbringing that discouraged open acknowledgment of the emotion. Pretending not to feel anger can be as harmful as aggressive outbursts, because it cuts off the chance to process and express it in healthier ways.

Another misconception is that **anger is uncontrollable**. The common phrase "I couldn't help it" suggests that once anger starts, it inevitably leads to explosion. Neuroscience shows otherwise. While anger does trigger powerful physical changes, including increased heart rate, blood pressure, and adrenaline release, people still have regulatory systems that can intervene. The prefrontal cortex can slow or redirect impulsive reactions when trained through practice. Evidence from cognitive-behavioral therapy demonstrates that individuals can learn to pause, evaluate, and choose assertive responses rather than aggressive ones. Believing anger is uncontrollable creates a self-fulfilling prophecy, making people less likely to try regulation strategies.

The idea that **anger and aggression are the same thing** is also misleading. Anger is an internal emotional state. Aggression is a behavior. You can feel angry without becoming aggressive, and you can behave aggressively without intense anger if other motives like dominance or frustration are present. Blurring these distinctions fuels stereotypes and prevents people from realizing they can channel anger in nonaggressive ways.

For example, a lawyer arguing passionately for a client's rights may be fueled by anger at injustice but expresses it through structured reasoning, not aggression. Recognizing that anger and aggression are separate helps dismantle the assumption that anger must always harm others.

A persistent myth insists that **anger only comes from external triggers**. While external events certainly matter, anger also emerges from internal interpretations. Two people can face the same traffic jam and react differently. One becomes enraged, another shrugs it off. The difference lies in cognitive appraisal, not the event itself. Believing anger is purely external removes responsibility, as if the outside world forces people into emotional states. In truth, anger is shaped by values, expectations, and thought patterns. Someone who interprets a colleague's late arrival as disrespect will feel angrier than someone who interprets it as unavoidable. This means people can change their experience of anger by shifting interpretations, not just by changing circumstances.

There's a common cultural story that **anger is stronger in men than women**. Stereotypes often suggest men are angrier or more prone to explosive reactions, while women are seen as more emotional in other ways. Research, however, doesn't support the idea of men being inherently angrier. Studies show that men and women experience anger at similar frequencies and intensities.

What differs is expression. Men are often socialized to externalize anger aggressively, while women may be taught to internalize or redirect it. This difference in expression feeds the stereotype, but the underlying emotion is universal. Recognizing this dispels gendered myths and prevents misinterpretation of behavior.

Some also believe that **anger disappears with age**. The assumption is that maturity brings calmness and wisdom that erases the fiery reactions of youth. While it's true that many people develop better regulation strategies as they grow older, anger itself doesn't vanish. Older adults still feel anger, especially when facing frustration, injustice, or loss of autonomy. The difference lies in how they channel it. Many have learned from past mistakes and now express anger with more patience and perspective. Others may still struggle, particularly if they've relied on suppression or aggression throughout life. Age changes physiology, but it doesn't erase emotion.

A damaging misconception is that **anger can't be positive**. Because the word is so often associated with harm, people forget its role in motivation and justice. Social movements throughout history have been fueled by anger at inequality. Individuals have stood up to oppression because anger refused to let them accept the status quo.

On a personal level, anger can drive someone to leave a toxic relationship, improve unfair workplace conditions, or push through challenges others told them to accept. Denying anger's potential benefits strips it of its complexity and power. It isn't about glorifying anger but recognizing that it can contribute to growth when directed wisely.

Finally, there's the myth that **anger disappears when ignored**. Many assume that if they simply wait it out, anger will fade on its own. While emotional arousal does decline over time, unprocessed anger often lingers in the form of grudges, bitterness, or sudden reactivations when similar situations arise.

Ignored anger doesn't resolve; it incubates. This incubation makes future reactions stronger because the brain connects current events with stored resentment. Addressing anger directly, through reflection or dialogue, prevents it from becoming a recurring burden.

These myths persist partly because anger is uncomfortable to witness and harder to manage than emotions like sadness or joy. People prefer simple rules, such as "never get angry" or "just let it out." Real understanding requires nuance. Anger is an ancient, deeply functional emotion, but it's surrounded by stories that oversimplify or distort it. The task is not to eliminate anger or pretend it never surfaces. The task is to recognize what's real and what's myth so that individuals can handle anger with accuracy rather than assumption.

The Biology of Anger: Hormones, Neurotransmitters, and the Brain

Anger isn't only a psychological experience. It's also a biological process that involves chemical messengers, electrical signals, and brain regions coordinating at remarkable speed. What people feel as a sudden rush of heat or tension in their chest is the outcome of a highly organized sequence inside the nervous system. To understand anger, it's essential to look at the hormones and neurotransmitters that generate and regulate the state, and to see how different brain areas cooperate or compete during those moments.

The first thing to recognize is that anger is part of the **stress response**. When a trigger is perceived, the brain quickly evaluates whether it represents a threat. The amygdala, a structure deep in the limbic system, acts as a rapid alarm system. Within milliseconds it sends signals that prepare the body for confrontation. This includes activating the **hypothalamic-pituitary-adrenal (HPA) axis**, which releases stress hormones into the bloodstream.

The most famous of these hormones is **adrenaline**, also known as epinephrine. Adrenaline increases heart rate, elevates blood pressure, and redirects blood flow toward muscles. That's why people often feel flushed or tense when angry. Adrenaline also sharpens attention, making individuals hyper-focused on the perceived source of threat or injustice. Alongside adrenaline comes **noradrenaline**, which boosts alertness and prepares the brain to respond quickly. Together they create the classic fight state that anger is designed to support.

Another key hormone involved is **cortisol**. While cortisol is typically associated with long-term stress, it also plays a role in anger. It helps sustain energy by mobilizing glucose and maintaining blood pressure. Short bursts of cortisol aid in responding to immediate threats, but chronic elevation caused by frequent anger episodes damages cardiovascular health and weakens immunity. This is why unmanaged anger has long-term physical consequences.

Hormones aren't the entire story. **Neurotransmitters**, the chemical messengers that allow nerve cells to communicate, also shape anger. **Serotonin** is particularly important. Low levels of serotonin are linked with impulsive aggression. Serotonin normally acts as a brake on excessive emotional arousal by calming circuits in the amygdala. When serotonin is deficient, that brake system weakens, making it harder to regulate rising anger. **Dopamine**, another neurotransmitter, also plays a role. It reinforces behavior by creating sensations of reward. Aggressive behavior can sometimes release dopamine, which unintentionally conditions the brain to repeat it. That's why people may find themselves exploding repeatedly even when they regret it afterward.

The brain's architecture helps explain why anger sometimes feels uncontrollable. The **amygdala** reacts quickly, often before the conscious mind has fully processed what's happening. The **prefrontal cortex**, particularly the ventromedial and dorsolateral regions, is responsible for reasoning, long-term planning, and impulse control. In moments of intense anger, activity in the amygdala surges while prefrontal cortex activity decreases. This imbalance explains why people sometimes say or do things they later regret. They're literally operating with reduced rational oversight while their emotional circuits dominate.

However, the prefrontal cortex isn't powerless. With practice in emotional regulation, people can strengthen these cortical pathways so they intervene more effectively. Mindfulness, cognitive reappraisal, and structured anger management techniques all rely on engaging the prefrontal cortex to reframe the trigger or slow the body's reaction. Neuroscience studies using imaging have shown that individuals trained in these methods display stronger connectivity between the prefrontal cortex and the amygdala, suggesting greater top-down control.

Another brain region involved is the **anterior cingulate cortex (ACC)**. This area monitors conflicts and errors. When someone feels torn between lashing out and holding back, the ACC is active. It works closely with the prefrontal cortex to weigh options and maintain social appropriateness. The **insula**, which processes internal bodily states, helps generate the physical sensations of anger like tightness in the chest or a flushed face. These interoceptive cues are part of what makes anger so compelling; the body and brain reinforce each other in a feedback loop.

The **hypothalamus** also contributes by coordinating the release of hormones and linking emotion to autonomic responses such as sweating and changes in heart rate. Damage to the hypothalamus in animal studies often alters aggression, underscoring its importance in anger expression.

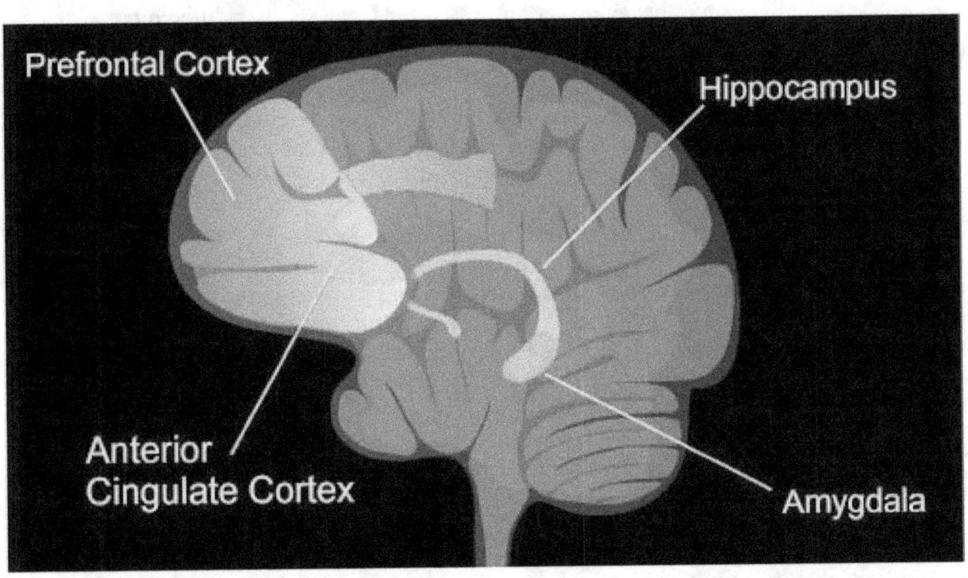

To bring these elements together, it's helpful to organize the main contributors in a clear overview:

System or Component	Function in Anger	Short-Term Effect	Long-Term Impact if Chronic
Amygdala	Rapid threat detection, emotional intensity	Quick surge of anger, heightened vigilance	Oversensitivity to minor threats

Prefrontal Cortex	Regulation, reasoning, impulse control	Calms or reframes response if engaged	Strengthened control with training, weakened if neglected
Anterior Cingulate Cortex	Monitors conflict between impulses and goals	Awareness of tension between acting out and restraint	Improved regulation with practice
Insula	Processes body sensations	Awareness of physical cues like flushing or tightness	Heightened sensitivity to bodily stress
Hypothalamus	Hormone regulation, links emotion and autonomic systems	Releases stress hormones, coordinates bodily readiness	Dysregulation contributes to hypertension
Adrenaline and Noradrenaline	Stress hormones for immediate response	Increased energy, focus, cardiovascular arousal	Chronic strain on heart and vessels
Cortisol	Sustains energy, blood pressure regulation	Maintains response to threat	Increases risk of heart disease and immune suppression
Serotonin	Neurotransmitter that regulates mood and impulse	Dampens excessive anger when levels are sufficient	Low levels linked with aggression and poor control
Dopamine	Reinforces behaviors through reward	Aggressive acts may feel satisfying	Conditioning of aggressive patterns

This table underscores how anger isn't the result of a single chemical or brain area but a network of processes working together. Each component has both adaptive and maladaptive effects depending on frequency and regulation.

Anger also shows up differently in the body depending on individual differences in biology. Genetic variations influence how strongly neurotransmitters function. For example, certain alleles in serotonin transporter genes are associated with greater risk of impulsive aggression. Hormonal differences also matter. Higher baseline testosterone levels can increase the likelihood of aggressive responses, particularly when combined with low serotonin. Testosterone doesn't cause anger by itself, but it can amplify competitive or confrontational tendencies.

The body's feedback systems shape how long anger lasts. When adrenaline surges, the body prepares for immediate action. If no action occurs, those stress hormones still need time to clear from circulation. That's why people often feel keyed up for minutes or even hours after an argument. The duration of anger isn't just psychological dwelling; it's also biochemical persistence. Training techniques that lower physiological arousal, such as slow breathing or relaxation exercises, help shorten this recovery period by signaling the body to halt the stress response.

The cardiovascular system bears the brunt of chronic anger. Every episode involves elevated heart rate and blood pressure. Over time, frequent surges contribute to stiffening of arteries and increased risk of heart disease. Researchers have documented higher incidence of myocardial infarction in individuals with chronic anger and hostility patterns. The immune system is also affected, as elevated cortisol suppresses immune responses and makes the body more vulnerable to infection. This shows that anger, while biologically adaptive in the short term, extracts measurable costs when it becomes a constant state.

Interestingly, not all biological consequences of anger are negative. Controlled anger expression can actually enhance resilience. Small, manageable stress responses build the body's capacity to adapt, a concept known as **hormesis**. In this sense, occasional anger expressed assertively and resolved constructively may strengthen cardiovascular flexibility and stress management systems. The problem arises when anger is either chronically suppressed, keeping the body in tension, or chronically aggressive, repeatedly overloading physiological systems.

Brain imaging studies shed light on the complexity of anger episodes. Functional MRI scans reveal that when people imagine or recall anger-inducing events, their amygdala activates strongly, but when they practice reappraisal strategies, prefrontal activation increases and amygdala activity decreases. This demonstrates that biological processes are dynamic rather than fixed. Regulation is possible, but it requires intentional cognitive engagement.

In short, the biology of anger is a sophisticated combination of hormones, neurotransmitters, and brain regions. It's an evolved mechanism designed to energize and protect, but it carries risks if left unchecked. Understanding this biological foundation emphasizes why anger management isn't about suppressing an emotion but about guiding biological responses with awareness and skill.

Environmental and Social Triggers of Anger

Anger is shaped by surroundings, circumstances, and the way people interact. While biological wiring primes the brain for anger, the spark usually comes from the environment or social context. These triggers range from crowded spaces and loud noises to interpersonal slights and cultural expectations. Recognizing them is crucial because anger management isn't only about internal regulation but also about understanding the conditions that fuel it.

One of the strongest environmental triggers is **crowding**. Human beings are highly sensitive to personal space. When that boundary is violated, tension rises quickly. In urban settings with dense populations, this leads to more frequent irritability. Studies show that traffic congestion, long lines, and cramped living conditions all increase the likelihood of anger. The brain interprets these intrusions as a loss of control, and control is a central component of emotional stability. Even when no one intends harm, the simple pressure of too many bodies in one place can set the stage for angry reactions.

Noise is another major factor. **Environmental noise pollution** has been linked to higher aggression. Loud, unpredictable sounds activate stress responses in the body. Sirens, machinery, shouting neighbors, or constant background noise interfere with concentration and sleep, lowering tolerance thresholds. When someone is already tired or stressed, the intrusion of noise makes them far more likely to lash out at minor irritations. This is one reason why anger episodes peak in environments like busy streets or crowded apartments, where noise is relentless.

Temperature also affects anger levels. Research consistently shows that **heat increases aggression**. Hot days correlate with higher rates of violent crime, a phenomenon sometimes called the heat hypothesis. The physiological discomfort of heat primes the body toward irritability. Sweating, fatigue, and dehydration strain the nervous system, making it easier for small provocations to trigger anger. Cold, in contrast, doesn't seem to produce the same widespread irritability. The link between heat and aggression highlights how even basic weather conditions shape emotional responses.

Social triggers are equally powerful. One of the most universal is **perceived disrespect**. When someone feels dismissed, insulted, or belittled, anger often rises sharply. Respect is tied to social identity, and threats to it activate defensive responses.

This is why insults often generate stronger reactions than physical inconveniences. A flat tire frustrates, but being mocked in front of peers provokes. The anger in such moments functions as a demand for recognition and fairness.

Another common social trigger is **injustice**. Whether at work, in relationships, or in society at large, people respond with anger when they perceive unfairness. A worker who sees a colleague promoted despite weaker performance, or a citizen who witnesses corruption, feels the same emotional spark. Anger here is moral in nature. It expresses a demand for fairness, not just self-interest. This moral component explains why anger often drives social change movements, where individuals rally together against perceived injustice.

Interpersonal triggers extend to **miscommunication**. Misunderstandings can escalate rapidly into anger because they create a sense of being unheard or invalidated. If someone believes their perspective is ignored, frustration builds.

Technology has amplified this trigger, since emails, texts, and social media often lack tone and nuance. A message intended as neutral can be interpreted as dismissive, sparking unnecessary anger. The rise of digital communication has therefore created new environments where anger thrives.

Family and intimate relationships also provide fertile ground for anger triggers. Expectations are higher in close relationships, which means disappointment cuts deeper. Partners often become angry not because of the size of the issue but because of accumulated minor grievances that feel magnified by emotional closeness. Parents and children trigger anger in one another through boundary testing, role expectations, and misaligned communication. These triggers aren't random; they're tied to the weight of emotional investment.

Workplaces add another layer. **Occupational stress** produces anger through deadlines, workload imbalances, and perceived unfair treatment by supervisors. Anger in professional contexts is often suppressed because open displays threaten reputations, but it still influences morale and productivity. When employees feel undervalued or controlled without respect, their anger may surface indirectly through decreased cooperation, absenteeism, or hostile attitudes. This shows how anger isn't limited to explosive outbursts but also shapes subtle patterns of resistance.

Cultural influences shape which triggers are most likely to ignite anger. In some societies, **honor cultures** heighten sensitivity to insult. Even minor slights provoke intense anger because they're perceived as challenges to personal or family reputation.

In contrast, collectivist cultures often prioritize harmony, so anger may be triggered more by betrayal of group obligations than by individual insults. Understanding these cultural frameworks helps explain why behaviors tolerated in one setting may spark fury in another.

Triggers also accumulate across time. Someone who faces repeated stressors without relief develops a **lower threshold for anger**.

For example, a person enduring chronic financial strain may become explosively angry at a small household mistake because their system is already overloaded. The anger isn't only about the immediate trigger but about accumulated tension. This cumulative effect means that environmental and social triggers can't be assessed in isolation. They build layers of pressure that eventually produce eruptions.

To see the diversity of triggers more clearly, it's helpful to map them across different contexts.

Category	Examples	Mechanism of Anger Activation
Physical Environment	Crowding, traffic, heat, noise	Perceived loss of control, physiological discomfort, sensory overload
Interpersonal Context	Insults, disrespect, miscommunication	Threats to identity and status, feeling unheard or invalidated
Family and Intimate Settings	Repeated grievances, boundary violations, unmet expectations	Heightened emotional investment, amplified disappointment
Workplace	Deadlines, workload imbalance, unfair promotions	Stress, perceived injustice, lack of recognition
Societal and Cultural	Corruption, discrimination, violation of cultural norms	Moral outrage, defense of group identity, honor sensitivity
Technology and Media	Online insults, misinterpreted texts, exposure to hostility	Lack of nuance, anonymity emboldening aggression, constant access to conflict

This table underscores how varied triggers can be, yet how consistently they tie back to themes of control, respect, fairness, and safety.

A factor that intensifies triggers is **expectation mismatch**. When people expect smooth travel but face delays, or expect loyalty from a friend and receive betrayal, anger spikes. The greater the gap between expectation and reality, the stronger the response. This explains why minor issues sometimes cause disproportionate anger: they violate deeply held assumptions. Someone who believes punctuality is essential won't just feel mild irritation at lateness, they'll experience it as disrespect and disregard for shared values.

Social learning also determines which triggers activate anger. Children who grow up watching parents react angrily to small frustrations learn to interpret those same events as worthy of anger. Over time, they internalize a broader range of triggers. Others raised in calmer environments may develop higher tolerance. This shows that anger triggers are partly conditioned. What sets off one person may barely register for another, not because biology differs but because experiences shaped their sensitivity.

Triggers are also connected to **power dynamics**. People are more likely to feel anger when they perceive themselves as disrespected by someone of equal or lower status.

When the same behavior comes from someone of much higher authority, fear may override anger. This explains why workers may grumble among themselves about a manager's decision but remain outwardly calm during a meeting. It also explains why anger often surfaces in settings where power feels contested, such as between siblings, colleagues, or rivals.

Chronic environmental stress amplifies the likelihood of anger, even from minor triggers. Living in high-crime neighborhoods, enduring poverty, or facing systemic discrimination creates constant vigilance. In these contexts, anger often functions as a protective shield, preparing individuals to defend themselves.

While this response is understandable, it also leads to exhaustion and ongoing tension. Over time, chronic exposure to such triggers reshapes the nervous system, lowering thresholds for arousal and making anger more frequent.

It's also important to consider the role of **technology-driven exposure**. Social media algorithms often highlight conflict and controversy because these grab attention. Repeated exposure to hostile debates, sensationalist headlines, and online insults normalizes anger triggers and creates a baseline of irritability. The anonymity of online interactions intensifies this because people say things they wouldn't in person, leading to more opportunities for perceived disrespect.

Triggers vary not only by context but also by individual vulnerabilities. Someone who values order may find mess and disorder highly triggering. Another who values loyalty above all may be especially sensitive to betrayal. Recognizing these individual triggers requires introspection and often journaling or therapeutic reflection. The task is not to eliminate triggers but to understand them well enough to anticipate and prepare for them.

Ultimately, anger is less about the objective event than about the **interpretation** of that event in the context of environmental and social cues. Noise, heat, or insult by themselves don't guarantee anger. They become triggers when filtered through personal expectations, cultural frameworks, and cumulative stress.

Managing anger requires both internal skills and external adjustments, such as reducing exposure to constant noise or creating clearer communication in relationships. Understanding triggers allows people to recognize when they're entering dangerous terrain and gives them a chance to redirect before anger spirals into destructive expression.

Short-Term vs. Long-Term Anger Patterns

Anger doesn't always follow the same trajectory. Sometimes it arrives in a flash and fades as quickly as it appeared. At other times, it lingers for days, months, or even years, shaping behavior and health in profound ways. Distinguishing between short-term and long-term anger patterns reveals why some people recover quickly after irritation while others carry grudges or develop chronic hostility. Understanding these patterns also helps explain the different consequences anger has for relationships, decision making, and physical health.

Short-term anger is often described as **acute anger episodes**. These arise in direct response to a specific event, such as being cut off in traffic, receiving rude service, or hearing an offensive remark. The experience is immediate and usually intense.

Physiological arousal surges quickly: adrenaline and noradrenaline flood the bloodstream, heart rate spikes, muscles tense, and attention narrows to the source of the trigger. The body prepares for immediate action, either through confrontation or some form of defensive expression.

In most cases, short-term anger dissipates once the event is resolved or reappraised. If the driver apologizes, if the waiter explains the mistake, or if the insult is reinterpreted as unintentional, the emotion often fades within minutes. The body gradually clears stress hormones and returns to baseline. For many, this form of anger is manageable and even functional, because it alerts them to boundaries and allows corrective action without lasting consequences.

However, even short-term anger can be destructive if expressed aggressively. A sudden fight in traffic or a heated argument with a colleague may cause damage far beyond the initial trigger. This reveals that while the duration of short-term anger may be brief, the intensity can still lead to disproportionate outcomes. What separates healthy short-term anger from harmful short-term anger is whether the individual regains regulation quickly or allows impulsive behavior to take over.

Long-term anger looks very different. It often takes the form of **chronic hostility**, **resentment**, or **rumination**. Instead of fading once the trigger passes, the anger persists, becoming part of a person's baseline emotional state. Someone who repeatedly replays past insults or injustices in their mind prolongs their physiological arousal. Stress hormones remain elevated, the cardiovascular system stays strained, and the brain becomes conditioned to expect and interpret more hostility in the environment.

Chronic anger is reinforced through **cognitive loops**. The person recalls the triggering event, feels anger again, and interprets new events through the lens of past resentment. This cycle makes even neutral situations feel provocative. For example, someone harboring long-term anger toward a coworker may perceive every neutral comment as sarcastic or undermining. Over time, this creates self-fulfilling patterns of conflict.

The consequences of long-term anger extend far beyond momentary discomfort. Physiologically, chronic anger is linked to higher rates of hypertension, heart disease, weakened immunity, and shortened lifespan. Psychologically, it contributes to anxiety, depression, and impaired concentration. Socially, it corrodes trust and intimacy because others experience the person as perpetually irritable or hostile. Unlike short-term anger, which often resolves naturally, long-term anger requires active intervention to break the cycle.

The difference between short-term and long-term anger patterns can be summarized through their features, effects, and regulation possibilities.

Pattern	Duration	Physiological Profile	Cognitive Style	Typical Consequences	Regulation Path
Short-Term Anger	Minutes to hours	Sharp spike in adrenaline and noradrenaline, quick return to baseline	Trigger-focused, situational	Boundary-setting, possible impulsive conflict, usually resolves	Breathing, reframing, apology, time-out
Long-Term Anger	Days to years	Prolonged cortisol elevation, chronic cardiovascular strain	Rumination, generalized hostility, threat expectation	Hypertension, depression, relationship erosion, chronic stress	Therapy, cognitive restructuring, lifestyle changes, forgiveness practices

This table shows that duration isn't just a matter of time but also of biology and psychology. Short-term anger uses the body's systems as intended, like a sprint. Long-term anger turns that sprint into a marathon the body isn't built to sustain.

Cultural norms influence which pattern dominates. Some communities normalize venting in the moment, which may create frequent but short anger episodes. Others discourage expression, leading individuals to carry resentment longer. Personality traits also matter.

People high in **neuroticism** are more prone to long-term rumination, while those high in **agreeableness** tend to resolve short-term conflicts more quickly. These differences highlight that while biology sets the framework, psychology and environment determine the pattern.

Long-term anger also manifests in subtler ways. It doesn't always appear as explosive rage. It can appear as cynicism, sarcasm, or chronic irritability. These expressions don't seem dramatic but reveal that the individual never fully resolves their underlying grievances. In relationships, this leads to what psychologists call **kitchen-sinking**, where every past grievance resurfaces in new arguments. The anger isn't about the current disagreement but about years of accumulated resentment.

Short-term anger, when handled constructively, can actually strengthen relationships. Partners who express irritation openly but respectfully resolve issues more quickly. Their anger signals importance, leads to clarification, and then fades. Long-term anger weakens relationships because it prevents resolution. When grievances are stored rather than addressed, trust erodes, and communication breaks down. This explains why some couples feel constantly stuck in cycles of tension even without overt fights.

Another distinction lies in memory. Short-term anger is event-specific and fades from memory once resolved. Long-term anger is reinforced by selective memory that retrieves past offenses to justify continued resentment. This biased recall strengthens anger's grip. Neuroscience studies show that during rumination, areas of the brain associated with memory and threat detection, like the hippocampus and amygdala, stay highly active. This makes long-term anger self-sustaining even without new triggers.

It's also worth noting the **social contagion** of long-term anger. Individuals who remain chronically hostile influence those around them. Families with one persistently angry member often develop defensive communication styles, walking on eggshells or responding with their own hostility. Workplaces with chronically angry leaders develop toxic cultures. Short-term anger can be disruptive, but long-term anger reshapes entire social environments.

Breaking long-term anger patterns requires more than momentary calming techniques. It involves altering cognitive habits, practicing forgiveness, and restructuring expectations. Some therapies focus on identifying rumination cycles and replacing them with problem-solving strategies.

Others use mindfulness to break the constant reactivation of angry memories. Biological interventions, such as medication that stabilizes serotonin, can also support regulation when anger is tied to neurotransmitter imbalances.

Short-term anger patterns can be managed with simpler techniques like deep breathing or taking time-outs. These strategies reduce immediate physiological arousal and create space for the prefrontal cortex to reassert control. Because the emotion is temporary, small interventions often suffice.

Long-term anger, however, requires sustained effort. It may involve addressing underlying trauma, changing environments, or rebuilding social connections. The complexity reflects the depth of the pattern.

Understanding the difference between these two patterns also helps explain individual differences. When people say they're "hot-headed," they may simply have frequent short-term anger spikes but return to calm quickly. Others who claim they're "holding a grudge" demonstrate long-term anger, where even after outward calm, inner hostility remains. Recognizing which pattern dominates allows for tailored strategies.

Ultimately, short-term anger is a natural biological reaction designed to address immediate threats or frustrations. It's intense but fleeting when managed properly. Long-term anger is a maladaptive extension, where the body and mind remain locked in confrontation long after the trigger is gone. One is like a firecracker, the other a slow-burning ember that smolders and damages everything nearby. Both demand attention, but they demand different forms of attention: quick cooling for the first, deep restructuring for the second.

The Costs of Unmanaged Anger: Health, Relationships, Career

Anger in itself is not destructive. What turns it into a burden is when it remains unmanaged, expressed impulsively, or suppressed until it warps behavior. When that happens, the costs appear across every dimension of life. The body suffers, relationships deteriorate, and professional futures are compromised. People often underestimate these costs because they unfold gradually, but the cumulative toll of unmanaged anger is immense.

The most visible cost is to **physical health**. Anger sets off a cascade of stress responses in the body, and if these responses repeat too often, they become corrosive. The cardiovascular system is particularly vulnerable. Every burst of anger raises heart rate, tightens blood vessels, and elevates blood pressure.

Occasional spikes aren't dangerous for most healthy people, but repeated surges stiffen arteries and increase the risk of atherosclerosis. Research has shown that people with chronic hostility patterns are more likely to suffer from heart attacks and strokes. For those already living with hypertension, unmanaged anger accelerates damage and complicates treatment.

The immune system also weakens under frequent anger. Elevated cortisol, the hormone that sustains the stress response, suppresses immune functioning over time. This leaves individuals more susceptible to infections and slows recovery from illness. Anger that festers in long-term patterns contributes to chronic inflammation, which has been linked to autoimmune disorders and even cancer progression. The irony is that anger evolved to protect survival in dangerous contexts, but when unchecked in modern life, it shortens survival instead.

Sleep is another victim of unmanaged anger. Heightened arousal makes it difficult to fall asleep or stay asleep. Insomnia becomes common when unresolved anger dominates a person's nights. Even when sleep occurs, it is often shallow and restless, leaving the individual fatigued. Fatigue, in turn, lowers tolerance thresholds, making fresh anger episodes more likely. The cycle reinforces itself, showing how unmanaged anger doesn't remain confined to a single domain but spreads across systems.

The psychological costs are just as heavy. Unmanaged anger distorts perception, narrowing attention toward threat and disrespect. People prone to chronic outbursts often misinterpret neutral cues as hostile, a bias that keeps them locked in cycles of conflict. The brain becomes conditioned to expect negativity, which heightens vigilance and maintains stress. This distorted perception damages problem-solving skills and increases impulsivity, leading to regretful decisions that reinforce guilt and shame. Over time, unmanaged anger contributes to depression and anxiety because the body and mind can't escape perpetual arousal.

Relationships often bear the brunt. **Aggressive anger** erodes trust quickly. Partners exposed to repeated yelling or intimidation lose a sense of safety. Children raised in households with unmanaged anger internalize either fear or imitation, developing their own difficulties with emotional regulation. Even friendships collapse when one person becomes known for volatility. People withdraw from those who lash out unpredictably because the cost of maintaining connection becomes too high.

Passive forms of unmanaged anger also corrode relationships. Silent treatment, sarcasm, and avoidance confuse and exhaust partners. The lack of open communication prevents resolution. Instead of extinguishing conflict, passive anger keeps it smoldering beneath the surface. Over years, resentment accumulates until the bond becomes brittle. Relationships don't always end because of dramatic blowups; they often wither slowly under the weight of unresolved hostility.

In intimate relationships, unmanaged anger is particularly destructive because it violates the expectation of emotional safety. Love depends on trust that vulnerabilities will not be weaponized. When anger is expressed aggressively, that trust evaporates. Couples may stay together out of obligation or fear, but the relationship becomes hollow. In other cases, unmanaged anger escalates to abuse, with severe consequences for both emotional and physical safety.

The costs also extend into **professional life**. Workplaces demand collaboration, composure, and communication. When anger is unmanaged, it interferes with all three. Colleagues avoid working with someone known for outbursts, which limits opportunities for collaboration and advancement. Supervisors hesitate to promote individuals who can't regulate emotions, fearing they'll damage team morale. A single outburst in a meeting can undo years of professional credibility.

Workplace studies show that employees with poor anger regulation are more likely to be disciplined or terminated. Their productivity often suffers because cognitive resources are drained by rumination and tension. Creativity also declines, since unmanaged anger narrows focus and limits flexible thinking. In fields where innovation and problem-solving are prized, this becomes a significant career obstacle. The costs aren't limited to the individual; organizations also suffer when unmanaged anger spreads toxicity through teams.

The financial consequences can be striking. Job loss, stalled promotions, and broken business relationships reduce income and limit opportunities. For entrepreneurs, unmanaged anger can alienate investors, clients, and partners, undermining ventures that depend on trust. Career trajectories bend downward not because of technical incompetence but because emotional regulation was neglected.

Another cost that cuts across health, relationships, and career is the effect on **reputation**. People known for unmanaged anger carry labels: hot-headed, unstable, difficult. Once these reputations solidify, they're hard to shake.

Others approach with caution or avoid altogether, reinforcing isolation. Social networks shrink, and opportunities for growth narrow. In some cases, unmanaged anger even brings legal consequences, through charges of assault or harassment, which create enduring records that shadow professional and personal life.

The difference between managed and unmanaged anger becomes even clearer when looking at long-term trajectories. People who regulate anger well often report stronger relationships, better physical health, and more stable careers. Those who don't find themselves isolated, unwell, and professionally stagnant. The following table summarizes the most significant costs of unmanaged anger across domains.

Domain	Immediate Impact	Long-Term Consequence

Physical Health	Elevated heart rate, blood pressure, insomnia	Hypertension, heart disease, immune suppression, chronic inflammation
Psychological State	Impulsivity, distorted perception, narrowed attention	Depression, anxiety, rumination, reduced problem-solving ability
Relationships	Erosion of trust, conflict, intimidation, avoidance	Divorce, family breakdown, social isolation, intergenerational patterns
Career	Damaged teamwork, conflicts with colleagues, lost opportunities	Stalled promotions, job loss, reputational damage, reduced income
Reputation and Social Standing	Labeling as volatile, avoidance by peers	Long-term stigma, diminished support networks, reduced opportunities
Legal and Financial	Aggressive outbursts, harassment, destructive acts	Legal records, financial losses, loss of professional licenses

This overview shows that unmanaged anger doesn't just cause momentary discomfort. It plants seeds that grow into lasting harm across every sphere.

There's also an **opportunity cost**. Every time anger consumes energy, it diverts resources from more productive pursuits. Hours spent ruminating could have been spent solving problems or building connections. Energy wasted in fights could have been invested in creativity or growth. Anger unmanaged doesn't just cause direct harm; it steals from the potential of what could have been.

It's important to recognize that unmanaged anger rarely isolates itself to one area. A health consequence may spill into relationships, as fatigue makes someone more irritable. A workplace conflict may carry over into home life, where residual tension sparks new fights. The domains interact, creating compounding effects. That's why unmanaged anger often feels overwhelming. It isn't one problem but a network of interconnected struggles, each reinforcing the others.

Unmanaged anger also influences identity. People begin to see themselves as "angry types" or "short-tempered" and stop believing change is possible. This internalization reduces motivation to improve, which locks them into the very patterns causing harm. Identity shaped by unmanaged anger is limiting because it defines the person by their worst moments rather than their capacity for growth.

The broader societal costs shouldn't be ignored either. Road rage incidents cause accidents and fatalities. Domestic violence rooted in unmanaged anger devastates families and burdens social systems. Workplace aggression decreases productivity and increases turnover, costing billions in lost economic output. Anger unmanaged is not just an individual problem but a collective one, with ripple effects far beyond the person experiencing it.

Despite the seriousness of these costs, many people underestimate them until consequences accumulate. They may dismiss frequent irritation as personality or justify aggressive outbursts as honesty. But biology, psychology, and social evidence converge on the same truth: unmanaged anger erodes wellbeing, weakens bonds, and blocks success. The costs are too broad and too deep to ignore.

Chapter 2: Recognizing Triggers and Early Warning Signs

Identifying Personal Triggers

Most people think of anger as something that happens suddenly, like a storm appearing without warning. In reality, there are patterns behind every outburst. These patterns come from **personal triggers**, the unique situations, words, or environments that ignite anger in one individual but may leave another unfazed. Learning to recognize and map these triggers is one of the most important steps in anger management because it moves anger from being a mysterious force to something predictable and controllable.

The Nature of Triggers

A trigger can be external, such as traffic congestion or a dismissive remark, or internal, like fatigue, rumination, or a painful memory. Both types are equally influential. What makes something a trigger isn't the event itself but the meaning attached to it.

A long line at the grocery store may frustrate one person because they associate it with wasted time, while another sees it as a chance to check emails. Triggers are subjective and deeply tied to values, expectations, and past experiences.

Triggers often cluster into categories: interpersonal conflict, feelings of disrespect, blocked goals, reminders of past trauma, and physical discomfort. These categories overlap, but seeing them clearly allows someone to identify patterns more quickly.

The Role of Beliefs and Interpretations

What happens after a trigger is just as important as the trigger itself. People don't react to raw events; they react to the interpretation of those events. **Cognitive appraisal** determines whether a situation is seen as insulting, threatening, or unjust. If a coworker interrupts you, you might think they're undermining your competence, or you might assume they're simply enthusiastic. Only the first interpretation sparks anger.

This is why two people can experience the same event and respond differently. Beliefs about fairness, respect, or authority filter every experience. Someone who strongly values punctuality will feel anger when others arrive late, while a person who views time more flexibly may not feel anything beyond mild inconvenience. Identifying triggers, therefore, requires understanding both the external stimulus and the internal story attached to it.

Early Life Experiences

Many personal triggers develop during childhood. If a child grows up in an environment where criticism was harsh, they may become hypersensitive to feedback in adulthood. If anger was modeled as a response to frustration, the person may unconsciously replicate that pattern later. Triggers often reflect the environments in which we learned to evaluate ourselves and others.

Family dynamics, cultural messages, and formative relationships all contribute. Someone who was bullied may be easily provoked by teasing, even when it's meant playfully. Another who grew up in a household where feelings were ignored may become angry when dismissed by a partner. Understanding these roots helps explain why some triggers feel so immediate and intense; they're linked to earlier wounds.

Physiological Sensitivity

Triggers are not only psychological. **Biological factors** influence how quickly someone reacts to stressors. People with high baseline arousal (measured in heart rate or cortisol levels) may perceive threats more quickly. Sleep deprivation, hunger, and hormonal fluctuations lower tolerance for stress. Even minor annoyances can seem intolerable when the body is already under strain.

This means that identifying triggers requires more than listing situations; it also involves tracking physical states. A person may notice they're more irritable when they haven't eaten or when they've been sitting in traffic after work. Recognizing the interaction between body and environment makes it easier to prepare for vulnerable moments.

Mapping Situational Patterns

The most effective way to identify triggers is to map them systematically. Keeping a daily **anger log** allows someone to track situations, thoughts, and physical responses. Over time, patterns emerge. Maybe arguments always happen after long workdays, or maybe specific words like "calm down" escalate tension.

A structured approach often includes:

1. The event (what actually happened).
2. Immediate thoughts (interpretations or judgments).
3. Emotions felt (not just anger but frustration, shame, or fear).
4. Physical sensations (tight chest, clenched fists, flushed skin).
5. Behavior that followed (raised voice, withdrawal, silence).

Once written out, the data often reveals surprising consistencies.

Common Categories of Triggers

Although triggers are personal, they often fall into recurring categories across individuals.

1. Disrespect or humiliation. Being ignored, belittled, or talked over can feel intolerable.
2. Blocked goals. Situations where progress is stalled, like waiting in traffic or facing bureaucracy, often elicit frustration.
3. Injustice. Perceptions of unfairness, whether at work or in relationships, frequently provoke anger.
4. Lack of control. When people feel powerless, anger can surge as a way of regaining influence.
5. Intrusion. Violations of personal space, privacy, or autonomy often become flashpoints.

The specifics differ, but the emotional themes are consistent.

The Interpersonal Dimension

Most anger episodes happen in the presence of others. This makes **relationships** central to understanding triggers. Family members, partners, colleagues, and even strangers often provide the spark. Triggers in relationships tend to be sharper because they tie into attachment needs: the need to feel respected, valued, and secure.

For example, when a partner doesn't respond to a text, one person may shrug it off while another feels dismissed and angry. The difference lies in how much importance is attached to responsiveness. Similarly, workplace hierarchy creates fertile ground for triggers, as issues of status and recognition are magnified.

The Influence of Culture

Culture shapes what is considered triggering. In collectivist cultures, disrespect toward family or group loyalty can provoke intense anger, while in individualist cultures, personal autonomy may be the more sensitive issue. Even within the same society, subcultures dictate what counts as offensive. A joke tolerated in one group may be viewed as deeply insulting in another.

Understanding cultural background helps individuals interpret their own reactions. Without that awareness, they may think their anger is irrational when it is actually rooted in cultural expectations.

The Role of Expectations

Unmet expectations are one of the most reliable triggers. When people expect courtesy, punctuality, or effort, and those expectations aren't met, anger often surfaces. The gap between what is imagined and what is experienced creates frustration.

For instance, if someone expects their colleague to prepare thoroughly for a meeting but finds them unprepared, the violation of standards becomes the source of anger.

This suggests that part of managing triggers involves questioning expectations. Are they realistic? Are they shared by others? Many conflicts arise not because of objective wrongs but because two people hold different assumptions about behavior.

Trigger Escalation Chains

A single trigger rarely stands alone. Often one event leads into another, creating a **chain reaction**. Someone cut off in traffic may arrive home irritated, snap at their partner, and then feel provoked by a small household annoyance. Each link in the chain is influenced by the previous one.

Learning to identify these escalation chains is essential because intervening early can prevent later explosions. Recognizing that traffic often sets the stage for irritability allows a person to pause before the next link in the chain forms.

The Role of Memory and Rumination

Sometimes triggers are not present in the moment but recalled from memory. **Rumination** (replaying past offenses) acts as a trigger in itself. Thinking about a past insult can elicit the same physiological and emotional response as the original event.

This is why unresolved conflicts tend to resurface repeatedly. Even in calm moments, recalling a fight can spark fresh anger.

Identifying rumination as a trigger helps people notice when their own mind is creating anger without external provocation.

A Table of Common Triggers and Interpretations

Category	Example Trigger	Common Interpretation	Typical Emotional Reaction
Disrespect	Being interrupted in a meeting	"They don't value my input"	Anger, resentment
Blocked goals	Long traffic jam	"My time is being wasted"	Frustration, agitation
Injustice	Unequal workload	"This isn't fair"	Irritation, indignation
Lack of control	Sudden policy change at work	"I have no say in this"	Powerlessness, anger
Intrusion	Partner reading texts	"My privacy is violated"	Anger, betrayal
Rumination	Recalling an old insult	"They got away with it"	Renewed anger, bitterness
Physical state	Lack of sleep	"I can't cope right now"	Irritability, short temper

Using Self-Monitoring Methods

Modern technology makes trigger identification easier. Journaling apps, wearable devices that monitor heart rate, and even digital mood trackers allow individuals to see correlations between events and reactions. These tools show, for example, that spikes in heart rate happen during arguments with a supervisor or after scrolling through negative news.

Such data provides objective evidence that can confirm subjective impressions. Instead of vaguely knowing "I get angry at work," someone can see that three out of four weekly incidents occurred after late afternoon meetings.

The Importance of Feedback from Others

Self-awareness has limits. People often miss their own triggers until others point them out. Feedback from partners, friends, or colleagues can reveal blind spots. Someone may not realize they always react angrily when given unsolicited advice until a friend highlights the pattern.

This feedback is most effective when received without defensiveness. It may feel uncomfortable, but others often see patterns more clearly because they observe repeated episodes from the outside.

Gradual Refinement

Identifying triggers is not a one-time exercise. It requires ongoing refinement. As life circumstances change, new triggers appear. Parenthood introduces triggers around children's safety, while career advancement may bring sensitivity to criticism. Aging, health changes, or shifting cultural contexts can also alter what feels provoking.

Over time, individuals build a more accurate internal map of their triggers. This map becomes a guide for anticipating and navigating challenging situations.

Integration with Coping Strategies

Awareness alone doesn't eliminate anger, but it lays the foundation for management. Once triggers are known, strategies like deep breathing, reframing, or setting boundaries can be applied at the right moment. Without identification, coping strategies are used reactively, often too late. With identification, they can be applied proactively, preventing escalation before it begins.

Why This Work Matters

People often say "that made me angry" as if the cause is external. Identifying triggers shifts the focus inward. It acknowledges that anger is not automatic but filtered through personal meanings, histories, and states of mind. This realization restores a sense of control. If you know what sets you off, you can prepare for it, alter your interpretation, or choose a different response.

Physical Cues That Signal Rising Anger

Anger begins as a physiological shift before it ever becomes an outburst. The body doesn't wait for the mind to catch up. Within seconds of perceiving a threat, the **sympathetic nervous system** activates, preparing you for confrontation. Heart rate accelerates, adrenaline pours into the bloodstream, and blood flow diverts to muscles that prepare for action. These responses evolved to keep humans alive in dangerous situations, but in modern life they often fire off during arguments, traffic jams, or workplace disagreements.

Some people feel the change as a wave of heat spreading across the chest or face. Others notice tension in the jaw or shoulders, or a buzzing in the ears.

These sensations aren't random. They're signals of the body gearing up to defend itself, whether the danger is physical or just perceived as disrespect. Recognizing these cues early is one of the most practical ways to keep anger from gaining momentum.

Shortness of breath is a common marker. Breathing becomes shallow because the body prioritizes speed over calm. This shallow breathing further raises anxiety and makes the mind feel cornered, which in turn intensifies anger. The cycle can escalate rapidly if unnoticed. People who learn to spot this change often catch their anger before it peaks, because deepening the breath immediately begins to slow the nervous system down.

Another early sign is **muscle tightening**. The body readies for action by contracting key muscle groups. The jaw clenches, fists close, or the shoulders rise unconsciously. These small adjustments are part of the fight response. Left unchecked, they prepare the body for aggression, even when aggression isn't necessary. Becoming aware of these subtle shifts makes it easier to interrupt the progression with deliberate relaxation or physical release.

Some individuals experience dizziness or lightheadedness. This happens because blood vessels constrict and blood pressure rises. For others, vision narrows. They describe it as tunnel vision, where peripheral awareness shrinks and attention locks onto the source of irritation. Both of these physical cues reflect how the body prepares to focus entirely on a perceived opponent. In an office argument, this can mean losing awareness of tone, context, or even allies in the room, which often worsens the situation.

Here's a table showing different physical signals, how they tend to manifest, and the kinds of outcomes they produce when ignored:

Physical Cue	How It Manifests	Outcome if Ignored
Increased heart rate	Feeling pulse in neck or ears	Reacting faster than intended, impulsive remarks
Shallow breathing	Shortness of breath, tight chest	Rising panic, quicker escalation
Muscle tension	Clenched fists, tight jaw, stiff posture	Aggressive body language, higher chance of lashing out

Heat sensations	Face turning red, warmth spreading	Loud voice, visible signs of anger others pick up on
Sweating	Damp palms, perspiration on forehead	Restlessness, fidgeting, difficulty focusing
Gastrointestinal changes	Upset stomach, nausea	Withdrawal, irritability, short fuse with small issues
Vision narrowing	Loss of peripheral sight, sharp focus	Tunnel thinking, inability to consider alternatives

Every person's body carries a signature set of cues. Some may show most of them at once, others may only experience two or three consistently. The challenge lies in learning to identify your unique pattern and catching it early. Once you know your signals, you can use them as an alarm bell to step back before the reaction overtakes you.

The intensity of cues often scales with the level of provocation. During minor irritations, you might only notice a slightly quicker heartbeat. As anger intensifies, your body recruits more systems into the response.

That's why people often describe the sensation of being "taken over" by anger. It's not just metaphorical. Physiological processes pile up until they dominate attention, narrowing your ability to choose a calm response.

One of the most overlooked cues is voice change. Even before shouting, the vocal cords tighten, pitch rises, and words come out faster. This shift signals to others that anger is brewing, which can either escalate or de-escalate depending on how they respond. If someone points out your voice is rising, instead of reacting defensively, you can treat it as useful feedback that your body has crossed into higher arousal.

Fatigue amplifies physical cues. When the body is tired, it struggles to regulate adrenaline efficiently. A small trigger can lead to exaggerated physical reactions, like a racing heartbeat or uncontrollable restlessness.

This explains why people often lose their temper at the end of the day over issues that wouldn't bother them in the morning. Tracking not just the cues, but also the conditions under which they intensify, provides better control.

Temperature sensitivity can also affect how anger shows up. Hot environments make the body work harder to cool itself, increasing baseline stress levels. Add a trigger, and physical cues appear faster. This is one reason aggression rates increase during heat waves. Recognizing the environmental context helps you separate what's happening inside from what's being imposed by the surroundings.

In some cases, physical cues show up long before the mind labels the feeling as anger. You might notice a throbbing temple or clenched fists without consciously feeling angry yet. By the time you acknowledge "I'm mad," your body has already been signaling it for minutes. Training yourself to pay attention to these earlier cues gives you a longer lead time to intervene.

Noticing physical cues doesn't mean suppressing anger. The goal isn't to deny the emotion but to manage its trajectory. If you feel your jaw clench, you can loosen it deliberately. If your breath shortens, you can take a slow inhale. These micro-adjustments don't erase anger, but they slow the body's escalation so the mind can regain balance. It's like applying brakes on a car rolling downhill.

Many people underestimate how quickly these cues escalate. The transition from mild irritation to full anger can occur in less than ninety seconds if the body isn't regulated. Recognizing cues within the first thirty seconds can change the outcome entirely. That small window makes the difference between walking away and exploding.

Physical cues are also useful for tracking progress over time. As you develop anger management strategies, you may still feel your heart race or your fists tighten, but the recovery time shrinks.

Instead of lingering for an hour, the cues dissipate in minutes. Documenting these changes gives tangible proof of improvement and reinforces the effort to stay aware.

The social impact of physical cues can't be ignored. People around you pick up on clenched fists, flushed faces, and sharp tones even before you say something harsh.

These signals influence how they respond, sometimes defensively, which escalates the conflict further. By calming the body early, you also shift the dynamic with others, preventing them from reacting to visible anger.

Children, in particular, are sensitive to adult physical cues. A parent may believe they're holding their anger in because they didn't yell, but their tightened posture and narrowed eyes send a message anyway. Learning to regulate these physical signs benefits relationships by reducing unspoken tension.

Developing awareness of these signals requires deliberate practice. Some people benefit from body scans, where they periodically pause and notice areas of tension or heat. Others track their reactions after stressful encounters, writing down the physical sensations they remember. Over weeks, the act of paying attention strengthens the connection between body and awareness.

What makes physical cues such an effective focus is their reliability. Thoughts can be slippery and subject to distortion, but the body tends to react consistently. If your chest tightens every time you're criticized, you can count on that cue appearing again. Anchoring your awareness to these reliable signals makes anger management less about guesswork and more about responding to predictable patterns.

Cognitive Distortions That Fuel Anger

Anger often feels like it's born from the outside world, but much of it comes from **distorted thinking patterns**. These distortions change the way you interpret situations, exaggerating offenses and making neutral events appear hostile. The mind runs stories that feel like facts, and once you believe those stories, the emotion intensifies. Understanding these distortions is essential because anger is rarely just about what happened. It's about how your thoughts frame the event.

One of the most common distortions is **mind reading**. This happens when you assume you know another person's intentions without any evidence. If a colleague doesn't say hello in the hallway, you might immediately think, "She's ignoring me because she doesn't respect me."

In reality, she may be distracted or preoccupied with her own stress. The distortion lies in taking limited information and filling in the blanks with the most negative interpretation. Once you've decided the action was deliberate, anger feels justified.

A closely related distortion is **personalization**. This is when you interpret neutral or ambiguous situations as personal attacks. Imagine someone cutting you off in traffic. Personalization turns that into, "He did that to me on purpose because he doesn't care about me." The truth is that drivers cut others off for many reasons, often because they're inattentive or in a hurry. But personalization transforms the event into an insult directed specifically at you. This distortion fuels anger by making the world feel constantly hostile.

Another distortion that magnifies anger is **catastrophizing**. Instead of seeing an event as inconvenient, the mind inflates it into a disaster.

For example, if your partner forgets to pick up groceries, catastrophizing sounds like, "This means they don't care about me, and our relationship is falling apart." The leap from a single oversight to a sweeping conclusion makes anger much more intense. Catastrophizing keeps you stuck in a cycle where small triggers spiral into overwhelming emotional responses.

Overgeneralization works in a similar way, but instead of inflating the severity of one event, it stretches a single instance into a pattern. If a friend arrives late once, overgeneralization creates the thought, "She's always disrespectful, she never cares about my time." This distortion erases nuance and ignores exceptions, locking you into rigid interpretations that breed resentment. When you believe "always" or "never" statements, anger becomes automatic because you're no longer judging isolated incidents.

Black and white thinking also contributes to angry reactions. This distortion divides situations into absolutes: right or wrong, respect or disrespect, friend or enemy. If someone doesn't support your idea, black and white thinking declares them against you. The lack of middle ground leaves no space for flexibility, and when people inevitably fall short of perfection, the only option left is anger.

Some distortions thrive in moments of comparison. **Unfairness bias** is the habit of constantly measuring your treatment against others and concluding you've been slighted. If a coworker gets praised in a meeting and you don't, you may instantly conclude, "They're overlooking me again, it's always unfair." This distortion feeds indignation because it interprets situations through the lens of injustice, even when there may be reasonable explanations.

What makes these distortions dangerous is how quickly they become automatic. Once your brain develops a habit of interpreting events through them, it takes little effort for anger to flare. You might not even notice the thought forming before the emotion surges. The cycle is so fast that people often mistake the emotion as purely instinctive, when in fact it was constructed by a distorted perception.

The table below shows common distortions, how they typically sound in thought form, and the impact they have when left unchecked:

Distortion	Thought Example	Impact on Anger
Mind reading	"He interrupted me because he thinks I'm incompetent."	Creates hostility without evidence, leads to defensive outbursts
Personalization	"She didn't call back because she doesn't respect me."	Turns neutral acts into insults, fuels resentment
Catastrophizing	"This mistake at work means I'll get fired."	Magnifies fear, drives explosive reactions
Overgeneralization	"They always ignore me, nobody cares."	Locks anger into a permanent state, dismisses positive experiences
Black and white thinking	"If he doesn't support me, he's against me."	Eliminates nuance, intensifies confrontations
Unfairness bias	"Others get away with everything, I'm singled out."	Builds chronic anger, nurtures grievance mindset

Recognizing distortions isn't about shaming yourself for having them. Every human mind uses shortcuts to interpret the world, and distortions are exaggerated versions of those shortcuts. The real task is catching them in action before they harden into unquestioned truth.

To weaken distortions, you can test them with questions. For mind reading, ask, "Do I have any proof of their intention, or am I assuming?" For catastrophizing, ask, "What's the most likely outcome, not just the worst-case scenario?" For overgeneralization, you might counter with, "Can I name a single example when this person acted differently?" Each time you question a distortion, you interrupt the automatic path to anger.

Another way to break distortions is by reframing. Instead of telling yourself, "She ignored me because she doesn't like me," you might reframe it as, "She might be tired, distracted, or dealing with her own issues." This doesn't excuse harmful behavior, but it opens up more possibilities and prevents you from locking into the angriest interpretation.

Context influences how distortions appear. When you're stressed, tired, or overwhelmed, the brain defaults to shortcuts. That's when distortions are most likely to run unchecked. A well-rested mind has more capacity to evaluate evidence, while an exhausted one jumps to conclusions. This is why anger management isn't only about monitoring thoughts but also about maintaining the conditions that reduce distorted thinking.

Distortions also interact with personal history. If you've experienced repeated rejection, your mind may lean toward personalization, seeing rejection even where it doesn't exist. If you grew up in a critical environment, you might be especially prone to black and white thinking, constantly scanning for whether you're "good enough." Understanding which distortions you're most vulnerable to helps target them more effectively.

Over time, unchallenged distortions shape identity. A person who repeatedly tells themselves, "Nobody respects me" eventually begins to live as though it's true, interpreting every event as confirmation. This creates a self-reinforcing cycle where distortions feed anger, and anger strengthens distortions. Breaking that cycle requires consistent awareness and correction, much like training a muscle through repetition.

Practical strategies often involve writing distortions down. When you put thoughts on paper, their flaws become clearer.

For example, "Everyone ignores me" looks exaggerated when compared against actual evidence. This externalization helps separate thought from truth. In therapy, this method is often used in **cognitive restructuring**, where the client identifies the distortion, challenges it, and replaces it with a more balanced perspective.

Even small shifts in language matter. Changing "always" to "sometimes" or "never" to "occasionally" reduces the distortion's intensity. These adjustments may seem minor, but they cut down anger by removing the sense of absolutes. Over time, this makes responses less extreme and more proportional.

The influence of distortions isn't only personal. They affect relationships and groups as well. In workplaces, mind reading can create toxic dynamics, where one person assumes hostility and responds with anger, leading to real hostility in return. In families, overgeneralization can trap members in roles they can't escape, like "He's always irresponsible." Recognizing distortions at the group level prevents conflicts from escalating unnecessarily.

What makes cognitive distortions particularly insidious is that they feel convincing. A racing heart might alert you that you're upset, but a thought like "They did this on purpose" feels factual in the moment. That conviction is what fuels angry responses. By training yourself to pause and ask for evidence, you chip away at the illusion of certainty. The more you practice, the less grip distortions have.

Addressing distortions doesn't mean eliminating anger altogether. Anger can be justified when real injustices occur. The goal is ensuring that anger aligns with reality rather than with exaggerated or imagined offenses. A distortion-free interpretation helps you respond with clarity, choosing whether anger is appropriate and how to express it constructively.

Situational Factors That Intensify Reactions

Anger never exists in a vacuum. It's not only about personal triggers or distorted thinking patterns. The environment you're in, the conditions surrounding you, and the context of the moment all contribute to how intensely you react. The same words said by a colleague can sting in one setting but roll off your back in another.

Understanding these **situational factors** gives you a clearer picture of why anger sometimes feels manageable and other times feels explosive.

One of the most significant amplifiers is **fatigue**. When the body and mind are tired, the brain's ability to regulate emotions weakens. The prefrontal cortex, which usually helps put the brakes on impulses, struggles to function effectively. That's why a small annoyance late at night can feel unbearable even though you would brush it off in the morning. Parents often recognize this in themselves and their children, noting that bedtime is when tempers flare most. Fatigue doesn't create triggers, but it magnifies them.

Hunger has a similar effect. Low blood sugar makes it harder for the brain to process situations rationally. Irritability rises, patience thins, and minor frustrations take on exaggerated importance. The term "hangry" has scientific backing. Glucose is the brain's primary energy source, and when it dips, self-control suffers. This is why timing matters. An argument that happens before lunch often feels sharper than one that occurs after a meal.

Stress accumulation also intensifies anger. Imagine carrying the weight of financial concerns, a looming deadline, and relationship tension all at once. Then someone bumps into you in a grocery store. Without the accumulated stress, you might laugh it off. With it, the bump can feel like a personal attack. Stress narrows your capacity, making even small triggers harder to absorb.

Public settings often raise the stakes. Being criticized in front of others carries a heavier sting than receiving the same feedback privately. Public embarrassment threatens social standing, which humans instinctively guard. Anger arises quickly when pride or reputation is challenged. This explains why meetings, classrooms, or group discussions can become heated faster than one-on-one conversations.

Environmental factors like heat, noise, or crowding contribute as well. High temperatures increase baseline irritability because the body is already under strain trying to regulate itself. Research consistently shows that aggression rates rise during hotter months. Noise operates differently. Constant exposure to loud or unpredictable sounds increases stress hormones. Even if you don't consciously register the noise as bothersome, it reduces tolerance for frustration. Crowding has a similar effect. Being packed in close quarters without personal space primes the nervous system for quicker emotional reactions.

The **timing of events** also influences how anger manifests. At the start of the day, your reserves of patience are usually higher. As the day wears on, each small stressor depletes those reserves. By evening, you may have little tolerance left. Timing interacts with other situational factors like hunger or fatigue, creating a perfect storm for explosive responses.

Alcohol or substance use further lowers inhibition. Under normal circumstances, you might feel irritation but stop yourself from reacting aggressively. With alcohol in your system, those filters weaken, and anger expresses itself more freely. This doesn't mean alcohol creates anger, but it strips away the restraint that normally keeps it contained.

Social dynamics have an important role. When you're around authority figures, anger might show up as simmering resentment held in check. Around peers, it may surface more openly. Around subordinates or children, it can emerge even faster because there's less fear of consequence. Social hierarchy shapes how and when anger is expressed. Recognizing this helps you understand why you may feel angrier in some relationships than others, even when the actual triggers are similar.

Technology adds another situational layer. Reading a curt text message without tone or facial cues can easily spark anger, especially if you're already stressed. Misinterpretations multiply in digital communication, where short responses often feel dismissive. The absence of context makes distortions more likely, and anger rises faster because the brain fills gaps with negative assumptions.

It's also important to consider **cultural context**. In some cultures, open disagreement is expected and doesn't provoke much anger. In others, even slight confrontation is seen as disrespectful. When cultural expectations clash, anger escalates because each party perceives the other's behavior through different lenses.

Situational factors can stack on top of each other. Imagine someone is hungry, sitting in traffic on a hot day, late for a meeting, and then gets cut off by another driver. Each element magnifies the next. What might normally be a small annoyance turns into road rage. Without considering the situation, it's easy to mislabel the anger as irrational. In reality, it's the product of multiple conditions converging.

To illustrate the interaction of factors, here's a table outlining some common conditions, how they intensify anger, and the likely behavioral outcomes when ignored:

Situational Factor	How It Intensifies Anger	Likely Outcome if Unchecked
Fatigue	Weakens impulse control, lowers tolerance	Overreacting to minor irritations
Hunger	Low blood sugar reduces patience	Snapping at others, irritability
Public criticism	Threatens social standing	Defensiveness, verbal escalation
Heat	Raises baseline stress	Quick temper, aggressive tone
Noise	Increases stress hormones	Difficulty concentrating, irritability
Crowding	Reduces personal space	Heightened aggression, restlessness
Alcohol	Lowers inhibition	Unfiltered expressions of anger
Stress accumulation	Narrows capacity to cope	Disproportionate reactions to small triggers
Digital miscommunication	Creates ambiguity	Misinterpretation, resentment

One subtle but important situational factor is **anticipation**. Waiting for something negative to happen can make anger appear faster. If you expect your boss to criticize you, you might enter a meeting already tense. When the criticism comes, even if it's mild, your reaction is more explosive because you've been stewing in anticipation.

Situational context also interacts with physical health. Chronic pain, illness, or hormonal changes can alter baseline mood. When the body is already dealing with discomfort, it takes less provocation to tip into anger. This connection often goes unnoticed, yet it explains why people recovering from injury or illness sometimes struggle with irritability.

Relationships create their own situational patterns. Couples often argue most during transitions, like arriving home from work.

The situational factor isn't the relationship itself but the shift from one environment to another, carrying stress across boundaries. Recognizing these predictable contexts allows for planning, such as creating short decompression rituals before engaging in conversation.

Another situational element is **perceived control**. When people feel trapped or powerless, anger rises quickly. Being stuck in traffic, waiting in long lines, or dealing with bureaucratic obstacles often provokes disproportionate anger because the situation highlights helplessness. The inability to change the environment intensifies frustration and narrows emotional options.

The presence of an audience can also influence anger differently depending on personality. Some people become more restrained when others are watching, while others flare up to display dominance.

In either case, the social presence alters the trajectory of anger. Recognizing whether you're someone who suppresses or amplifies emotions in front of others gives insight into how situations shape reactions.

Time pressure compounds the intensity of anger. Being late for a meeting, rushing to catch a flight, or trying to finish a task under deadline primes the body with stress hormones. When an obstacle arises in those moments, anger feels immediate and justified. Without time pressure, the same obstacle might be met with calm problem-solving.

Situational factors don't excuse angry outbursts, but they explain why reactions vary so much. The same person can appear patient in one scenario and explosive in another, depending on the surrounding conditions. By identifying these factors, you gain the ability to anticipate vulnerable moments and prepare responses before anger takes hold.

Practical steps often involve adjusting the environment when possible. Eating regularly, scheduling breaks, reducing background noise, and setting realistic deadlines all reduce the load that situational factors place on your emotional system. While you can't control every condition, you can minimize the ones that amplify anger most consistently for you.

Reflection after angry episodes often reveals patterns. You may notice that outbursts happen more frequently when meetings run long without breaks, when arguments occur late at night, or when conflicts arise in front of others. These aren't coincidences but examples of situational amplification. The more you identify these conditions, the more prepared you are to defuse them.

The ultimate insight is that anger is rarely just about the event itself. It's about the event interacting with the situation in which it occurs. If you only focus on triggers or thoughts without considering context, you miss a large part of the picture. Recognizing situational factors adds depth to your understanding and increases your ability to manage responses effectively.

Journaling and Tracking Patterns

Anger can feel unpredictable in the moment, but when you record it over time, patterns start to appear. **Journaling** gives you a way to externalize what happened, how you felt, and how you reacted. This practice turns raw emotions into concrete information. Instead of remembering only the intensity of the outburst, you see the sequence of events that led up to it. That sequence holds the key to understanding and eventually changing your responses.

The value of journaling lies in detail. A vague note like "got mad at work" doesn't provide much insight. A more specific entry such as "became angry when a coworker interrupted me in the 10 a.m. meeting, noticed my jaw tightening, thought 'they don't value my input,' raised my voice, silence followed" captures the trigger, the physical cues, the thought, the behavior, and the outcome. Each element matters. Together they form a map of your anger episode.

Consistency makes the map clearer. One entry might show you lost your temper in traffic. Another reveals a similar reaction after being interrupted. A third shows irritability at home after a long day.

The common thread may be loss of control, feeling dismissed, or simple exhaustion. Without recording, the link stays invisible. With journaling, you begin to see that your anger doesn't erupt randomly. It clusters around specific triggers and contexts.

The act of writing slows the mind down. Anger is fast and impulsive, but journaling forces reflection. By the time you write the words, the heat of the moment has passed, and you can analyze it more calmly. Over time, this repeated analysis strengthens awareness. You start noticing physical cues earlier, distorted thoughts faster, and situational factors more clearly. Journaling becomes not just a record but a practice that reinforces self-monitoring.

Some people prefer narrative entries, while others find structure more helpful. A simple template organizes information and ensures that nothing is overlooked. It also allows you to compare episodes more easily. Here's a sample table you might use:

Date	Situation	Trigger	Physical Cues	Thoughts	Reaction	Outcome

7/10	Work meeting	Interrupted while speaking	Heat in face, clenched jaw	"They never respect me"	Raised voice	Awkward silence, regret
7/12	Traffic jam	Car cut me off	Heart racing, sweaty palms	"People are selfish"	Honked repeatedly	Arrived still tense
7/13	Evening at home	Kids loud during call	Stomach tightness, shallow breath	"They never listen"	Yelled	Guilt, strained evening
7/15	Grocery store	Long line moving slowly	Tapping foot, sighing	"This is unfair"	Complained aloud	Embarrassment, tension lingered

This table does more than catalog behavior. It highlights repeating themes. In this example, the thoughts often involve respect or fairness. The physical cues vary, but the underlying triggers revolve around control and recognition. Once you spot those themes, you can prepare strategies specifically for them, such as reframing thoughts about respect or practicing relaxation in situations where patience is tested.

Patterns also emerge around timing. You might notice your outbursts cluster at the end of the day, before meals, or during transitions between work and home. This information is actionable.

If evenings are difficult, you can plan decompression time before engaging with family. If hunger amplifies irritability, keeping a snack on hand can prevent escalation. The goal isn't to eliminate every trigger but to build awareness that helps you intervene earlier.

Journaling helps with accountability. When anger strikes, memory often blurs. You may downplay how loud you were or exaggerate how badly others behaved. Writing it down shortly after the event creates a more accurate record. Looking back, you can't easily escape the fact that you yelled or that your thought was "they never listen," even though you know that's an exaggeration. The written word holds you responsible in a way memory alone doesn't.

For those working with a therapist, coach, or support group, a journal provides material for discussion. Instead of describing anger in general terms, you can bring specific examples. This makes guidance more practical and targeted. It also helps others see progress. If your early entries show yelling every time and later entries show you stepping outside or pausing before reacting, the improvement is visible.

It's important not to treat journaling as a punishment or constant reminder of failure. The purpose isn't to dwell on mistakes but to create a tool for growth. Progress is often slow and uneven. You may have several calm days followed by a blowup. That doesn't mean journaling isn't working. It means you're gathering more data about the conditions that challenge you most.

Some people combine journaling with rating scales. You might score the intensity of anger on a scale from 1 to 10, or note how long it took to calm down afterward. These numbers provide another way to track progress. Over time, you may notice that while triggers remain the same, the intensity drops from an 8 to a 5, or the recovery time shrinks from an hour to fifteen minutes. That's measurable improvement.

You can also experiment with adding notes about what you tried to de-escalate. Did you take deep breaths, leave the room, or reframe your thought?

Recording what you attempted, even if it didn't fully work, creates a log of strategies. Reviewing it later shows which techniques help most reliably. It prevents the common mistake of forgetting what worked in calmer moments.

Digital tools can make the process easier. Apps designed for mood tracking allow you to log entries quickly, tag triggers, and generate charts that reveal trends. Some people prefer handwriting because it forces them to slow down, while others value the efficiency of typing on a phone. The format matters less than the consistency. Choose whichever method you'll realistically maintain.

Journaling also helps shift perspective over the long term. When you look back at older entries, you may realize how often you interpreted situations through distortions. What once felt justified may now seem exaggerated. This retrospective view reinforces the idea that anger is shaped by perception and situation, not just by the events themselves.

The process can even uncover hidden triggers you didn't recognize. If multiple entries show anger during transitions, such as leaving work or starting chores, you might realize that shifting contexts stresses you more than you thought. Without documentation, that insight might never surface.

In the end, journaling isn't about eliminating anger altogether. It's about **pattern recognition**.

The more clearly you see the threads connecting triggers, cues, thoughts, and outcomes, the better equipped you are to change the story before it reaches a breaking point. Anger becomes less of an uncontrollable force and more of a process you can anticipate and influence.

Chapter 3: The Science of Emotional Regulation

The Role of the Prefrontal Cortex in Self-Control

The experience of anger feels fast, overwhelming, and sometimes impossible to stop. That sense of urgency comes from the way the brain is wired. The amygdala, a small structure buried deep in the temporal lobe, reacts to threat almost instantly. Its job is to keep you safe, and it doesn't take chances. A raised voice, a dismissive gesture, or an insult can all be registered as threats, even though none of them carry physical danger.

As mentioned earlier, what stands between that raw emotional surge and your behavior is the **prefrontal cortex**, the part of the brain located just behind your forehead. This region is responsible for regulating impulses, judging consequences, and weighing long-term goals. Without it, anger runs unchecked.

The prefrontal cortex isn't one single piece of tissue working alone. It contains different regions that cooperate to manage self-control. The dorsolateral prefrontal cortex allows you to hold thoughts in working memory, which helps you balance what just happened against what matters in the long run. The ventromedial prefrontal cortex connects emotions with values, guiding you toward choices that protect relationships or reputations. The orbitofrontal cortex specializes in evaluating social outcomes, letting you recognize that yelling at your boss may feel good in the moment but will damage your career. These regions work together to apply restraint and perspective, giving you options beyond immediate retaliation.

The main difficulty comes from timing. The amygdala reacts in about 20 milliseconds, while the prefrontal cortex needs a few hundred milliseconds to respond. That gap explains why anger feels like it erupts before you think. By the time the prefrontal cortex engages, your heart is already pounding, your muscles are tight, and adrenaline is circulating. The challenge of self-control lies in shortening the delay and allowing frontal circuits to influence behavior before the body commits to action.

Everyday conditions can weaken the prefrontal cortex. Sleep deprivation reduces its activity and heightens amygdala reactivity, which is why even minor annoyances feel unbearable when you're tired. Alcohol has a direct dampening effect on the frontal lobes, lowering inhibition and letting emotional impulses dominate.

Chronic stress has a longer-term effect. Prolonged exposure to cortisol shrinks prefrontal gray matter and strengthens amygdala connections, creating a brain that reacts quickly and struggles to restrain itself. Even adolescence shows the same imbalance in a different form. The amygdala matures earlier than the prefrontal cortex, which doesn't fully develop until the mid-twenties. Teenagers therefore experience strong emotions with less ability to regulate them.

The encouraging part of the story is that the prefrontal cortex can be trained. The brain is plastic, meaning it changes with use. Cognitive reappraisal, the practice of reframing how you interpret events, reliably increases prefrontal activation. If someone criticizes you and you think "He attacked me," anger flares. If you reframe it to "He may be venting his own frustration," the frontal lobes engage and the amygdala's reaction weakens. Each time you use reappraisal, you reinforce circuits that make future regulation easier. Mindfulness practices work in a similar way. Brain scans of long-term meditators show thicker prefrontal cortices and stronger connections with emotional centers. Controlled breathing also helps by sending calming signals to the nervous system, giving the frontal lobes more time to deliberate.

Working memory exercises strengthen the prefrontal cortex as well. If you can hold multiple perspectives at once, you're less likely to act on impulse. When you remember both the offense and the consequence, restraint is easier. A parent, for example, may feel the urge to yell when a child ignores instructions. Holding in mind the goal of teaching patience alongside the immediate frustration allows the prefrontal cortex to override the impulse to shout.

Real-world examples show how this works. Imagine a colleague dismisses your idea in a meeting. The amygdala interprets it as a threat to your standing, and your body reacts within seconds. If the prefrontal cortex engages, you might think, "If I respond aggressively, I'll look defensive. If I ask for clarification, I might expose his weak reasoning." That shift turns an outburst into a strategic response.

In families, the same process happens when parents resist the urge to yell at children. Regulation doesn't remove anger but channels it into action that protects relationships rather than damaging them.

When the prefrontal cortex is damaged or weakened, the consequences are obvious. Patients with frontal lobe injuries often show poor judgment and uncontrolled anger. The famous case of Phineas Gage, who survived an iron rod passing through his frontal lobes in the 19th century, demonstrated how profound the change can be. Once calm and responsible, he became irritable and reckless, illustrating how essential the prefrontal cortex is for regulating impulses. Modern studies show similar patterns in individuals with violent histories, where reduced frontal volume correlates with difficulty restraining aggression.

To support prefrontal health, lifestyle factors matter. Consistent sleep, limited alcohol, regular exercise, and stress management all help frontal regions function effectively. Practices like reappraisal, mindfulness, and deliberate breathing strengthen the neural pathways that link the prefrontal cortex with the amygdala. Each pause, each reframed thought, each moment of restraint builds the brain's regulatory capacity. Over time, these small acts accumulate into structural and functional changes that make self-control more reliable.

The prefrontal cortex doesn't eliminate anger, and it isn't meant to. Anger can carry useful information, pointing to injustice or unmet needs. The task of regulation is to let the emotion surface without dictating the behavior. A strong prefrontal response means you can express anger calmly, set boundaries effectively, and act without damaging your long-term goals. Without it, you're at the mercy of milliseconds of emotional circuitry. With it, you gain the ability to respond instead of react.

Condition	Effect on Prefrontal Cortex	Impact on Anger
Adequate sleep	Maintains strong regulation	Calmer responses to triggers
Sleep deprivation	Weakens regulation, boosts amygdala	Heightened irritability, quick outbursts
Alcohol	Suppresses inhibition	Aggression and impulsivity
Chronic stress	Shrinks gray matter, weakens connections	Lower threshold for anger
Cognitive reappraisal	Activates frontal areas	Reduced intensity of emotion
Mindfulness practice	Strengthens prefrontal circuits	Greater ability to pause and choose

The science is clear: the prefrontal cortex is the control center that lets you manage anger without suppressing it entirely. Each effort to pause, reflect, and respond strengthens this region's authority. With time, the balance shifts away from uncontrolled eruptions toward thoughtful responses. That shift isn't abstract; it's built into the brain's wiring and can be cultivated deliberately.

Stress Response and Anger: Fight-or-Flight Explained

When people describe anger as coming over them like a wave, they're usually talking about the stress response. The moment you sense threat, whether physical or social, a cascade of biological processes begins almost instantly. At the center of this process is the **hypothalamic-pituitary-adrenal axis**, which links the brain to the endocrine system. The hypothalamus signals the adrenal glands, sitting above the kidneys, to release adrenaline and cortisol. These chemicals prepare the body for immediate action.

This is what's known as the **fight-or-flight response**.

Anger often emerges as the "fight" branch of this system. The body gears up to confront, push back, or defend against what it perceives as danger. Your heart rate jumps, blood pressure rises, blood vessels narrow, and oxygen-rich blood gets redirected toward large muscle groups. Even digestion slows so more energy can fuel quick movement. All of this happens within seconds of the perceived threat. You don't decide to become angry in that moment; your body sets the stage before conscious thought can even weigh in.

The amygdala is the brain structure that kicks this process off. It specializes in rapid threat detection, scanning incoming sensory data for signs of danger. If it perceives a threat, it activates the hypothalamus without waiting for confirmation. This is efficient in life-or-death situations, but in modern life, it creates problems. The amygdala doesn't distinguish between a lion in the grass and an insult in a meeting. Both receive a similar biological reaction. That's why the stress response feels disproportionate to the situation.

Adrenaline acts within moments, speeding up heartbeat and sharpening awareness. Cortisol enters slightly later but sustains the response, keeping you on edge for minutes or even hours. Adrenaline is the sprint, cortisol is the marathon. Together, they make sure your body is primed for survival. The downside is that these hormones don't just heighten readiness. They also narrow focus.

This is why anger often produces **tunnel vision**. You lose awareness of broader context and fixate entirely on the source of frustration.

The physical sensations of the stress response are familiar: heat rushing to the face, clenched fists, sweaty palms, shallow breathing. These are evolutionary signals, preparing you for combat. Yet when these reactions occur in traffic or during a disagreement at work, they no longer serve survival in a literal sense. Instead, they push you toward actions that may damage relationships, reputations, or even physical safety.

An overlooked aspect of the fight-or-flight system is how it differs among individuals. Some people naturally lean toward the fight response. They're quick to raise their voice, argue, or push back physically. Others default toward flight. They withdraw, go silent, or physically remove themselves. Both patterns are products of the same stress machinery, just expressed differently.

Neither is inherently better, but each carries risks. A fight response can escalate conflict unnecessarily, while a flight response can bury anger until it resurfaces later in more destructive ways.

Modern research also highlights the **freeze response**, a kind of paralysis that occurs when neither fighting nor fleeing seems possible. In this state, people may feel overwhelmed, unable to speak, or frozen in place.

While it doesn't look like anger, the freeze response can mask it. The body is still flooded with stress hormones, and once the freeze subsides, anger often emerges suddenly and explosively.

Situations that repeatedly activate fight-or-flight change the brain over time. Chronic stress strengthens amygdala circuits while weakening the prefrontal cortex. This rewiring makes the stress response easier to trigger and harder to regulate. That's why people under prolonged stress often feel "on edge" and more prone to anger. Their bodies have adapted to constant readiness, making even minor irritations feel threatening.

There's also a reward element built into this system. The adrenaline rush associated with fight responses can feel energizing, even intoxicating. Some people unconsciously seek conflict because it delivers stimulation. That doesn't mean they enjoy the consequences, but their bodies have learned to crave the hormonal surge. Recognizing this helps explain why some individuals seem to manufacture anger-inducing situations.

To understand how this process unfolds, imagine being cut off in traffic. The amygdala detects the sudden movement as a potential threat. Adrenaline spikes, making your heart race and hands tighten on the wheel. Cortisol follows, keeping you agitated even after the car has moved ahead. Without intervention, you may honk, shout, or drive aggressively. Yet the danger was minimal. The stress response mobilized as if your survival was at stake.

The timeline of the stress response is important. Adrenaline peaks quickly but fades within a few minutes. Cortisol lingers much longer. This means the initial explosion of anger often fades quickly, but the sense of irritability remains. Many people mistake this lingering cortisol-driven tension as proof that the original offense was severe, when in reality it's just biology keeping the body alert.

Repeated activation of the stress response damages health. Chronic cortisol elevation contributes to hypertension, cardiovascular disease, weakened immunity, and weight gain. Anger, when expressed frequently, isn't just a social problem; it becomes a medical one. The link between unregulated anger and heart attacks is well established, with episodes of intense anger doubling the risk of cardiac events in the following hours.

The context of the trigger determines how the stress response unfolds. If you're in a public setting, social evaluation amplifies the fight response. Being criticized in front of others feels more threatening than in private. The body mobilizes more intensely because social standing has evolutionary importance. If you're already fatigued or hungry, the stress response also escalates more quickly. Energy depletion reduces the brain's ability to apply restraint.

You can see the stress response as a chain: stimulus, amygdala activation, hormone release, physiological changes, emotional experience, behavior. Each link provides a point of possible intervention. If you wait until behavior, the chain is almost complete, and stopping it requires enormous effort. If you intervene earlier, recognizing physical cues or reframing thoughts, you prevent the cascade from reaching full intensity.

Here's a way to organize how the fight-or-flight system interacts with anger:

Stage of Stress Response	What Happens in the Body	Impact on Anger
Threat detection	Amygdala flags danger	Immediate sense of being provoked
Hormonal surge	Adrenaline released, cortisol follows	Rapid arousal, readiness for action
Physical preparation	Heart rate, blood pressure, muscle tension increase	Feels like a wave of anger building
Cognitive narrowing	Tunnel vision, loss of context	Fixation on offense, reduced perspective
Emotional labeling	Body sensations interpreted as anger	Justifies aggressive response

Behavioral action	Shouting, aggression, withdrawal	Determines outcome of the conflict

By breaking it down, it becomes clear that anger isn't just an emotion but a biological sequence. Each stage provides opportunities for awareness and regulation. Recognizing a racing heartbeat as an early warning signal can give you a chance to breathe deeply and engage the prefrontal cortex before behavior is set in motion.

Different strategies target different stages. Breathing exercises lower physical arousal, calming the body so the prefrontal cortex can catch up. Reappraisal works at the cognitive stage, shifting interpretation from "he disrespected me" to "he's stressed and lashing out." Physical removal targets the behavioral stage, reducing the chance of escalation when earlier interventions weren't possible.

Even though the stress response is automatic, it isn't fixed. People who train regularly in awareness techniques show reduced amygdala activation and quicker prefrontal engagement.

Over time, the brain learns to react less intensely to the same triggers. This doesn't eliminate the stress response but makes it less overwhelming.

In children, the stress response develops gradually. Younger children have strong amygdala reactions but weaker prefrontal control, so tantrums are essentially unregulated fight responses. As children grow and the prefrontal cortex matures, they gain more ability to manage these surges. Adults, however, can regress under stress. When the frontal cortex is overtaxed, even grown individuals can display tantrum-like anger, driven by the same primitive system.

Understanding fight-or-flight also clarifies why anger sometimes feels disproportionate to the situation. The body mobilizes as if survival is at stake. The mismatch between the actual threat and the biological response is what makes anger so destructive in modern contexts. By learning to recognize this mismatch, you can begin to separate the physical surge from the decision of how to act.

The fight-or-flight response is universal, but its expression varies. Some cultures encourage direct confrontation, channeling fight responses into open anger. Others discourage outward displays, pushing responses inward and increasing the likelihood of chronic stress. Neither approach eliminates the underlying biology. What changes is how the stress-driven anger is expressed and whether it damages health or relationships.

The science of fight-or-flight shows that anger isn't just a matter of "bad temper." It's a product of ancient systems working in modern contexts. Knowing how these systems work allows you to anticipate, interrupt, and redirect anger before it becomes destructive.

Emotional Awareness vs. Emotional Suppression

Anger is one of the most difficult emotions to manage because it comes with both mental and physical intensity. The question most people struggle with is what to do once it arrives. Some people attempt to notice and understand it, while others try to push it away and deny it. These two strategies, **emotional awareness** and **emotional suppression**, have radically different outcomes for the mind and body. Understanding the difference between them, and the science behind each, is central to managing anger in healthy ways.

Awareness begins with acknowledgment. When you say to yourself, "I feel anger in this moment," you've already created space between you and the emotion. This simple step matters because it activates regions of the brain associated with self-regulation, particularly the prefrontal cortex. Research using fMRI scans has shown that labeling emotions reduces activity in the amygdala, the part of the brain that generates raw fear and anger responses. By noticing and naming the emotion, you prevent it from overwhelming your ability to think clearly. Suppression works in the opposite direction. It doesn't decrease the amygdala's activity, but it increases physiological arousal in the body.

When people suppress anger, they often appear calm on the surface, but heart rate, blood pressure, and muscle tension remain elevated. The nervous system continues to operate in fight-or-flight mode even though the outward signs are hidden.

Over time, this hidden activation damages the cardiovascular system, raises the risk of hypertension, and keeps the body in a state of chronic stress. Awareness avoids this problem because it doesn't require hiding the emotion. It allows the body to process what's happening without creating additional strain.

The choice between awareness and suppression has consequences for relationships as well. When you're aware of anger, you can express it in controlled ways, such as stating calmly that you felt dismissed or disrespected. This type of expression communicates needs while preserving the relationship.

Suppression, on the other hand, often leads to **leakage**. The anger doesn't disappear; it seeps out in sarcasm, passive-aggressive remarks, or sudden explosive outbursts. Partners, colleagues, and friends usually sense the tension, even if you think you've hidden it.

An important distinction lies in energy expenditure. Suppression requires constant effort, like holding a beach ball underwater. The moment your focus slips, the anger bursts through. Awareness requires less effort. By acknowledging the emotion and observing it, you allow it to rise and fall naturally. The energy that would have gone into suppression can instead be used for problem-solving, empathy, or constructive action.

The difference is stark when examined in experimental settings. In one study, participants asked to suppress anger during a film showing disturbing content showed increased physiological stress, while those asked to label their emotions showed calmer responses. Suppression also impairs memory because holding emotions down consumes cognitive resources that could be used elsewhere. Awareness doesn't burden memory in the same way because it integrates the emotion into conscious thought rather than hiding it.

Awareness doesn't mean indulgence. Some people fear that acknowledging anger will make it stronger. In fact, awareness allows the emotion to be observed without judgment, which reduces its intensity. The practice of **mindful attention** illustrates this. When individuals notice anger as a wave of sensations (heat in the chest, tightness in the jaw, rapid breathing) they often find it loses some of its grip. It becomes an experience they can watch rather than a force that controls them. Suppression lacks this benefit because it denies those sensations and resists them, which paradoxically keeps them alive longer.

Suppression also tends to backfire socially. In workplaces, suppressed anger often emerges in gossip, subtle undermining of colleagues, or withdrawal from team efforts. Leaders who habitually suppress anger create climates of tension because employees can sense the unspoken hostility. Awareness allows for more direct, respectful conversations about frustrations, which build trust rather than erode it. Families operate in a similar way. Suppressed anger between partners creates a background of irritability that children notice. Awareness, even if uncomfortable, models honesty and teaches children how to recognize emotions without shame.

Suppression carries another hidden cost: it distorts communication. When you hide anger, your words often conflict with your nonverbal signals. You might say "I'm fine" while your tone, posture, or facial expression communicates irritation. This mismatch confuses others, leading to misunderstandings. Emotional awareness reduces this dissonance. When you acknowledge anger openly, your words and body language align, which improves clarity and reduces conflict.

The physiological differences between awareness and suppression can be organized in a clear way:

Strategy	Brain Activation	Body Response	Social Consequence	Long-Term Effect
Awareness	Engages prefrontal cortex, lowers amygdala activity	Reduced arousal over time	Clearer communication, healthier relationships	Builds resilience and emotional intelligence
Suppression	Sustains amygdala activity, reduces prefrontal engagement	Elevated heart rate, blood pressure, muscle tension	Passive aggression, sudden outbursts	Increases risk of stress-related illness

Anger management programs often teach awareness as a first step. Journaling, for example, forces you to notice emotions and put them into words. This act alone reduces intensity because it requires prefrontal engagement. Breathing exercises also encourage awareness. By focusing on the rise and fall of your breath, you notice how anger affects your body in real time. This awareness then provides a chance to intervene before the emotion drives behavior. Suppression, by contrast, delays intervention until the pressure becomes too great, at which point it bursts uncontrolled.

Awareness also creates opportunities for learning. When you notice and record your anger, you start seeing patterns. You may discover that interruptions, disrespect, or certain environments consistently provoke strong reactions. With this knowledge, you can anticipate triggers and prepare responses. Suppression hides these patterns, because if you deny the anger, you also deny the chance to study it. Over time, suppression keeps you blind to the roots of your own reactions.

Culturally, suppression has often been encouraged. Many workplaces and families reward people who appear calm no matter what. In some cases, people are told that anger itself is unacceptable, which reinforces suppression.

The result is that anger doesn't disappear; it moves underground. This cultural tendency makes awareness difficult because people fear judgment if they admit to being angry. Yet cultures that normalize awareness and direct expression show lower rates of chronic stress and healthier conflict resolution.

Awareness isn't comfortable, though. Facing anger means confronting feelings of vulnerability, shame, or fear that often lie underneath. For many, suppression feels easier in the moment because it avoids this discomfort. But the price of comfort is high. Suppression may spare short-term awkwardness, but it multiplies long-term consequences. Health deteriorates, relationships suffer, and self-understanding weakens.

Children provide a clear window into this difference. A child taught to notice anger learns to say, "I'm mad because you took my toy." This statement gives parents a chance to address the problem constructively. A child taught to suppress anger may stay silent, then lash out later by breaking the toy or hitting a sibling.

Adults mirror this same dynamic. Suppression produces delayed, often disproportionate expressions of anger, while awareness makes immediate but manageable communication possible.

Awareness also interacts with memory in important ways. When you acknowledge an emotion, your brain integrates it into memory with context. You recall not just that you were angry but why. Suppression fragments memory. People who habitually suppress often struggle to recall the reasons behind their outbursts. They only remember the explosion, not the buildup. This makes growth harder because you can't adjust what you don't remember.

In clinical contexts, suppression is associated with depression and anxiety. The constant effort to hide emotions creates internal conflict and drains mental energy. Awareness, in contrast, is associated with improved mental health outcomes, greater resilience, and better problem-solving skills. This is why therapies like cognitive behavioral therapy and mindfulness-based stress reduction emphasize awareness rather than suppression.

The biology behind suppression shows why it's so costly. When you suppress, the sympathetic nervous system stays activated, keeping heart rate and blood pressure high. The parasympathetic system, which calms the body, doesn't get a chance to do its job. Awareness allows the parasympathetic system to engage, slowing breathing and lowering arousal. This isn't just subjective calmness; it's measurable physiological recovery.

Anger management, then, isn't about eliminating the emotion but choosing awareness over suppression. Awareness allows anger to be experienced, understood, and directed. Suppression denies anger, magnifies its impact on the body, and undermines relationships. The choice between them determines whether anger becomes destructive or constructive. By training awareness through labeling, mindfulness, and reflection, you build a foundation for healthier responses.

Breathing and Physiological Regulation Techniques

Anger is not just an emotion that lives in the mind. It is a whole-body event that mobilizes muscles, accelerates heart rate, changes blood chemistry, and sharpens attention in ways that prepare for confrontation.

When the body reacts this way, the mind follows. This is why efforts to regulate anger that only focus on thoughts often fail. The body must be addressed directly. Breathing is the most accessible and reliable way to influence physiology in real time. It gives you leverage over systems that usually operate automatically, such as heart rhythm and stress hormone release.

The science of breathing begins with the autonomic nervous system. This system has two major branches: the sympathetic branch, which activates during stress and triggers fight-or-flight, and the parasympathetic branch, which promotes recovery and calm. Breathing links both systems.

When you inhale, the sympathetic branch becomes more active. When you exhale, the parasympathetic branch strengthens its influence. This means that slowing and lengthening your exhalations tilts the body toward calm, directly counteracting anger's arousal.

The vagus nerve acts as the main highway for this influence. Running from the brainstem through the heart, lungs, and digestive system, the vagus nerve carries signals that regulate bodily states. When you breathe slowly and deeply, sensors in the lungs send messages through the vagus nerve that tell the brain to ease up on the stress response. Heart rate slows, blood pressure drops, and muscles relax. This chain reaction makes it possible to shift from explosive anger to manageable irritation, creating space for the prefrontal cortex to take control.

Different breathing techniques tap into these mechanisms in distinct ways. One of the simplest is **diaphragmatic breathing**. Instead of shallow breaths from the chest, which reinforce stress, diaphragmatic breathing involves expanding the belly and filling the lower lungs. This maximizes oxygen exchange, slows respiration rate, and sends stronger calming signals to the brain. People practicing diaphragmatic breathing often notice within minutes that their heart rate steadies and their mind feels less pressured.

Another technique is **box breathing**, named because the pattern resembles four equal sides. You inhale for a set count, hold, exhale for the same count, then hold again. A common pattern is four seconds for each stage. The rhythm creates structure, which the brain interprets as stability. Military and law enforcement personnel often use box breathing to stay calm in high-stress environments. For anger regulation, it provides a disciplined way to interrupt escalating physiological arousal.

A variation that focuses more directly on anger is **extended exhalation breathing**. You inhale briefly, then exhale slowly for twice as long. For example, a three-second inhale followed by a six-second exhale. This heavily engages the parasympathetic system because long exhalations emphasize vagal influence. It works particularly well in moments when you feel your chest tightening or your pulse racing. The extended exhale signals to the body that the danger has passed, even if the situation remains tense.

Breathing is most effective when practiced regularly, not just in moments of crisis. Training your body to respond to slow breathing creates familiarity. Over time, the association between controlled breathing and calm becomes automatic, making it easier to use when anger rises.

Athletes, musicians, and performers already use this principle. They practice breathing routines outside of competition or performance so that the skill is ingrained when pressure mounts. Anger management benefits from the same rehearsal.

One challenge people face when using breathing techniques is remembering to apply them in the middle of anger. The surge of adrenaline narrows focus, and controlled breathing may not come to mind. This is why cues are helpful. Some people set reminders on their phones or place sticky notes in common trigger locations like cars or desks. Others practice short breathing sessions several times a day, so it becomes second nature. The more automatic the response, the more likely it will surface during anger.

There is also value in combining breathing with posture. When anger rises, the body tends to hunch, shoulders tighten, and muscles brace. If you straighten your posture, relax your shoulders, and then breathe deeply, the calming effect is amplified. This works because posture itself influences the nervous system. A tense body tells the brain that threat is present. A relaxed body tells the brain that the environment is safe enough to lower arousal.

Another physiological regulation technique linked to breathing is **heart rate variability training**. Heart rate variability, or HRV, refers to the natural variation in time between heartbeats. High HRV reflects strong parasympathetic influence and resilience to stress. Low HRV reflects vulnerability to emotional overload. Breathing at a pace of about five to six breaths per minute maximizes HRV. Devices and apps now provide feedback, showing users in real time how their breathing influences HRV. People who train this way report greater emotional stability and less frequent angry outbursts.

The influence of breathing extends beyond the immediate calming effect. Regular practice changes brain structure. Studies show that long-term mindfulness practitioners who emphasize breath awareness have thicker prefrontal cortices and stronger connections between the prefrontal cortex and amygdala. This means their brains are literally rewired to regulate anger more effectively. Breathing practice becomes not just a temporary intervention but a long-term investment in emotional regulation capacity.

Some might argue that breathing is too simple for such complex emotions. But simplicity is the strength. In the middle of conflict, you can't always step away to analyze cognitive distortions or consult a journal. You always have your breath. It's portable, requires no equipment, and works quickly. That reliability makes it indispensable for anger management.

To appreciate the difference between regulated and unregulated breathing, consider this scenario. You're in traffic, already running late, and another driver cuts you off. Your heart jumps, jaw tightens, and your hands grip the wheel.

If you continue breathing shallowly from your chest, your body interprets the situation as a battle, fueling further anger. If you deliberately shift to slow belly breathing with long exhalations, your heart rate begins to drop. Within a few cycles, your perspective changes. The offense is still irritating, but it no longer feels like a personal attack requiring retaliation. The physiological shift creates space for mental flexibility.

Breathing also interacts with language. If you pause to take a deep breath before speaking, you delay the impulse to lash out. That pause is not just symbolic. It's physiological time for cortisol to begin receding and for the prefrontal cortex to weigh in. Many conflicts escalate not because of the initial feeling of anger but because of words spoken too quickly under its influence. A few controlled breaths change the trajectory of the interaction.

Children can learn these techniques as well. Teaching a child to "blow out candles" on their fingers or to imagine inflating a balloon in their belly creates a playful approach to diaphragmatic breathing. These methods give children tools to regulate before tantrums peak. Adults benefit from similar simplicity. You don't need elaborate routines. Even one slow inhale and exhale can begin to shift physiology in the right direction.

Below are several techniques and their specific effects on anger regulation:

Technique	How It Works	Physiological Effect	Application
Diaphragmatic breathing	Expands belly and lower lungs	Slows heart rate, increases oxygen exchange	General daily practice and acute anger
Box breathing	Equal inhale, hold, exhale, hold	Stabilizes nervous system, creates rhythm	High-stress situations requiring focus
Extended exhalation	Inhale shorter, exhale longer	Activates parasympathetic system strongly	Rapid anger surges, panic moments
HRV training	Breathing at 5–6 breaths per minute	Increases heart rate variability, resilience	Long-term regulation capacity building
Posture combined with breath	Relax shoulders, open chest, deep breaths	Reduces muscle tension, signals safety	Social conflicts, meetings, family disputes

Breathing is not the only path to physiological regulation, but it is the foundation. Other techniques build on it. Progressive muscle relaxation involves tensing and releasing muscle groups while breathing steadily, which releases stored tension from anger. Cold exposure, like splashing water on the face, activates the diving reflex that lowers heart rate and resets the nervous system. Exercise burns through adrenaline and cortisol, restoring balance after an angry episode. Yet each of these works best when combined with controlled breathing.

The effectiveness of breathing has been demonstrated in diverse contexts. Police officers use it to stay calm during confrontations. Surgeons use it to maintain steady hands in the operating room. Athletes use it to recover focus under pressure. If it can regulate performance in these high-stakes environments, it can certainly regulate anger in everyday life.

The habit of breathing also shapes perception. When you breathe slowly, you notice more details in your environment. This broader awareness counters the tunnel vision of anger.

You begin to see not only the offense but also the other person's stress, the overall situation, and your own long-term goals. The breath doesn't just calm the body; it opens the mind to alternatives.

Breathing is sometimes dismissed as a cliché recommendation, but in the science of anger management, it is a precise intervention targeting the autonomic nervous system. It interrupts the chain of escalating physiology and buys time for the prefrontal cortex to engage. The simplicity of the practice is matched by its depth of impact. It is not about pretending the anger doesn't exist but about creating the conditions where anger can be expressed constructively rather than destructively.

The bottom line is that breath is the lever through which you influence your body's readiness for anger. With shallow, rapid breaths, you intensify it. With slow, deep, deliberate breaths, you ease it. Over time, practicing controlled breathing rewires both body and brain for calmer responses. It is the bridge between physiology and self-control, always available, always effective, and always worth practicing.

Building Tolerance to Frustration

Anger often emerges when expectations collide with reality. Someone drives too slowly when you're late, a colleague doesn't deliver on time, or technology malfunctions at the worst possible moment.

These situations trigger frustration, which acts like dry kindling for anger. When frustration tolerance is low, the smallest obstacle feels unbearable and the stress response ignites. Building tolerance to frustration is therefore one of the most practical ways to reduce anger's grip.

Frustration is different from stress. Stress comes from overload, while frustration comes from blockage. You have a goal or need, and something stands in the way. That obstacle can be external, like traffic, or internal, like fatigue or lack of focus. The brain perceives blocked goals as threats, activating the same systems that respond to danger. The amygdala fires, adrenaline surges, and the prefrontal cortex must decide whether to escalate or regulate. The lower your tolerance for frustration, the more often escalation wins.

Children illustrate this clearly. A toddler denied a toy will throw a tantrum because their tolerance is underdeveloped. Adults who never strengthen frustration tolerance behave in similar ways, though usually in subtler forms. They snap at cashiers, curse at traffic, or lash out at coworkers. These reactions reveal an inability to endure blocked goals without melting into anger. Fortunately, tolerance is not fixed. It can be expanded through deliberate practice.

One pathway to tolerance lies in expectation management. When expectations are rigid and absolute, frustration rises quickly. If you believe every meeting should run smoothly and end on time, you will be perpetually annoyed. If you recognize that delays and disruptions are normal, frustration decreases. Adjusting expectations doesn't mean lowering standards. It means building flexibility into your thinking so that obstacles aren't treated as catastrophes.

Another pathway is emotional regulation training. When you face frustration, your body sends physical signals: tight chest, clenched jaw, heat in the face. By practicing awareness of these cues, you can intervene before anger peaks.

Techniques like diaphragmatic breathing or pausing before responding don't erase frustration but allow you to endure it without exploding. The more often you practice this endurance, the larger your frustration tolerance becomes.

Deliberate exposure also builds tolerance. Psychologists call this **stress inoculation**. You place yourself in mildly frustrating situations and practice calm responses. Waiting in longer lines intentionally, driving in traffic without turning on music, or attempting difficult puzzles all serve as training. Each time you stay composed, your brain learns that frustration can be endured. Over time, your threshold rises, and situations that once provoked anger barely register.

Cognitive strategies help as well. Many frustrations are magnified by distorted thoughts. Overgeneralization turns one delay into "nothing ever goes right." Personalization transforms a traffic jam into "the universe is against me." By identifying and correcting these distortions, you reduce the intensity of frustration. Thought restructuring takes practice, but it becomes automatic with repetition.

Social skills influence tolerance too. People who lack assertive communication often feel powerless, which makes frustration more painful. If you can calmly state needs and set boundaries, obstacles feel less overwhelming.

For example, if a colleague consistently misses deadlines, assertiveness allows you to address the issue directly rather than stewing in silent anger. Communication becomes a release valve for frustration before it erupts.

Resilience research shows that tolerance also depends on lifestyle. Sleep, nutrition, and exercise strengthen the prefrontal cortex, improving regulation. When you are well rested, nourished, and physically active, you can withstand more frustration without breaking down. When you are depleted, even small obstacles provoke disproportionate anger. Tolerance is partly about mindset, but it is also about biology.

Relationships provide constant opportunities to practice frustration tolerance. No partner, friend, or coworker will always meet your expectations. The ability to accept imperfections without reacting angrily determines the quality of those relationships. People who demand perfection create tension. People who allow room for mistakes build trust. Tolerance doesn't mean ignoring repeated problems, but it means addressing them with calm persistence rather than angry outbursts.

The workplace offers another training ground. Projects run late, clients change requirements, and colleagues disagree. Low tolerance leads to frequent conflict and poor collaboration. High tolerance allows you to absorb obstacles and redirect energy toward solutions. Managers who model tolerance set the tone for their teams, reducing anger contagion in group settings.

Frustration tolerance can be understood in stages. At the first stage, even small obstacles provoke immediate anger. At the second stage, you feel frustration but delay reaction briefly. At the third stage, you can endure longer delays or repeated obstacles without escalation. At the fourth stage, you reframe frustration as part of growth or challenge. People can move through these stages with practice. The key is consistency and reflection.

The following table outlines strategies and their direct effects on tolerance:

Strategy	Mechanism	Effect on Frustration Tolerance
Expectation flexibility	Reduces rigidity of thought	Lowers frequency of frustration
Awareness of physical cues	Detects escalation early	Creates opportunity to regulate
Stress inoculation	Gradual exposure to obstacles	Expands threshold for endurance
Cognitive restructuring	Corrects distorted thinking	Reduces exaggerated reactions
Assertive communication	Restores sense of control	Prevents buildup of hidden anger
Healthy lifestyle	Supports brain regulation	Strengthens ability to stay calm

Tolerance is not about becoming indifferent. It is about increasing the space between trigger and response. In that space lies the ability to choose action rather than be driven by impulse.

Each time you resist snapping in traffic, you lengthen that space. Each time you breathe instead of yelling, you expand your threshold. **Over weeks and months**, this accumulation makes frustration less threatening.

It is also important to recognize limits. Tolerance should not mean enduring abuse or chronic injustice. Anger can be appropriate in the face of genuine harm. The purpose of tolerance is not to erase anger but to prevent it from erupting at every inconvenience. It ensures that anger is reserved for situations that truly require it rather than being wasted on minor frustrations.

Children raised with guidance on tolerance develop better emotional regulation later in life. Teaching a child to wait for a turn, to lose a game gracefully, or to complete a task without immediate reward strengthens their tolerance. Adults can practice the same skills by delaying gratification, resisting distractions, and working through challenges without shortcuts. These small acts build a foundation for enduring larger frustrations without anger.

Frustration tolerance is closely tied to patience. Patience is not passive waiting but active endurance. It involves recognizing that obstacles are temporary and that reacting with anger will not remove them faster. Patience grows from the repeated decision to remain composed under strain. The more often you practice patience, the stronger your tolerance becomes.

In the end, building tolerance to frustration is less about suppressing feelings and more about training endurance. It is a skill, like lifting weights. Each repetition of staying calm under stress strengthens the neural circuits that regulate anger. Over time, situations that once triggered outbursts become manageable. What changes is not the world but your capacity to endure it without losing control.

Understanding Emotional Thresholds

Every person has a limit, a point at which accumulated stress, frustration, or provocation tips over into anger. That point is the **emotional threshold**. It functions like a container. Some people have large containers, able to absorb many irritations before reacting. Others have smaller ones that overflow quickly. Understanding your own threshold, and what raises or lowers it, is essential for managing anger effectively.

Thresholds are not fixed. They vary day to day depending on sleep, nutrition, stress, environment, and even recent experiences. A person who slept well, exercised, and ate a balanced meal may tolerate a long line at the grocery store without issue. That same person, running on little sleep and skipping breakfast, might explode at a minor delay. The difference is not personality but threshold capacity.

The nervous system governs much of this variation. The sympathetic branch primes the body for action, while the parasympathetic branch restores balance. If sympathetic activation dominates, thresholds lower because the body is already on high alert. If parasympathetic influence is strong, thresholds rise, giving more room to absorb provocation before reacting. This balance can shift rapidly depending on circumstances.

Past experiences also shape thresholds. People who grew up in volatile households may develop lower thresholds because their nervous systems became conditioned to respond quickly to threat. Others raised in calmer environments may have higher thresholds because they never learned to perceive everyday stressors as urgent. Thresholds therefore carry both biological and learned components.

Awareness of thresholds starts with noticing patterns. Do you lose patience more quickly at certain times of day? Do specific people lower your tolerance faster than others? Do accumulated small irritations lead to one large outburst? Recognizing these patterns is the first step toward managing thresholds.

A useful way to conceptualize thresholds is as a **bank account of emotional energy**. Each stressor is like a withdrawal. Sleep, rest, and recovery are deposits. If you enter a situation with a depleted account, even a small withdrawal can overdraft, triggering anger. If you enter with a full account, you can withstand multiple withdrawals without losing composure. This analogy emphasizes the importance of daily habits in raising thresholds.

Nutrition, exercise, and sleep directly impact threshold capacity. Low blood sugar makes the brain less effective at regulating impulses, lowering tolerance. Exercise releases endorphins and strengthens regulation circuits, raising tolerance. Sleep restores prefrontal cortex function, which acts as the brake on impulsive reactions. When these elements are neglected, thresholds shrink.

The environment plays a major role as well. Crowding, noise, heat, and constant stimulation all drain emotional energy. They reduce the margin of error and make anger more likely.

By contrast, quiet, spacious, and orderly environments replenish energy and raise thresholds. This explains why vacations often feel calming even if nothing dramatic changes in life circumstances. The environment itself raises the threshold.

Another dimension of thresholds is accumulation. One frustration may not reach the tipping point, but repeated frustrations accumulate until the threshold is crossed. People often misinterpret the final event as the cause of anger when it was actually the accumulation of many smaller irritations. Recognizing this accumulation prevents misplaced blame.

Individual differences also matter. Some people naturally have higher thresholds due to temperament. These individuals tend to be less reactive, more adaptable, and slower to anger. Others are more reactive by nature, with lower thresholds and faster emotional surges. Both types can learn regulation skills, but the starting point differs.

You can measure thresholds informally by observing how long it takes before anger shows up under provocation. Journaling can reveal this over time. For example, if you record three minor irritations before losing your temper one day and seven on another, you begin to see how conditions affect your threshold. This helps you anticipate vulnerable periods. **There's also a link between thresholds and health**. Chronic illness, pain, or fatigue lower thresholds because the body is already under stress. Hormonal fluctuations can produce similar effects. This means that thresholds must be understood not only as psychological but also as physiological.

Coping strategies increase threshold capacity. Techniques like controlled breathing, mindfulness, and reappraisal all raise the amount of provocation you can tolerate before anger emerges. Social support also increases thresholds. People who feel supported by friends, partners, or colleagues can endure greater stress without breaking down, because they know help is available. Isolation reduces thresholds because every stressor feels heavier when carried alone.

The following table illustrates how various factors influence thresholds:

Factor	Effect on Threshold	Mechanism

Sleep quality	Raises threshold when adequate, lowers when deprived	Restores prefrontal regulation
Nutrition	Stable blood sugar raises threshold, low glucose lowers	Supports brain function and impulse control
Exercise	Raises threshold	Releases endorphins, reduces baseline stress
Environment	Calm and quiet raises threshold, noise and crowding lower	Alters baseline arousal
Social support	Raises threshold	Provides emotional buffering
Chronic stress	Lowers threshold	Strengthens amygdala, weakens prefrontal cortex
Accumulation of irritations	Lowers threshold	Builds until tipping point

Threshold awareness also helps in relationships. If both partners recognize when their thresholds are low, they can avoid difficult conversations until conditions improve. Saying, "I've had a draining day, let's talk later," prevents conflict by acknowledging a low threshold. Without this awareness, minor disagreements can escalate into full arguments simply because tolerance was depleted.

In workplaces, threshold management determines culture. Leaders with low thresholds create climates of fear and reactivity, where employees walk on eggshells. Leaders with high thresholds create stability, absorbing pressure without passing it down. This stability improves collaboration and reduces turnover. Teams benefit when members understand not only their own thresholds but also those of colleagues.

Cultural expectations influence thresholds too. Some cultures encourage emotional expression, which can provide small releases that prevent thresholds from being breached. Others encourage suppression, which allows pressure to build until it explodes. The cultural model of emotional expression shapes how thresholds are managed at a group level.

An overlooked dimension is recovery. After anger, thresholds take time to reset. If recovery is incomplete, thresholds remain lower, making the next outburst more likely. This creates cycles where frequent anger shortens thresholds even further. Rest, exercise, and reflective journaling are necessary to restore capacity.

Children again provide a clear example. A child may tolerate losing one game but not two in a row. With coaching and reassurance, the child learns to handle repeated frustrations, raising their threshold over time. Adults undergo the same process when they practice endurance, patience, and reappraisal in frustrating situations.

Raising thresholds doesn't mean never getting angry. It means pushing the tipping point further away, giving you more time to choose how to respond. A raised threshold transforms anger from an immediate explosion into a manageable feeling. With practice, thresholds can be expanded steadily, turning volatile reactivity into stable composure.

Chapter 4: Practical Techniques for Calming Down

Progressive Muscle Relaxation

When anger builds, the body doesn't stay neutral. Muscles tighten, posture stiffens, and tension spreads from the jaw to the shoulders to the chest. This physical readiness for confrontation happens automatically, part of the body's preparation for action.

Progressive muscle relaxation, or PMR, gives you a direct way to counter that buildup by engaging the body's natural rhythm of tension and release. It works by deliberately tightening specific muscle groups, holding them for a short period, and then releasing them while noticing the sensation of relaxation. What makes PMR effective for anger is that it directly interrupts the physical state that fuels aggressive thoughts.

The technique was first developed in the 1920s by Edmund Jacobson, a physician who believed that physical relaxation could reduce emotional stress. His research showed that people who learned to contract and release muscles systematically experienced lower levels of anxiety, irritability, and physical complaints.

Over time, PMR became widely used in clinical settings, from stress management to chronic pain treatment. In anger regulation, the technique provides a structured method for calming the body before emotions escalate beyond control.

The process begins by focusing on one muscle group at a time. You might start with the hands, clenching them tightly for about five seconds. During this phase, tension builds, mimicking the natural tightness anger creates. Then, you release completely, allowing the hands to relax for ten to fifteen seconds. The contrast between tension and release trains the nervous system to recognize what relaxation feels like. You then move systematically through the body, covering arms, shoulders, face, chest, stomach, legs, and feet. By the time you finish, the entire body has shifted from readiness for confrontation to a state of calm.

The science behind PMR connects to the autonomic nervous system. Contracting muscles activates the sympathetic branch, the same branch that powers the fight response. Releasing them, especially with awareness, activates the parasympathetic branch, which calms the body. Cycling through tension and release essentially gives the body a rehearsal of anger's physical arousal followed by an intentional downshift. Over time, this builds faster access to calm in real situations.

People often underestimate how much anger is carried in the face. Jaw clenching, brow furrowing, and tight lips all intensify the feeling of being on edge. PMR specifically targets these muscles. For example, you can press your lips together firmly, hold, then release. Or raise your eyebrows as high as possible, hold, then let them fall. These small exercises reduce the subtle muscle activity that reinforces the emotional experience of anger.

Consistency matters. Practicing PMR daily trains the nervous system to shift gears quickly. At first, it may take twenty minutes to complete the full sequence. With practice, you can run through a shortened version in two or three minutes during stressful situations. Some people eventually learn to focus on a single muscle group, like shoulders, to trigger a whole-body calming response. This becomes particularly useful in meetings, arguments, or public settings where time is limited.

One benefit of PMR is that it provides feedback. When you tense and release muscles, you often realize how much unconscious tension you carry. Many people discover they keep their shoulders lifted or their jaw tight without noticing. By making the contrast explicit, PMR raises awareness of physical states that feed anger. Once noticed, these patterns can be interrupted throughout the day.

Clinical studies have shown measurable effects. People practicing PMR regularly report reduced blood pressure, lower resting heart rate, and improved sleep quality.

In anger management programs, PMR is often introduced early because it gives participants a tangible skill. Even those skeptical about meditation or therapy often find value in the physical routine of tightening and releasing muscles.

The technique is versatile. You can use a long form, moving systematically from head to toe, or a short form focusing on key areas like jaw, shoulders, and fists. You can also adapt it to context. At a desk, you might tense and release your legs discreetly. In a heated conversation, you might relax your shoulders while taking a slow breath. The flexibility of PMR makes it usable in many environments.

Parents sometimes teach children simplified versions, such as pretending to squeeze lemons in their fists, then dropping them. This playful framing helps children connect with the idea of tension and release. Adults benefit from similar imagery. Imagining squeezing stress out of muscles as you release can deepen the calming effect.

The process of PMR also overlaps with mindfulness. When you focus on the sensations of tension and release, your attention stays anchored in the body. This prevents rumination on angry thoughts. The body becomes the focus, giving the mind a chance to reset. For people who find traditional meditation difficult, PMR offers a concrete, physical entry point to the same calming effect.

There are challenges too. Some people find it hard to remember the sequence during moments of anger. Others feel self-conscious doing the exercises in public. This is why practice in calm settings is important. Rehearsing the technique at home or during daily routines builds familiarity so it surfaces automatically when needed.

The following table outlines different ways PMR can be practiced and what each variation achieves:

Variation	How It's Done	Effect on Anger Regulation

Full body sequence	Tense and release all major muscle groups from head to toe	Produces deep overall relaxation, best for daily practice
Short sequence	Focus on 3–4 groups like jaw, shoulders, fists	Calms body quickly in stressful moments
Targeted release	Relax one tense area such as shoulders while breathing deeply	Prevents escalation during conversations or meetings
Guided PMR	Use audio instructions to follow sequence	Enhances focus for beginners or during high stress
Child-friendly version	Use imagery such as squeezing lemons or making robot muscles	Teaches children frustration control early

PMR also integrates well with other anger management techniques. When paired with breathing, it accelerates calming because both the muscular and respiratory systems send safety signals to the brain. When combined with visualization, it helps you imagine releasing not just tension but also the grip of anger itself. This layering of techniques creates stronger and faster results.

In long-term practice, PMR does more than prevent explosions. It recalibrates the baseline. People who use PMR regularly often describe feeling less irritable overall. Their container of tolerance becomes larger, meaning their threshold for anger rises. This effect emerges because the nervous system learns to spend more time in calm states and less time in readiness for conflict.

PMR also shows the link between body and mind. Many assume anger is only about thoughts, but the body carries equal weight. By intervening physically, you remind yourself that emotions are embodied experiences.

This realization broadens your options. If you can't think your way out of anger in a given moment, you can act your way out by relaxing the body.

For people dealing with chronic anger, PMR offers hope because it demonstrates that change is possible through practice. Anger doesn't have to dictate the body's state indefinitely. With deliberate cycles of tension and release, the body learns new patterns, and those patterns influence emotions. The process requires consistency but yields measurable shifts in both physiology and behavior.

PMR may look simple, but its impact runs deep. It taps into the body's wiring, trains awareness, and builds resilience. Used daily, it prepares you for stressful situations by giving you a reliable method to step back from the edge. Used in the heat of anger, it provides a lifeline back to calm. The technique illustrates one of the central truths of anger management: by learning to regulate the body, you gain control over the mind.

Mindful Breathing and Meditation Practices

When anger surges, most people try to reason their way out of it. They argue with themselves, attempt to silence the inner dialogue, or push the feeling aside. The problem is that anger doesn't begin in thoughts alone. It begins in the body with rapid heartbeats, shallow breathing, and tightened muscles. To calm anger effectively, the body must be addressed directly, and the most immediate doorway is through **breath**. Breathing is both automatic and voluntary. You don't need to think about it, but you can control it whenever you choose. This unique feature makes it the fastest route to influencing the nervous system and opening the mind to calmer responses.

Mindful breathing isn't just about slowing down. It's about paying attention to each inhalation and exhalation with full awareness. The act of noticing the breath anchors attention in the present moment.

Anger often pulls you into the past, replaying insults or offenses, or into the future, imagining consequences and retaliations. Breath awareness brings you back to now, where you have more control. The simple instruction, "Breathe in, know you're breathing in. Breathe out, know you're breathing out," interrupts mental spirals and re-centers awareness.

The nervous system responds quickly. Inhalation activates the sympathetic branch, which increases alertness. Exhalation activates the parasympathetic branch, which calms. When you extend and slow the exhale, the parasympathetic influence grows stronger, reducing heart rate and muscle tension.

Within a few cycles, the entire body shifts from readiness for confrontation to recovery. This isn't speculation. Studies measuring heart rate variability, blood pressure, and cortisol levels consistently show reductions after even five minutes of mindful breathing.

Meditation builds on this principle. While breathing is the anchor, meditation trains the mind to notice thoughts and emotions without reacting to them. Anger thrives on reactivity. A thought appears ("He insulted me") and the body launches into arousal. Meditation introduces a pause. You notice the thought as a thought, not as an absolute truth. That pause is the opening where self-control lives. Without it, anger has free rein. With it, you can choose your next move.

One common practice is **breath counting meditation**. You count each inhale and exhale up to ten, then begin again. When anger distracts you and you lose track, you return to one. The counting provides structure, helping you stay focused when the mind tries to wander back to the offense.

Another practice is **noting**. When a thought of anger arises, you simply label it: "anger, anger." Labeling activates the prefrontal cortex, reducing the amygdala's intensity. It doesn't deny the feeling but puts it into perspective.

Meditation also strengthens brain circuits over time. Imaging studies show that regular meditators have thicker prefrontal cortices and reduced reactivity in the amygdala. This structural change translates into functional resilience. The more you meditate, the less easily anger hijacks your system. The practice rewires the brain to support calm responses even in situations that once triggered explosive reactions.

Daily meditation doesn't need to be lengthy to create benefit. Ten minutes of focused breath practice can reset the nervous system and build long-term tolerance. What matters most is consistency. Anger management requires skills that surface

(The benefits of meditation have been known since ancient civilizations, where practices in India, Tibet, and China taught individuals to regulate anger through disciplined attention and breath control. These traditions viewed emotional restraint not as suppression but as mastery, training the mind to observe anger without acting on it and maintain inner stability.)

automatically in heated moments, and automaticity comes from repetition. Just as athletes drill simple moves until they're instinctive, meditators practice daily until calm responses emerge without conscious struggle.

Some people worry that meditation means suppressing anger, but that's a misunderstanding. Meditation isn't about pushing anger away. It's about observing it fully without immediately reacting. By seeing anger clearly, you reduce its control.

For example, in meditation you might notice heat in the chest, tightness in the jaw, and the thought, "They don't respect me." You don't push these away. You note them, breathe with them, and let them shift on their own. This observation weakens the compulsion to act destructively.

Meditation can also be combined with visualization. One practice involves imagining anger as a storm passing through. You observe clouds forming, wind rising, then slowly settling. Another involves picturing the breath as a calming wave washing tension out of the body. These images help translate abstract emotions into experiences the mind can relate to physically, making them easier to regulate.

Below let's summarize different forms of mindful breathing and meditation and their direct benefits for anger regulation:

Practice	How It's Done	Immediate Effect	Long-Term Effect
Simple breath awareness	Focus on inhalation and exhalation	Anchors attention, slows arousal	Builds capacity for present-moment focus
Extended exhale breathing	Inhale normally, exhale twice as long	Strong parasympathetic activation	Faster recovery from anger episodes
Breath counting	Count breaths from 1 to 10, repeat	Reduces distraction, provides structure	Improves sustained attention under stress
Noting practice	Label thoughts or feelings as they arise	Activates prefrontal cortex, reduces reactivity	Builds habit of observing rather than reacting
Visualization with breath	Imagine waves, storms, or calming images with each breath	Adds imagery to relaxation	Increases resilience by linking calm states to symbols

In real situations, mindful breathing can shift outcomes dramatically. Imagine you're in a heated argument. Your heart races, voice rises, and fists clench. If you continue unchecked, words will likely be spoken that can't be taken back. If, instead, you pause, lower your shoulders, and take three slow breaths with long exhalations, your body begins to calm. That pause may be enough to shift your words from attack to explanation. The conflict softens because the physiology behind it has been interrupted.

Mindful practices extend beyond formal sessions. Micro-meditations (pausing for one slow breath before answering the phone, walking to a meeting with awareness of each step, or noticing the rise and fall of breath while waiting in line) build cumulative calm. Each micro-practice raises your baseline tolerance, making anger less likely to surge later.

Children can learn mindful breathing through simple imagery. Asking them to imagine blowing up a balloon in their belly or smelling a flower and blowing out a candle introduces the mechanics of diaphragmatic breathing. Adults benefit from the same simplicity. You don't need elaborate instructions to regulate anger. A single deep inhale and a slow exhale, done with awareness, is often enough to create space for choice.

Meditation also helps with the aftermath of anger. After an outburst, many people feel shame or regret, which can spiral into more frustration. Sitting quietly, noticing breath, and observing these secondary emotions helps prevent them from compounding. Instead of suppressing regret, you observe it, which allows it to pass more quickly. This prevents cycles of self-criticism that often sustain anger over time.

Group meditation amplifies the effect. Practicing in a class or community provides structure and accountability. It also normalizes the experience of struggling with distraction or irritation during practice.

People often find it easier to persevere when they see others working through the same challenges. In anger management groups, meditation sessions create shared calm that carries over into discussions.

There are limitations too. In moments of extreme anger, it can be difficult to remember to breathe mindfully. The surge of adrenaline pushes the body toward action, not reflection. This is why practice during calm periods is essential. With repetition, mindful breathing becomes automatic, surfacing even under intense pressure. Without prior practice, it may feel inaccessible when needed most.

Meditation doesn't need to be spiritual or tied to any belief system. While many traditions include it, the practice itself is secular and evidence-based. It is simply the training of attention and awareness. Framing it in scientific terms often helps those skeptical of mindfulness engage with it as a practical technique rather than a mystical one.

In professional settings, mindful breathing has been shown to improve emotional regulation among nurses, teachers, and law enforcement officers. These roles involve constant exposure to stress and potential conflict. Workers who practiced daily breathing meditation reported fewer angry reactions and more patient interactions. The practice doesn't change external stressors but changes the internal capacity to meet them calmly.

Ultimately, mindful breathing and meditation practices give you leverage over anger at its root. By regulating breath, you calm the body. By observing thoughts, you free the mind from automatic reactivity.

Together, they expand the space between trigger and response, turning moments of potential explosion into opportunities for deliberate choice. With consistent practice, anger shifts from an uncontrollable force to an emotion you can experience fully without being ruled by it.

Visualization and Mental Reframing

Anger is often fueled by the pictures you hold in your mind and the way you interpret what those pictures mean. Someone cuts you off in traffic, and your brain immediately paints them as an arrogant person who disrespects you. A co-worker interrupts you, and your mental image becomes one of deliberate sabotage.

These mental frames generate emotional fuel, and once the picture locks in place, the anger feels justified.

Learning to **visualize differently** and to **reframe mentally** is one of the most effective ways to calm down because it changes the story before the body commits to full arousal.

Visualization works because the brain reacts to imagined events almost as strongly as to real ones. Athletes have long used imagery to improve performance, but the same mechanism can regulate emotion. If you repeatedly picture yourself responding calmly to provocation, your nervous system rehearses that calmness. When the moment arrives, the body follows a pattern it already knows. By contrast, if you constantly imagine exploding in rage, that's the script the body rehearses. Changing the inner film changes the outer response.

One of the simplest visualizations involves imagining anger itself as a **physical substance** leaving the body. Some people picture steam venting from the top of their head with each exhale. Others imagine a dark cloud dispersing from the chest. The brain registers this image as release, and muscles loosen in response. Another approach is to visualize a safe, calming environment. A beach, forest, or quiet room works, as long as it carries personal meaning. By mentally transporting yourself into that setting, you give the nervous system cues of safety, which reduce the drive to fight.

Mental reframing adds another layer. While visualization changes inner imagery, reframing changes interpretation. A common trigger for anger is the assumption of **intentional harm**.

For instance, when someone doesn't return a call, it's easy to frame it as disrespect. Reframing means deliberately considering other explanations. Maybe the person was overwhelmed, distracted, or dealing with something unseen. This doesn't excuse the behavior, but it shifts the meaning from personal attack to situational difficulty. The moment you reframe, the anger loses some of its intensity.

Reframing also applies to self-talk. Many people interpret mistakes as catastrophic and respond with anger toward themselves. Reframing turns "I failed again" into "I learned something useful." This change of frame doesn't erase accountability but replaces destructive anger with constructive motivation. Self-directed anger often lingers longer than outward anger, and reframing is essential for interrupting those cycles.

In high-stakes environments, reframing has proven measurable effects. Police officers trained in reframing suspect behavior report fewer escalations in confrontations. Instead of interpreting every act of defiance as deliberate disrespect, they practice seeing it as fear, confusion, or miscommunication. The physiological difference between those frames is enormous. Disrespect prompts adrenaline surges, while miscommunication prompts problem-solving. The shift prevents unnecessary force and preserves emotional stability.

Visualization and reframing also work together. Consider a scenario where you receive a critical email late at night. The first image that may arise is the sender smirking with superiority. Anger surges. You can replace that image with a visualization of the person under pressure, typing quickly, exhausted. Then you reframe the act, telling yourself, "This might not be about me at all." The combination weakens the original anger and leaves space for measured action.

The table below outlines several visualization and reframing strategies with their distinct effects on anger:

Technique	How It Works	Example	Emotional Effect
Releasing imagery	Imagine anger leaving the body as steam, smoke, or color	Exhaling a dark mist with each breath	Creates sense of physical relief
Safe-place imagery	Picture a calming environment with sensory detail	Visualizing walking along a quiet forest path	Signals safety, reduces fight-or-flight
Role reversal	Visualize being the other person in the conflict	Seeing the situation through their eyes	Increases empathy, reduces hostility
Alternative story reframing	Replace negative interpretation with situational explanation	"They ignored me" becomes "They might be overwhelmed"	Lowers perceived threat, reduces anger
Self-talk reframing	Change inner dialogue from self-blame to learning	"I blew it again" becomes "I'll try a different approach next time"	Shifts anger into problem-solving energy
Forward projection	Visualize the consequences of acting in anger	Seeing the fallout of yelling at a partner	Inhibits impulsive response

Role reversal is particularly striking. When you deliberately picture yourself as the other person, occupying their body and seeing through their eyes, anger often softens. This doesn't mean you excuse harmful behavior, but the exercise highlights the humanity on the other side. Even imagining being a driver in traffic who didn't see your car can reduce road rage significantly. The act of perspective-taking rewires the experience from personal offense to shared fallibility.

Another useful visualization is **forward projection**. Anger thrives on short-term focus. You want to lash out now. Projecting forward forces you to imagine the next hours, days, or weeks. If you visualize yourself shouting, then replay the likely fallout —strained relationships, regret, lingering tension—the mind registers the cost. The urge weakens because you see beyond the immediate release. Conversely, if you visualize yourself staying calm and resolving the conflict, you reinforce the benefits. This practice trains the brain to weigh outcomes before acting.

Visualization is flexible. It can be practiced formally, sitting with eyes closed and focusing for ten minutes, or informally, in the heat of the moment.

At work, if a colleague's comment sparks irritation, you can silently imagine placing the anger into a box and setting it on a shelf. That image gives just enough distance to respond without edge. In family disputes, picturing loved ones as younger versions of themselves (children vulnerable and learning) can soften harsh reactions. The imagery shifts perspective in ways logic alone can't.

Mental reframing benefits from language precision. Words like "always" and "never" exaggerate events and magnify anger. Reframing replaces them with concrete descriptions. Instead of "You never listen," you might reframe to "You didn't listen this time." The difference is dramatic. The first frame implies permanent disrespect; the second points to a solvable event. Cognitive therapists often teach clients to spot absolute words and replace them with situational phrasing to reduce anger intensity.

Cultural reframing can also help. In some traditions, anger is viewed not as personal failure but as an energy to be transformed. Reframing anger as energy rather than defect changes how people engage with it.

Energy can be redirected, while defect leads to shame. By shifting from "I shouldn't feel this way" to "I can redirect this energy," people maintain dignity while calming down.

Reframing is most effective when paired with bodily awareness. If you feel your shoulders rising and breath quickening, you can reframe the physical signals themselves. Instead of saying, "I'm losing control," you reframe to "My body is preparing to act, but I don't need to act yet." This interpretation prevents panic about the feeling of anger and reduces secondary frustration.

Children can learn reframing through storytelling. When a child says, "He pushed me because he hates me," you can guide them to consider, "Maybe he wanted the toy too." The reframing doesn't remove accountability but broadens interpretation. Adults use more complex narratives, but the principle is identical: shifting meaning reduces anger's grip.

In negotiation settings, reframing can change outcomes entirely. If one side interprets firmness as hostility, the discussion derails. By reframing firmness as commitment to values, negotiators prevent anger escalation. Mediators often function as reframing guides, translating hostile statements into constructive frames. Observing this process shows how much emotional tone depends on the lens through which events are interpreted.

Another advanced visualization involves **color breathing**. You imagine inhaling a calming color, such as blue or green, and exhaling a harsh one, like red or black. The imagery ties directly to cultural associations with color, and the brain reacts to the symbolic shift. This practice has been used with trauma survivors to reduce anger flare-ups during therapy, giving them an accessible tool in moments of high stress.

Mental reframing isn't about lying to yourself. It's not pretending harmful actions are acceptable. It's about widening interpretation to reduce automatic hostility. If you're cut off in traffic, reframing doesn't mean saying, "That was fine." It means saying, "I don't know their story, and it may not be personal." The difference matters, because when you drop the assumption of personal attack, anger loses its sharpest edge.

Some people find reframing easier when writing. Keeping a journal of anger triggers, then rewriting the story from a different perspective, strengthens reframing skill. For example, an entry might begin with, "My colleague humiliated me in front of the team." The reframed version could be, "My colleague interrupted because they were anxious to prove themselves." Reading both versions side by side reveals how dramatically interpretation alters emotional tone.

Visualization and reframing are not always immediately effective in extreme anger, just as mindful breathing may feel inaccessible in the heat of the moment. For this reason, practice during calm states is critical. By rehearsing images of release and reframing stories when calm, you build a library of responses that surface more naturally when needed. Anger management depends on preparation, not improvisation.

Over time, consistent use of visualization and reframing changes the baseline of anger reactivity. Instead of defaulting to hostility, the mind defaults to alternative stories and calming images. The shift isn't about never feeling anger. It's about preventing anger from dictating behavior. With these practices, you become able to experience the surge without being swept away by it.

Counting and Time-Out Strategies

Anger thrives on speed. It pushes the body to act before the mind has caught up, which is why so many people regret their words or actions once the moment passes. Slowing the process even slightly can make all the difference between escalation and calm. That is the logic behind **counting techniques** and **time-out strategies**, two classic methods that interrupt anger by giving space for reflection. Both are simple, but their effects on physiology and thought are powerful.

Counting is often introduced in childhood, yet many adults underestimate its depth. The basic instruction is to **count slowly to ten** before reacting. While simple, the practice combines cognitive redirection, rhythmic breathing, and impulse control in one motion. Each number spoken or thought creates a micro-pause, giving the prefrontal cortex time to weigh options instead of letting the amygdala dictate a reflexive response. The slow cadence also encourages longer exhalations, which naturally activate the parasympathetic nervous system. Counting isn't childish; it is a neurological brake.

Different versions of counting exist. Some people prefer to count backward from ten to one, which requires slightly more mental effort and therefore diverts attention more effectively from the trigger. Others count in pairs, such as "one and one, two and two," which extends the rhythm and deepens the pause. Advanced variations involve synchronizing each number with a breath, stretching the process into a miniature meditation. The numbers themselves don't matter. What matters is that the mind becomes occupied with structure instead of spiraling in anger.

Time-out strategies extend the principle of slowing down into physical space. Taking a **time-out** doesn't mean avoiding conflict forever. It means deliberately leaving the immediate setting long enough to cool down and return with clarity. Research shows that when people step away from an anger-inducing situation for as little as twenty minutes, physiological arousal such as heart rate and adrenaline levels drop substantially. Once those markers fall, rational thought improves and the likelihood of aggression decreases.

Time-outs can be structured or informal. A structured time-out is common in therapy, especially in couples counseling. Partners agree on a signal word or phrase, such as "pause," which means both commit to disengage temporarily rather than continue fighting. This agreement prevents one partner from interpreting withdrawal as abandonment. Instead, both know the pause is a commitment to return calmer. Informal time-outs can be as simple as walking outside, going to another room, or taking a short drive. The principle is consistent: create distance between the trigger and the reaction.

Counting and time-outs reinforce each other. Counting works when the body is still but the mind is racing. Time-outs work when the environment itself is too stimulating for thought to settle. A heated argument in a crowded living room may need both: first count to avoid blurting something damaging, then take a time-out to reduce physiological arousal.

Below are several approaches to counting and time-out strategies and their specific effects:

Strategy	How It Works	Example	Effect on Anger
Counting forward	Simple sequential count to ten	Silently counting "one... two... three..."	Creates pause, slows reaction
Counting backward	Requires extra focus, engages working memory	Counting down from 10 to 1	Distracts brain from trigger, enhances control
Counting with breathing	Syncing each number with an inhale or exhale	Inhale "one," exhale "two"	Combines rhythm with calming breath
Extended counting	Repeating numbers or using longer sequences	"One and one, two and two"	Deepens pause, lengthens delay
Mini time-out	Brief withdrawal from trigger for a few minutes	Stepping outside after a tense remark	Reduces immediate arousal
Extended time-out	Longer removal until full calm returns	Taking an hour apart during conflict	Allows physiological reset
Prearranged signal	Shared agreement to pause conflict	Saying "pause" during heated discussion	Prevents escalation, ensures mutual understanding

Counting is effective because it restores the gap between stimulus and response. Psychologists often refer to this as the **freedom interval**. Without it, anger decides. With it, choice returns. Each second spent counting is a reclaimed fragment of freedom. The repetition also reinforces a sense of self-control. Even if the anger remains, the knowledge that you managed to delay its expression builds confidence. Over time, this reduces the fear of being overwhelmed by emotion.

Time-outs have additional layers. Physical withdrawal not only calms the body but also alters perspective. Conflict often feels absolute when you are in the middle of it. Stepping outside, hearing different sounds, or seeing a different view resets context. What felt unbearable indoors can feel manageable with distance. This shift doesn't erase the issue but reduces the emotional charge enough to approach it with less hostility.

Critics sometimes claim that time-outs are avoidance. That perception is only true when people never return to address the problem. A healthy time-out has a clear endpoint. The goal is to come back and continue the conversation with clarity. Couples who misuse time-outs by storming out indefinitely create more tension. Those who treat time-outs as part of respectful dialogue report greater relationship satisfaction.

Counting and time-outs also train the brain for **delayed gratification**, a skill strongly tied to emotional regulation. When you count or step away, you resist the short-term satisfaction of an angry outburst in favor of long-term outcomes such as preserved relationships or professional reputation. Neuroscience shows that the same circuits involved in resisting an impulse to spend money or eat unhealthy food are engaged when resisting anger. Practicing delay strengthens those circuits across domains.

Practical integration of these methods depends on environment. In professional settings, overt time-outs may be difficult. Counting silently during a tense meeting can serve as a hidden form of regulation. Even a short pause before responding to an aggressive email counts as a digital time-out. In family life, explicitly teaching children to use counting helps normalize it. Parents who model counting aloud when frustrated teach regulation through example.

One advanced adaptation is **layered time-outs**. This involves taking several pauses at increasing intervals. For instance, if anger flares, you might count to ten, then take a five-minute break, then revisit the issue after an hour. The layers ensure that no single pause must fully resolve the anger. Instead, each pause reduces intensity, allowing gradual descent from peak arousal.

Counting can also be linked to **visualization techniques** for greater impact. A person might picture a traffic light while counting. At "one," the light is red, representing stop. By "five," it shifts to yellow, signaling caution. At "ten," the light turns green, meaning it's safe to move forward with words or action. The imagery reinforces patience and aligns with a familiar symbol of control.

In high-stress professions such as emergency medicine or law enforcement, time-outs may not always be possible. Here, micro time-outs are useful. Taking three controlled breaths, closing eyes briefly, or focusing on a neutral object for ten seconds functions as a compressed time-out without leaving the scene. These micro strategies demonstrate that time-outs are not about duration alone but about intentional interruption.

Counting and time-outs can fail if misapplied. Counting too quickly or with sarcasm ("one, two, three!" shouted in anger) defeats the purpose. Time-outs used as punishment or silent treatment damage trust.

The key is intention. Counting must be slow, deliberate, and tied to calm breathing. Time-outs must be framed as opportunities to cool down, not weapons to control or punish.

The strength of these methods lies in accessibility. They require no equipment, no special training, and no lengthy preparation. They can be practiced in a boardroom, classroom, or kitchen. Their simplicity makes them easy to dismiss, but simplicity is exactly why they work. Anger is impulsive, fast, and blunt. The antidotes are pauses, space, and time.

Children often adopt counting first, but adults refine it with maturity. A child may loudly count to ten when upset, while an adult may silently count backward from fifty while taking measured breaths.

Both are using the same principle: slowing the surge. Parents who reinforce counting as legitimate rather than childish help children retain the tool into adulthood.

In relationships, time-outs are best paired with communication agreements. For example, partners may agree that any time-out must be followed by a check-in after thirty minutes. This creates accountability and reassures both sides that withdrawal isn't abandonment. Over time, the practice builds trust because both partners know escalation can be halted without permanent rupture.

In personal growth, these strategies contribute to broader resilience. People who master the pause report fewer regrets, fewer damaged relationships, and less self-directed anger.

The pause becomes a symbol of autonomy: proof that you are not bound by emotion alone. This sense of mastery encourages further emotional growth, reinforcing the cycle of self-regulation.

Counting and time-outs show that anger management doesn't always require complex techniques or extended therapy. Sometimes it requires nothing more than patience measured in numbers or a short walk outside. The brain, given even a sliver of time, is remarkably good at cooling itself. By choosing to count or step away, you invite that cooling process to unfold.

Using Physical Activity to Dissipate Anger

Anger is an energy-loaded emotion. When it rises, the body releases adrenaline, heart rate quickens, and muscles tense as if preparing for a fight. If this energy has nowhere to go, it lingers, fueling rumination and making small triggers feel larger than they are.

Physical activity provides a safe outlet for this surge of energy, helping to restore balance to both body and mind. Rather than trying to suppress anger or letting it explode outward, moving the body transforms that internal pressure into motion that reduces tension.

Exercise changes anger physiology almost immediately. When you walk, run, or engage in another activity that raises the heart rate, your breathing becomes deeper and steadier. This activates the parasympathetic nervous system, which calms the fight-or-flight response. Muscles that were tense begin to loosen, blood vessels dilate, and stress hormones start to drop.

Endorphins, the body's natural pain relievers and mood elevators, also release during exercise. This chemical shift moves the body out of a state of agitation and into one of recovery.

Different types of physical activity can serve different purposes. **Aerobic exercise** such as jogging, cycling, or swimming is particularly effective because it mimics the body's natural response to stress. Since anger prepares the body for action, completing a bout of sustained movement gives the nervous system closure, as if the "prepared for battle" state has finally been completed and resolved. Even a brisk 15-minute walk can shift the intensity of anger to a calmer baseline.

Strength training can also be helpful, but in a different way. Lifting weights or doing pushups channels anger into bursts of effort. The strain on muscles gives a direct outlet for tension that often builds up when frustration simmers. People who feel a need to "burn off" anger often find that pushing against physical resistance provides relief that's both immediate and satisfying.

Mind-body practices like yoga, tai chi, or martial arts offer another angle. These combine controlled movement with breath regulation and mental focus, teaching people to stay grounded in their bodies even while releasing energy. A person who's angry may begin a yoga session feeling tight and restless but leave with a calmer mind because each pose demanded both strength and balance. Martial arts can be especially effective since they provide structure, discipline, and movement patterns that simulate aggression in a controlled environment without harm.

The act of walking is one of the simplest and most accessible forms of using movement to dissipate anger. Taking a walk outdoors adds extra benefits because of exposure to natural light, fresh air, and changing scenery. These cues help the brain shift attention away from ruminative thoughts. When the mind loops on "what they said" or "what I should have done," rhythmic movement paired with new surroundings interrupts that loop, creating mental distance from the trigger.

Some people worry that vigorous activity while angry will intensify the emotion. This can happen if the exercise becomes an outlet for dwelling on hostile thoughts. For example, punching a bag while replaying insults may strengthen the sense of grievance rather than reduce it. The key is to focus on the physical act itself—how muscles feel, how breath steadies, how movement unfolds—rather than mentally rehearsing the cause of anger. When exercise is done with awareness, it acts as a release rather than a rehearsal of hostility.

The social dimension of physical activity also matters. Joining a sports team, running group, or workout class creates a supportive environment where energy is shared and directed. Anger often isolates people, making them withdraw or lash out. Exercising with others offers connection, distraction, and shared effort, which can replace the lonely intensity of anger with a sense of belonging. Even casual conversations during or after a game can help diffuse lingering irritation.

The role of **routine** should not be underestimated. Regular exercise builds a buffer against chronic anger by lowering overall stress levels and improving mood stability. People who exercise consistently report fewer outbursts and recover more quickly when conflicts arise. The body learns to process adrenaline more efficiently, and the mind develops a habit of release instead of suppression. This means that exercise isn't only a short-term fix but also a long-term strategy for anger management.

Physical activity can also be paired with reflection once the intensity has cooled. For example, after a run, the brain is more capable of rational thought and problem solving because the immediate storm has passed. At that point, someone can revisit the situation with more clarity, perhaps deciding whether to address the conflict assertively or let it go. The exercise acts as a bridge, carrying the person from raw emotion to thoughtful action.

The relationship between anger and physical activity can be visualized in this table:

Activity Type	How It Helps	Best For
Aerobic exercise (running, cycling, swimming)	Reduces adrenaline, releases endorphins, calms nervous system	Quick relief from acute anger
Strength training (weights, pushups, resistance bands)	Channels tension into controlled exertion	People needing an outlet for physical frustration
Mind-body practices (yoga, tai chi, martial arts)	Combines breath, focus, and movement to restore balance	Long-term regulation and emotional awareness
Walking or light activity	Provides mental space, shifts attention, lowers stress hormones	Everyday triggers and mild anger
Group activities (sports, fitness classes)	Adds social support, distraction, and shared energy	Preventing isolation and prolonged rumination

Physical activity also interacts with sleep and recovery. Anger often interferes with sleep by keeping the body in a state of alertness. Exercise earlier in the day can improve sleep quality, which in turn makes people less vulnerable to irritability and emotional volatility. This creates a reinforcing cycle where exercise lowers anger, better sleep protects against anger, and both combine to build resilience.

In some cases, people may need to adapt activity to their circumstances. For example, someone at work may not be able to leave for a run when anger spikes. In those moments, smaller physical actions like stretching, taking the stairs, or stepping outside for deep breaths with a short walk can be enough to shift physiology. Even five minutes of movement is often better than none.

Over time, using physical activity to dissipate anger teaches the body and mind that strong feelings don't have to dominate behavior. Instead of shouting or bottling up resentment, energy is converted into motion, and motion restores calm. This approach respects the biological roots of anger, acknowledges its intensity, and transforms it into a tool for growth and resilience.

Distraction and Redirecting Focus

When anger floods the mind, it narrows attention to a single source of irritation. The brain locks on, replaying events and building arguments that reinforce the emotion. This mental loop strengthens the anger, making it feel larger and more consuming.

Distraction breaks that loop by shifting attention away from the source of anger toward something that absorbs mental energy in a different direction. Redirecting focus doesn't erase the cause of anger, but it interrupts the escalation long enough for the body and mind to cool down.

One reason distraction works is that attention is limited. The brain can't give equal weight to multiple demanding tasks at the same time. When you immerse yourself in an activity that requires thought or effort, the mind diverts energy away from ruminating on what made you angry. This change in focus gives the nervous system time to return to baseline. Heart rate begins to slow, muscles loosen, and adrenaline clears more quickly.

Simple mental distractions can be surprisingly effective. Working through a puzzle, doing quick math in your head, or recalling the lyrics to a favorite song draws focus away from the trigger. Some people use humor as a form of redirection, watching a short comedy clip or remembering something absurd to weaken the seriousness of the moment. These aren't solutions to the underlying problem, but they buy time for the heat of anger to fade.

Physical distractions work differently but with equal impact. Engaging the senses or the body pulls attention outward. Cleaning a desk, organizing a drawer, or cooking a meal shifts focus into tactile movement. Walking into another room or stepping outside to notice colors, sounds, or the feel of the air diverts mental energy into new sensory input. When the brain receives fresh stimulation, it has less room to recycle hostile thoughts.

There's also the option of **goal-directed distraction**. This involves channeling attention into a productive or creative outlet that requires full engagement. Writing in a journal, painting, gardening, or even coding can absorb anger by demanding concentration. The satisfaction of progress in another area replaces the spiral of resentment with accomplishment. These activities don't just occupy the mind, they also produce positive feedback, giving the person a sense of control rather than helplessness.

The effectiveness of distraction depends on timing. Redirecting focus works best before anger reaches its peak. Once someone is shouting or shaking, it's harder to shift gears. Recognizing early signs like clenched jaws, shallow breathing, or racing thoughts creates an opportunity to apply distraction techniques before intensity takes over. This requires awareness, but practice makes the recognition easier over time.

Distraction also has limits. If it becomes the only strategy, problems that triggered anger may never get addressed. For instance, someone who distracts themselves every time a colleague disrespects them might avoid outbursts but never resolve the underlying conflict.

Distraction is most effective as a short-term regulator, giving enough space for calmer reflection and deliberate problem solving later. It's not avoidance but rather a temporary reset.

Here's a way to organize how different forms of distraction work:

Type of Distraction	Example Activities	Best Use Case
Mental tasks	Math problems, word puzzles, recalling song lyrics	Interrupting rumination quickly
Sensory shifts	Stepping outside, noticing sounds, touching a textured object	Grounding attention in the present moment
Physical tasks	Cleaning, cooking, organizing, walking	Channeling restless energy constructively
Creative outlets	Writing, painting, music, gardening	Replacing anger with focused accomplishment
Humor and entertainment	Watching a comedy clip, remembering a funny story	Reducing the seriousness of anger spikes

Technology adds both opportunities and risks for distraction. A quick game on a phone, a podcast, or a playlist can redirect thoughts, but scrolling through social media might worsen anger if the content fuels irritation. Choosing distractions with intention matters. Activities that engage and calm are effective; those that provoke or overstimulate keep anger alive.

Redirecting focus can also involve attention to others. Volunteering, calling a friend, or helping someone with a task directs energy outward. This not only distracts from anger but also changes the emotional context entirely. Instead of being consumed by resentment, the mind receives cues of connection, usefulness, and empathy.

A practical example: someone feels furious after a tense meeting. Instead of replaying the discussion, they walk to a nearby café, order a drink, and sketch ideas for a personal project in a notebook.

The physical movement, sensory shift, and creative focus combine to redirect energy. When they return to work, the sharp edge of anger is gone, and they're better prepared to handle the next step.

Children often learn distraction techniques before adults formalize them. Parents hand them toys, tell stories, or introduce games to redirect tantrums. Adults benefit from the same principle but with more deliberate choice. The skill lies in picking an activity that fully absorbs attention, not one that leaves space for the mind to wander back to the grievance.

Over time, distraction and redirection can become automatic. Instead of spiraling into arguments, someone develops a reflex of shifting to music, walking, or reorganizing tasks. This creates a mental habit of stepping away rather than sinking deeper. The habit doesn't minimize anger's importance, but it prevents it from becoming overwhelming.

Chapter 5: Communication and Conflict Resolution Skills

Assertive vs. Aggressive Communication

When people think about handling anger in conversations, they often confuse **assertiveness** with **aggressiveness**. On the surface, both can look similar because each involves speaking directly and strongly. The difference lies in intent, delivery, and respect for others. Assertive communication acknowledges one's needs without trampling on the rights of others, while aggressive communication pushes those needs at the expense of someone else.

One way to understand the distinction is to look at control. Assertiveness seeks control over oneself: control of emotions, clarity of thoughts, and steadiness of delivery. Aggressiveness, in contrast, seeks control over the other person, using volume, intimidation, or force of personality to dominate. That difference shifts not only the outcome of the exchange but also the long-term relationship between the two people.

Aggressive communication often emerges when anger has been allowed to build without expression. Someone who stays silent until they boil over is more likely to lash out, raising their voice, interrupting, or using cutting words. Assertive communication requires earlier intervention. It works best when someone notices their irritation rising and chooses to speak before resentment spills into hostility. This timing matters because once the adrenaline rush has peaked, aggression tends to feel like the only available outlet.

Consider an example. A manager who's frustrated by repeated late arrivals might respond aggressively with "You're always late, you don't care about anyone's time, and this has to stop now." This puts the employee immediately on the defensive. An assertive alternative would be "I need you to arrive on time because when meetings start late, it affects the entire team's schedule." The first statement assigns blame and attacks character. The second communicates an expectation tied to a specific impact without insulting the person. Both convey urgency, but only one invites change without resistance.

Tone and delivery also set assertiveness apart. Assertive communication uses a calm, steady tone, with words chosen to state facts and needs directly. Aggressive communication often includes exaggerated terms like "always" or "never," heavy sarcasm, or threats. The body language that accompanies aggression (leaning in too close, pointing, clenching fists) reinforces the hostility. Assertive body language looks different: upright posture, steady eye contact without glaring, and open gestures that signal confidence rather than intimidation.

It helps to compare the two styles along several dimensions:

Dimension	Assertive Communication	Aggressive Communication
Goal	Express needs clearly while respecting others	Win, dominate, or silence the other person
Tone	Calm, firm, measured	Loud, hostile, sarcastic, or threatening
Language	Uses "I" statements, specific examples	Uses accusations, exaggerations, insults
Focus	Problem-solving and mutual respect	Blame, control, or venting anger
Body language	Relaxed but confident posture, steady eye contact	Intrusive gestures, glaring, clenched fists
Effect on relationship	Builds trust, invites cooperation	Damages trust, creates resentment

People sometimes shy away from assertiveness because they mistake it for being harsh or rude. In reality, avoiding assertiveness often creates bigger problems.

Suppressed anger tends to leak out in **passive-aggressive** ways: sarcasm, subtle digs, or silent treatment. That approach confuses others and undermines relationships. Assertiveness, by contrast, provides clarity and reduces the need for guessing games.

Developing assertiveness requires practice. It doesn't come naturally to everyone, especially those raised in environments where open disagreement was discouraged. A practical method involves starting small: stating preferences in low-stakes situations. Saying "I'd prefer this restaurant tonight" instead of going along silently builds the muscle for larger conversations later. Over time, this strengthens confidence to express anger without aggression.

Anger itself can be a signal that assertive communication is necessary. If someone feels a rush of irritation when a boundary is crossed, the anger isn't the problem, it's information. The challenge lies in how it gets expressed. Aggression lets anger drive the words, while assertiveness allows the message to be filtered through reflection. By treating anger as a cue rather than a command, people can direct it into assertive statements that preserve respect.

Timing influences whether communication comes out assertive or aggressive. Addressing a frustration immediately after it happens can prevent exaggeration and resentment. But sometimes waiting is better, especially if adrenaline is still high. In those cases, a short pause or a request to revisit the discussion later prevents aggression from taking over. The difference between saying "I need a moment before we talk about this" and exploding on the spot can decide whether the conflict moves toward resolution or escalation.

Assertiveness also extends to listening. It's not just about stating needs, but about allowing others to express theirs. Aggression shuts down dialogue by interrupting or overpowering. Assertiveness, in contrast, creates space for both voices. This balance communicates strength without hostility. Someone who listens carefully, acknowledges the other's point, then restates their own boundary models assertive behavior. For example, "I hear that the deadline feels tight for you. At the same time, we need to deliver on schedule, so let's look at how to divide the work."

Cultural background shapes how people interpret assertiveness. In some cultures, direct statements may feel disrespectful, while in others, anything less than directness is seen as weak. Being sensitive to these differences matters. What's considered assertive in one setting might be read as aggressive in another. Recognizing this helps adjust delivery without compromising clarity.

An overlooked aspect of assertive versus aggressive communication is **self-talk**. Before words are spoken aloud, they're rehearsed internally. If someone tells themselves "They're disrespecting me, they'll never change, I need to shut this down," their outward tone leans toward aggression.

If instead the inner framing is "This is frustrating, but I can make my expectations clear," assertiveness is more likely. Self-regulation starts with the story we tell ourselves about the other person's behavior.

There's also a biological factor at play. Aggression activates the body's fight response, which narrows focus and primes the body for confrontation.

Assertiveness, on the other hand, requires keeping the nervous system steady enough to allow reasoning and measured speech. Practicing breathing techniques, grounding exercises, or even rehearsing phrases in advance helps someone stay in the zone where assertiveness is possible.

In workplace settings, assertiveness strengthens leadership. Leaders who express needs clearly without hostility earn respect and cooperation. Aggressive leaders may get compliance in the short term, but over time, their teams disengage or retaliate silently. The difference affects productivity, morale, and even employee retention. In families, the same pattern holds: assertive communication builds trust between partners or parents and children, while aggression breeds distance and fear.

One of the most practical exercises for shifting from aggression to assertiveness involves rewriting statements. Take a sentence like "You're useless, you never do what I ask." Change it to "I feel frustrated when tasks aren't completed because it adds pressure to my schedule. I need us to find a system that works." This exercise shows that the core frustration remains, but the delivery transforms the impact. Over time, this practice reshapes habits and makes assertive phrasing more automatic.

Active Listening Techniques

When anger rises, the instinct is often to talk louder, defend harder, and interrupt more quickly. Yet the ability to calm conflict often depends less on what you say than on how well you listen. **Active listening** means more than hearing the words that leave someone's mouth. It's about tracking tone, body language, and emotional cues, then showing the speaker you've absorbed what they said. People in conflict rarely calm down because they were told to. They calm down when they feel heard.

Anger narrows attention. Both people in a heated exchange are likely rehearsing counterarguments instead of taking in the other person's point. Active listening breaks that cycle by redirecting focus outward. It's a skill that requires intention, because the brain resists listening when emotions surge. Think of it like steering against a current: the default flow pulls you toward reaction, but discipline allows you to hold steady.

One way to understand active listening is to contrast it with passive hearing. Hearing is effortless, like catching background noise at a café. Active listening is deliberate, like turning toward someone and signaling with your whole body that their words matter. This difference changes how people respond, because most conflicts aren't fueled by the facts themselves but by the sense that no one respects or understands the perspective involved.

An essential component of active listening is **nonverbal attention**. Eye contact communicates presence, but it has to be steady rather than piercing. Nods, slight forward leans, and an open posture show that you're engaged without saying anything. Conversely, crossed arms, looking at your phone, or scanning the room signal disinterest and escalate anger further. When someone's angry, every small cue gets magnified, so attentive body language matters as much as verbal responses.

Reflective listening, sometimes called **paraphrasing**, is another cornerstone. This involves restating what the other person has said in your own words to confirm you've understood.

If a partner says, "You never help around the house," reflecting might sound like, "You're feeling overwhelmed because you think I'm not contributing enough at home." This doesn't mean you agree, but it demonstrates that you're trying to understand. The immediate benefit is de-escalation. The longer-term benefit is trust, because the other person starts to believe that future concerns won't be ignored.

There's a fine line between reflecting and parroting. Simply repeating the other person's words can sound robotic or mocking. Effective reflection shows you've processed the content and emotion. For example, if someone says, "I'm tired of covering shifts because nobody else steps up," repeating that word-for-word won't soothe them. Saying, "It sounds like you feel taken advantage of when shifts get dumped on you," communicates comprehension of both message and feeling.

A related technique is **validation**. Validation isn't agreement. It acknowledges that the other person's feelings make sense given their perspective.

Telling someone, "I understand why that situation made you angry" doesn't mean you condone their anger, but it signals recognition. Without validation, people often feel dismissed, which intensifies frustration. With validation, even harsh truths become easier to deliver, because the emotional charge gets reduced.

Interruptions erode listening. When two angry people talk over each other, no one feels heard. Active listening requires resisting the urge to jump in, even if the speaker exaggerates or misrepresents your behavior. That's hard, because adrenaline creates urgency to correct the record.

But corrections delivered too early rarely land. Letting someone finish not only clarifies their full thought but also makes your eventual response more effective, because it shows discipline and control.

Questions deepen active listening. Asking clarifying questions communicates that you want to understand details rather than assume. These questions must be open-ended and curious rather than loaded. Asking "Why are you always overreacting?" invites defensiveness. Asking "Can you tell me what part of this feels unfair to you?" draws out specifics that guide a calmer discussion. The act of questioning itself can cool tempers, because it shifts the focus from accusation to exploration.

There's also a timing factor. Silence used strategically can enhance listening. Short pauses after someone speaks give space for them to add thoughts they might have withheld. Many people in anger-driven conversations don't say what matters most until after an initial outburst. If you rush to respond, you might miss the deeper issue. Allowing silence communicates patience and confidence, qualities that contrast with the volatility of aggression.

One of the overlooked aspects of active listening is **tone mirroring**. People unconsciously match each other's vocal energy. If someone speaks at a rapid, sharp pace, responding with calm, steady speech naturally slows them down. This works because nervous systems attune to each other through a process called **emotional contagion**. Matching anger escalates. Matching calm steadies. The listener's choice of tone can shift the entire rhythm of the exchange.

Below we compare listening behaviors and their likely effects in heated conversations:

Listening Behavior	Example	Effect on Conflict
Reflecting/paraphrasing	"So you're saying you felt left out when I didn't consult you?"	Shows understanding, reduces defensiveness
Validating	"I can see how that situation would frustrate you."	Affirms feelings without agreement
Clarifying questions	"What part of this is most difficult for you right now?"	Encourages detail, slows escalation
Strategic silence	Pausing after they speak	Signals patience, invites deeper sharing
Tone mirroring	Lowering voice and slowing speech	Helps regulate emotional intensity
Nonverbal attention	Steady eye contact, nodding	Communicates respect and presence
Interrupting	Cutting off mid-sentence	Fuels defensiveness, intensifies anger
Distracted behavior	Checking phone, crossing arms	Signals disinterest, escalates tension

Active listening also requires awareness of **internal distractions**. Even if you stay silent, your mind might still be crafting rebuttals. This internal monologue leaks out in subtle cues like eye rolling or sighs. The discipline of active listening involves quieting internal chatter long enough to give real attention. Techniques like focusing on breathing while the other person speaks can anchor your mind in the present.

It's worth noting that active listening doesn't mean tolerating abuse. If someone's yelling insults or threatening, the priority shifts to safety and boundaries. In those cases, you can listen enough to acknowledge the emotion but still state limits. For instance, "I hear that you're angry, but I won't continue this conversation while being shouted at. Let's take a break and return to it later." That blend of listening and boundary-setting protects both dignity and safety.

In professional settings, active listening improves not just conflict resolution but also decision quality. Meetings often stall when participants talk past each other. Leaders who practice reflective listening ensure everyone's perspective is understood, which reduces later resistance.

In therapy, active listening forms the basis of treatment, because patients often improve when they feel deeply heard even before solutions appear. These examples show that listening is not a passive stance but an active influence on outcomes.

The emotional benefit of active listening can't be overstated. Anger narrows perception, creating tunnel vision where people misinterpret neutral actions as hostile. When someone feels truly listened to, that tunnel begins to widen. They regain perspective. This shift doesn't erase disagreement, but it lowers the emotional intensity enough for problem-solving to begin.

Practicing active listening takes effort. One exercise involves pairing up and having one person speak for two minutes while the other only listens, then repeats back what they understood. The speaker then rates how accurate the reflection was. Over time, this exercise reveals how often we miss emotional nuance even when we think we're listening. It also builds the muscle for staying quiet longer than feels comfortable.

Technology makes listening harder. Phones, email alerts, and background screens split attention. In conflict conversations, these distractions signal disrespect. Deliberately putting devices aside, turning the body fully toward the speaker, and eliminating multitasking sends a strong message: the conversation matters. The effort itself reduces anger, because it contrasts with the dismissiveness many people expect in heated exchanges.

"I" Statements and Expressing Needs Clearly

Arguments often spiral because people frame their complaints as accusations. Saying "You never listen" or "You always screw this up" instantly sparks defensiveness. The other person feels attacked, and the conversation shifts from solving the issue to protecting their pride.

A different approach is to use **"I" statements**, which shift focus from blame to personal experience. Instead of pointing a finger, you reveal how the situation affects you. This doesn't guarantee agreement, but it reduces the chance that the other person will shut down or lash out.

An "I" statement has three elements: the behavior, your feeling, and the impact. For example, "I feel frustrated when meetings start late because it pushes my work into the evening." The structure is simple, but the effect is powerful. It names a feeling, identifies the trigger, and explains why it matters. Compare this with "You're always late to meetings." The first builds understanding, the second invites retaliation.

The psychology here is clear. People respond better to vulnerability than to attack. Expressing how you feel requires courage, but it also disarms aggression. When you say "I feel ignored when my suggestions aren't considered," you're sharing something personal rather than swinging an accusation. The other person may not agree, but they can't argue against the fact that you feel what you feel. This creates space for dialogue instead of escalating conflict.

Clarity is essential. Vague complaints like "I feel bad about how things go around here" don't move the discussion forward. Effective "I" statements specify the exact situation. "I felt anxious yesterday when the schedule changed without notice" is more constructive because it links emotion with a clear event. The listener knows what to address instead of guessing. The sharper the focus, the higher the chance of resolution.

Tone matters as much as words. If "I" statements are delivered sarcastically or with hostility, they lose their effect. Saying "I feel like you're an idiot" isn't an "I" statement at all, even if it starts with "I." The purpose isn't to disguise blame but to communicate genuine feelings and needs. Anger may still show in your voice, but aiming for calm delivery makes it easier for the other person to stay engaged.

One of the challenges is identifying the true need behind the feeling. Feelings point to unmet needs. Anger often masks hurt, insecurity, or fear of rejection. By naming the underlying need, you give the other person a chance to respond constructively. If you say, "I need more notice before plans change so I can adjust," you're offering a pathway to improvement rather than leaving the other person guessing.

The distinction between **requests** and **demands** is important here. A request invites cooperation, while a demand pressures. "I need you to check in before making changes" is a request. "You'd better check in before making changes" is a demand. The first preserves autonomy, the second provokes resistance. Both communicate a need, but the style determines whether the other person feels respected.

Below we look at examples of ineffective versus effective "I" statements:

Situation	Ineffective phrasing	Effective "I" statement
Partner forgets an errand	"You never care about what I ask you to do."	"I felt disappointed when the groceries weren't picked up because I planned dinner around them."
Colleague interrupts	"You're so rude."	"I felt overlooked when I was interrupted, and I need space to finish my thought."
Teen misses curfew	"You don't respect my rules."	"I felt worried when you came home after midnight, because I didn't know if you were safe."

Friend cancels plans	"You always let me down."	"I felt hurt when plans were cancelled at the last minute, because I was looking forward to seeing you."
Roommate leaves a mess	"You're lazy."	"I feel stressed when dishes pile up, because the kitchen feels unusable."

"I" statements are also effective for preventing escalation in workplaces. Managers who phrase criticism through their own perspective reduce defensiveness in employees. Instead of saying, "You don't prioritize properly," a manager might say, "I feel concerned when deadlines slip, because it affects the team's progress." The shift seems small, but it lowers resistance while still addressing the issue.

Even in personal relationships, clarity about needs helps prevent recurring conflict. If you always get angry when someone is late, but you never explain why it bothers you, the problem will repeat.

By saying, "I feel anxious when you're late because I don't know if something went wrong, and I need you to text me if you'll be delayed," you identify both feeling and solution. Over time, this improves trust and reduces cycles of resentment.

There's also an important difference between expressing needs and expecting them to be met every time. No one can meet another person's needs perfectly. "I" statements invite collaboration but don't guarantee outcomes. The benefit is that they create transparency. The other person can weigh your needs against their own and work toward compromise. Without clear expression, compromise isn't possible because the needs remain hidden.

Some people resist "I" statements because they feel unnatural. In the heat of conflict, it's easier to spit out blame. Training yourself to pause and reframe takes practice. One method is to catch accusatory phrases and flip them.

If you hear yourself saying, "You never listen," stop and rephrase: "I feel ignored when I don't get a response." Over time, this re-patterns how you communicate, making constructive language more automatic.

It's also worth noting that cultural factors shape how direct people feel comfortable being. In some cultures, indirect communication is the norm, and direct "I need" statements may feel confrontational. In those cases, softening with context can help. Instead of bluntly stating, "I need you to respect my boundaries," one might say, "I'd feel more comfortable if we could keep this between us." Both express needs, but the style adjusts to context.

Technology has introduced new challenges. Text-based communication strips away tone and body language, making "I" statements even more important. In a short message, it's easy for "Why didn't you call?" to sound harsh. "I felt worried when I didn't hear from you, because I wasn't sure if you were okay" provides clarity and reduces misinterpretation. The extra words create context that replaces missing cues.

Using "I" statements doesn't mean suppressing anger. It means channeling it productively. Anger signals that something matters to you, and expressing that through clear statements gives others a chance to respond instead of fight. This approach takes discipline, but it reshapes conflict from a battlefield into a problem-solving session. People may not always agree, but they'll better understand your position, and understanding is the starting point for resolution.

De-Escalating Tense Conversations

When emotions rise, conversations can flip from constructive to destructive in seconds. De-escalation isn't about winning or shutting the other person down, it's about guiding the exchange back to a level where people can think clearly. Anger floods the body with adrenaline, narrows attention, and makes threats feel larger than they are. If both parties stay in that state, the conflict intensifies. The ability to **de-escalate** is the difference between an argument that resolves and one that scars relationships.

The first step is to manage your own state. If you can't keep yourself calm, you won't help calm the other person. Taking a slower breath, lowering your voice, or even pausing briefly before responding changes the dynamic. People unconsciously match energy levels, so when you steady yourself, the other person often begins to regulate too. This doesn't mean suppressing feelings, it means not letting them dictate your tone or words.

Language choice carries enormous weight. Absolutes like "always" or "never" intensify defensiveness. Compare "You always cut me off" to "I felt cut off during our last conversation." The second focuses on a specific instance, which is easier to discuss. Similarly, inflammatory words trigger escalation. Replacing "That's ridiculous" with "I see this differently" avoids insulting the other person's intelligence while still disagreeing.

Tone often determines whether a conversation cools down or ignites further. A neutral or softer tone signals safety, while sarcasm or mockery signals attack. People rarely notice how much their voice shifts under stress. Recording yourself in conflict may be uncomfortable, but it reveals patterns you can change. Lowering volume and slowing pace gives the impression of control, which calms both sides.

Sometimes the best move is silence. Not every statement requires an immediate rebuttal. Pausing allows emotions to settle before you respond. A five-second pause can feel long, but it prevents reflexive comments that inflame the situation.

Silence also communicates that you're listening, not simply preparing your counterargument. This creates space for the other person to expand on their feelings instead of hardening their stance.

Physical environment influences tension as well. Conversations in crowded or noisy places often escalate faster because distractions add to stress. When possible, moving to a quieter spot reduces the sensory load and makes it easier to focus on the words rather than the surroundings. Seating arrangements matter too. Facing someone head-on across a table can feel confrontational. Sitting at an angle or side by side reduces that intensity.

Nonverbal signals are powerful. **Body language** communicates openness or hostility before words are even processed. Crossing arms, pointing fingers, or standing too close increases threat perception. Relaxed posture, steady eye contact without glaring, and an open stance reduce perceived aggression. Even nodding occasionally shows engagement, which lowers the sense of opposition.

A key tactic is to reflect what you hear. Phrases like "So what I'm hearing is that you felt left out when that decision was made" both validate the emotion and confirm understanding. This doesn't mean agreement. It means acknowledging the other person's perspective, which reduces their need to repeat it with greater intensity. Validation often diffuses anger more quickly than explanation.

Timing matters. Trying to resolve a conflict when someone is at peak anger usually fails. Recognizing when to step back temporarily is part of de-escalation. Suggesting, "I think we both need a short break before we continue" prevents irreversible statements said in the heat of the moment. Returning later with calmer energy makes problem-solving possible.

Below we look at specific tactics and the reasoning behind them:

Strategy	Why it works	Example in practice
Lowering voice	Signals calm, disrupts escalation cycle	Speaking at a slower pace during an argument
Pausing before responding	Reduces impulsive statements, allows emotions to cool	Waiting a few seconds before answering a harsh remark
Reflecting feelings	Validates the other person, decreases defensiveness	"It sounds like you felt excluded from that choice."
Adjusting environment	Removes triggers that heighten stress	Moving discussion from a noisy kitchen to a quiet room
Open body language	Reduces perceived threat	Uncrossing arms, leaning slightly forward
Avoiding absolutes	Prevents exaggerated blame	Saying "This situation frustrated me" instead of "You always frustrate me"
Suggesting a break	Stops escalation before it peaks	"Let's take 10 minutes and come back to this."

De-escalation doesn't mean giving up your perspective. It means creating conditions where your perspective can actually be heard. If the other person feels attacked, they won't process logic or facts. But if they feel understood, they're more open to considering alternatives. The discipline lies in not matching intensity with intensity. It takes strength to respond to heat with steadiness rather than matching fire with fire.

A useful mindset is to separate the person from the problem. Even if their behavior is frustrating, labeling them as "selfish" or "impossible" entrenches conflict. Instead, treat the behavior as the issue. "I was upset when the report wasn't submitted" targets the action, not the identity. This distinction preserves dignity while still addressing the problem.

It also helps to introduce future-focused language. Conversations that dwell on past wrongs often spiral. Shifting to what can be done going forward creates movement. Saying, "How can we prevent this from happening again?" opens a collaborative path. It turns energy toward solutions instead of blame.

Some conflicts escalate because of misunderstandings, not malice. People often interpret tone or phrasing in ways that weren't intended.

Asking clarifying questions prevents assumptions from solidifying. "Did you mean that as a criticism, or were you just pointing it out?" gives the other person a chance to clarify before tempers flare further.

Physical self-regulation supports verbal tactics. Relaxing your shoulders, unclenching fists, or adjusting breathing patterns lowers physiological arousal. Anger primes the body for fight, but consciously signaling relaxation tells the brain it's safe. This makes it easier to think clearly and choose words wisely.

Not every attempt at de-escalation will succeed. Some people remain combative no matter how calm you are. Even then, maintaining your composure protects you from being pulled into destructive cycles. Walking away when necessary isn't weakness, it's recognition that resolution requires both sides' willingness.

When practiced consistently, de-escalation changes not only conflict outcomes but also how people perceive you. Those known for keeping their cool are trusted with leadership, sensitive negotiations, and difficult conversations. The skill builds over time, starting with small disagreements and gradually extending to more heated situations.

Negotiation and Compromise Strategies

Negotiation isn't limited to business deals or formal contracts. It takes place in marriages, friendships, workplaces, and even small daily interactions. Whenever two people want different outcomes and need to find a way forward, negotiation begins. The ability to negotiate well depends on understanding both your own priorities and the other person's. Compromise often follows, but it isn't about losing. It's about balancing interests so that both sides feel heard and satisfied enough to move forward.

The first element in negotiation is preparation. Walking into a conflict without clarity about what matters most often leads to giving up too much or pushing too hard. A useful way to prepare is to identify **non-negotiables** and **flexible areas**. Non-negotiables are the boundaries you can't cross without undermining your core needs or values. Flexible areas are preferences you'd like but can give up if it helps reach agreement. People who fail to separate these two often either refuse to budge or give up on essentials, both of which create resentment.

Framing matters just as much as preparation. How you present your case influences whether the other person views you as an adversary or as a partner in problem-solving. Framing an issue around **shared interests** increases cooperation. For example, in a workplace dispute over deadlines, saying "We both want this project to succeed" creates common ground. From there, specifics can be debated without threatening the relationship.

Listening actively is another cornerstone of negotiation. Many people focus so much on persuading that they miss critical information being offered by the other side. Listening isn't passive silence; it involves clarifying questions, summarizing what was said, and checking whether you understood correctly. This not only provides useful details but also signals respect, which lowers defensiveness. When people feel heard, they're more open to adjusting their stance.

Power dynamics often shape negotiations, but influence doesn't always come from formal authority. **Leverage** can arise from expertise, relationships, or even timing. Understanding what gives you leverage helps you decide how assertive to be. At the same time, overplaying leverage backfires if it humiliates the other party. Good negotiators aim to preserve relationships while reaching agreements, not to dominate at all costs.

The use of language during negotiation matters deeply. Absolutes, threats, or exaggerated claims tend to push the other person into resistance. Phrases like "You must" or "This is the only way" rarely bring cooperation. Instead, conditional and collaborative language works better: "If we can adjust the timeline, then I can take on the extra task." This frames concessions as part of an exchange rather than as submission.

A negotiation is rarely linear. People move forward, backtrack, and sometimes introduce new issues midway. The ability to stay flexible without losing sight of core objectives distinguishes effective negotiators. Rigidity may feel safe, but it often blocks creative solutions. Flexibility allows discovery of outcomes that neither side initially imagined.

Emotions surface in nearly every negotiation. Ignoring them is unwise because emotions drive behavior as much as rational arguments. Anger, fear, or frustration can derail progress, while curiosity and optimism keep dialogue constructive. Acknowledging emotions doesn't mean indulging them. Simply stating, "I sense this is frustrating, let's slow down" diffuses tension and prevents escalation.

Compromise often emerges once positions are clarified. Compromise isn't simply splitting the difference. It involves identifying which elements matter most to each party and trading accordingly. If one side values speed while the other values quality, they might agree to extend deadlines for certain tasks while tightening them for others. Each side gains something they care about most.

The table below illustrates how negotiation strategies align with real-world applications:

Strategy	Purpose	Example in practice
Identify non-negotiables	Prevents sacrificing core needs	Refusing to work overtime every weekend but open to occasional late nights
Frame shared interests	Builds cooperation	"We both want the team to meet its targets."
Active listening	Gains information and lowers defensiveness	Summarizing the other side's concerns before responding
Balanced leverage	Uses influence without damaging relationships	Highlighting expertise while inviting collaboration
Conditional language	Makes concessions part of exchange	"If you take on client calls, I'll handle the reports."
Trade priorities	Moves beyond splitting difference	Offering faster delivery in exchange for reduced scope
Acknowledge emotions	Maintains constructive tone	"I can see this issue is upsetting, let's pause for a moment."

Timing shapes negotiations more than many realize. Approaching someone at the wrong moment, such as when they're under stress or distracted, reduces chances of success. Choosing a setting where both people can concentrate and feel comfortable increases the likelihood of constructive dialogue. Time pressure also shifts outcomes. Deadlines can push agreement, but they can also lead to rushed compromises that don't hold up later.

Another tactic is to expand the options on the table. People often lock into either/or thinking, which limits creativity. By brainstorming multiple possibilities, negotiators avoid zero-sum standoffs.

For instance, instead of arguing whether a budget should go to marketing or training, exploring partial allocations or phased funding might satisfy both priorities. Expanding the pie often reveals unexpected alignments.

The psychology of fairness strongly influences acceptance of outcomes. Even if an agreement is objectively beneficial, if one side feels cheated, resentment lingers. Fairness isn't just about equal distribution; it's about transparency of process. When people see that their concerns were considered, they're more likely to accept less-than-ideal outcomes.

Preparation also involves anticipating the other side's objections. Thinking through likely counterarguments allows you to craft responses without defensiveness. This reduces surprise and prevents derailment. If you can articulate the other person's position better than they can, you gain credibility and often soften their resistance.

Compromise sometimes requires short-term concessions for long-term gains. Skilled negotiators know when to yield on a smaller issue to secure goodwill for future interactions. This is especially relevant in ongoing relationships like workplaces or families. Winning every point may satisfy temporarily, but it weakens trust over time.

Cultural context influences how negotiation unfolds. In some cultures, direct confrontation is acceptable, while in others, indirect approaches maintain harmony.

Sensitivity to cultural norms prevents missteps that might be interpreted as disrespect. Even within the same culture, individual preferences vary widely, so observing cues and adjusting your style is essential.

Silence can also be a negotiation strategy. When someone makes a demand, pausing rather than responding immediately creates discomfort that often leads them to soften their position. Silence conveys thoughtfulness rather than aggression if combined with steady body language.

Technology has changed modern negotiations. Virtual meetings reduce some cues like body language, which makes tone and word choice even more important.

Misunderstandings arise more easily when people rely only on text, so clarifying intentions explicitly becomes critical. In digital contexts, written summaries of agreements prevent disputes later.

Ethical boundaries must guide all negotiation. Manipulation or deceit might secure short-term advantage, but it damages credibility. Once trust is broken, future negotiations become nearly impossible. Transparent reasoning and consistent follow-through strengthen long-term influence.

Negotiation also benefits from perspective-taking. Imagining the situation from the other person's vantage point reveals hidden motivations. For instance, a colleague resisting a deadline extension might not simply be stubborn but may fear appearing unreliable to upper management. Recognizing this allows you to address the underlying concern rather than the surface objection.

In highly charged situations, involving a neutral third party can help. Mediators bring distance and structure, allowing both sides to save face while finding compromise. Even informal mediators, like a trusted colleague, can diffuse defensiveness and keep dialogue constructive.

The best compromises are those that people can implement without resentment. Agreements that look good on paper but leave one party feeling forced rarely last. Sustainability comes from balance, clarity, and mutual respect. The aim isn't to get everything, it's to get enough for both sides to feel the exchange was worthwhile.

Managing Tone and Body Language

The way words are delivered often matters more than the words themselves. In conflict or negotiation, **tone** and **body language** become powerful tools that shape meaning, influence perceptions, and either escalate or calm situations. A raised voice, a dismissive shrug, or even a long silence can alter the entire course of a conversation. People tend to respond less to logic in heated moments and more to the cues that tell them whether they're safe, respected, or threatened. Learning to manage both tone and body language allows you to maintain control of interactions while encouraging cooperation from others.

Tone is a combination of volume, pitch, speed, and inflection. When these elements are misaligned with your intention, your message can easily be misunderstood. A statement like "I hear you" can sound empathetic when spoken with warmth but sarcastic when delivered with flat or exaggerated inflection. **Neutral tones** are often the most useful in conflict. They prevent defensiveness while leaving room for calm discussion. However, neutrality should not be confused with coldness. A completely flat voice might seem detached, which can be taken as a lack of concern. The goal is balance, where the voice carries calm authority but also care.

Body language carries an equally heavy weight in communication. Humans instinctively read posture, gestures, and facial expressions for cues about intentions. Crossing arms, avoiding eye contact, or leaning too far forward can communicate defensiveness, disinterest, or aggression even when none is intended. On the other hand, open postures, steady but non-intimidating eye contact, and relaxed gestures signal confidence and receptivity. In negotiation or conflict resolution, people are more willing to trust and cooperate when they see nonverbal signs that you're approachable yet firm.

One of the strongest links between tone and body language is **congruence**. When your words and physical signals don't match, people believe the body over the words. Saying "I'm listening" while glancing at your phone undermines credibility. Smiling while expressing frustration creates confusion. Consistency between verbal and nonverbal cues builds trust, while inconsistency breeds suspicion.

Table: Practical applications of tone and body language strategies

Technique	Purpose	Example in practice
Lowering voice volume	Reduces escalation and signals control	Speaking softly during an argument to bring tension down
Slowing speech	Encourages reflection and calm	Pausing between points in a heated meeting
Open posture	Conveys receptivity and confidence	Keeping arms relaxed at your sides rather than crossed
Steady eye contact	Signals respect without intimidation	Looking at the speaker while they finish their thought
Mirroring	Builds rapport subtly	Leaning slightly forward after the other person does
Congruence of cues	Builds credibility	Saying "I understand" while nodding sincerely
Neutral tone	Prevents defensiveness	Speaking evenly rather than raising pitch during disagreement

Tone also shapes perceptions of authority. Leaders who consistently speak in overly harsh tones may achieve compliance but at the cost of long-term trust. Conversely, those who always soften their tone may struggle to be taken seriously. The skill lies in adjusting tone based on context. Firmness is appropriate when boundaries need to be reinforced, but warmth is better when cooperation is sought.

Pacing is another subtle dimension of tone. People who rush through sentences in conflict often appear anxious or dismissive, while those who drag out their words risk sounding condescending. Measured pacing signals thoughtfulness. Even short pauses after a key point can give the impression of confidence and allow others time to absorb the message.

Silence itself is a powerful tool of both tone and body language. Used intentionally, silence signals that you're considering what was said or waiting for the other person to elaborate. It also disrupts cycles of escalation because it removes the fuel of reactive words. However, silence can also be misread as stonewalling or indifference if combined with closed body language. To prevent misinterpretation, pair silence with nonverbal cues like nodding or steady eye contact.

Cultural background influences how tone and body language are perceived. In some cultures, direct eye contact signals respect, while in others it's considered rude or aggressive.

Loud voices may be normal in one context and a sign of anger in another. Sensitivity to cultural norms avoids accidental offense. When in doubt, erring on the side of calm tone and open but non-intrusive body language tends to be safest.

Stress often disrupts tone and body language control. Under pressure, voices rise, bodies tense, and gestures become exaggerated. Awareness is the first step in countering this. Noticing that your shoulders are tightening or your speech is quickening gives you a chance to consciously relax and reset. Techniques like controlled breathing or grounding yourself by pressing your feet firmly into the floor can restore composure and prevent reactive escalation.

The role of body language in negotiations extends beyond personal control. Observing others' cues provides valuable insight. Signs of discomfort like fidgeting or avoiding eye contact may signal disagreement even when words suggest consent. Recognizing these discrepancies allows you to address hidden concerns before they turn into obstacles. Similarly, when the other person mirrors your gestures or leans in, it often means rapport is building, which is the ideal time to introduce compromises.

Managing tone and body language also involves recognizing triggers. Some words or gestures inflame situations regardless of intent. A dismissive wave of the hand, rolling eyes, or sighing can provoke anger instantly. Even if you don't mean disrespect, these cues are often read as such. Eliminating these habits requires deliberate practice. Recording yourself during conversations or asking trusted colleagues for feedback can reveal unconscious signals that need adjustment.

Training in tone and body language should not aim for perfection but for **awareness and adaptability**. Mechanical efforts to control every gesture look artificial, which erodes trust. Instead, the aim is authentic alignment between internal state and external expression. When calm and clarity are genuine, they naturally shape tone and body language in ways that promote resolution.

In tense conflicts, grounding your tone in curiosity works better than in judgment. Phrasing questions with gentle intonation, such as "Can you tell me more about what concerns you?" invites openness. The same words delivered with sharp inflection can sound like interrogation. Similarly, leaning slightly forward with relaxed shoulders conveys genuine interest, while leaning in aggressively communicates pressure.

Technology introduces new challenges to managing tone and body language. In video calls, cameras capture limited body language, so facial expressions and vocal tone carry even more weight. Neutral lighting, eye-level camera placement, and careful modulation of voice help maintain professionalism and connection. In text-based communication, tone is hardest to convey, which is why clarifying intent explicitly becomes crucial. A simple statement like "I want to be clear this isn't criticism, just a suggestion" prevents misinterpretation that body language might otherwise have clarified.

Repairing tone mistakes is possible and often strengthens credibility. If you notice you snapped or used a sarcastic tone, acknowledging it openly can disarm tension. Saying, "I realize my tone came across more sharply than I intended" demonstrates self-awareness and care for the relationship. Similarly, if your body language has signaled disinterest, small corrections like adjusting posture or reestablishing eye contact quickly restore balance.

Children and adolescents are particularly sensitive to tone and body language, often more than adults. A calm explanation delivered with a reassuring posture has more impact on a child than logical reasoning delivered with visible frustration. In workplaces, supervisors who deliver feedback in calm tone and supportive posture see better motivation than those who rely solely on the content of their words.

At the heart of managing tone and body language is the principle of **emotional regulation**. If you can't manage your internal state, your external signals inevitably reveal agitation or hostility. Developing habits of emotional awareness, such as noticing early signs of frustration, makes it easier to prevent these signals from leaking into your tone and gestures. Over time, self-regulation becomes second nature, creating consistency between what you feel and what you express.

The integration of tone and body language creates presence. Presence isn't about dominating a room but about projecting calm authority and attentive openness. People who manage these cues effectively draw respect without demanding it. They influence not because they shout the loudest but because they convey steadiness and sincerity.

In negotiation and conflict resolution, what people remember most often isn't the exact words exchanged but how they felt during the interaction. If your tone and body language made them feel respected and safe, they'll be more willing to cooperate, even if they didn't get everything they wanted. By contrast, if they felt dismissed or attacked, resentment will linger regardless of agreements reached.

Tone and body language are skills, but they're also reflections of deeper qualities like patience, empathy, and confidence. The more you cultivate these inner qualities, the more naturally your external signals align with constructive communication.

With practice, you can use tone and body language not as manipulation but as genuine tools to foster understanding, deescalate conflict, and create durable agreements.

Chapter 6: Cognitive and Behavioral Strategies

Cognitive Restructuring to Challenge Angry Thoughts

When anger rises, it's rarely just about the event itself. It's about the **thoughts that interpret the event**. Cognitive restructuring is the process of catching those thoughts, evaluating their accuracy, and replacing distorted patterns with more balanced interpretations. The technique comes from cognitive behavioral therapy, and it's one of the most direct ways to reduce both the intensity and duration of anger.

Anger often starts with **automatic thoughts**. These are rapid mental reactions that jump to conclusions before reason has a chance to intervene. For example, if someone cuts you off in traffic, you might instantly think, "That guy disrespected me on purpose." Notice the leap: you assume intent, even though you know nothing about the driver's motives. Automatic thoughts frequently contain errors called **cognitive distortions**, and these distortions fuel emotional escalation.

Several distortions commonly appear during anger episodes.

Mind reading is one, where you assume you know what someone else is thinking. **Catastrophizing** exaggerates the impact of an event, turning a minor slight into a life-defining insult. **All-or-nothing thinking** frames situations in extremes, like "If my colleague doesn't respect my idea, then no one ever will." These distortions aren't just inaccurate, they also create a feedback loop where anger reinforces the thought, and the thought keeps anger alive.

The first step in cognitive restructuring is to **identify the thought**. Most people miss this because they focus on the emotion itself, not the underlying idea. Writing down angry thoughts as they occur is surprisingly effective.

A simple log of situations, triggers, and the sentences that popped into your head can reveal patterns you never noticed before. Someone might see that every time they feel dismissed, they default to "Nobody respects me," which becomes the match that lights the fire.

Once you've identified the thought, the next step is **challenging it with evidence**. Evidence-based questioning works like a courtroom cross-examination. Ask: "What facts support this thought? What facts contradict it? Could there be other explanations?" If you thought, "That driver cut me off on purpose," you might counter with, "Do I know their intentions? Could they have been distracted, or maybe they didn't see me?" The point isn't to excuse behavior but to dismantle the certainty of distorted assumptions.

The third step is **reframing the thought**. Instead of simply tearing down the distortion, you create a replacement that's more realistic and less incendiary. This isn't about positive thinking, it's about accurate thinking. A balanced reframe of the traffic example could be: "That was reckless driving, but it doesn't mean they targeted me personally." The difference in phrasing prevents the spiral of personalization that drives rage.

Cognitive restructuring is not about suppressing anger. Suppression pushes the emotion underground, where it lingers and leaks out later. The goal is to **transform the meaning of the event**, which reduces anger naturally because the brain no longer perceives the same level of threat or disrespect.

One of the most effective formats for practicing restructuring is a **thought record table**. It organizes the process into clear steps, making it easier to repeat until it becomes habit.

Situation	Automatic Thought	Distortion Present	Evidence For	Evidence Against	Balanced Reframe
Driver cut me off	"He disrespected me on purpose"	Mind reading, personalization	He swerved quickly into my lane	I don't know him, maybe he didn't see me	"It was careless driving, but not necessarily directed at me."
Boss criticized my report	"She thinks I'm incompetent"	All-or-nothing thinking	She pointed out errors	She's given me positive feedback before	"She found problems with the report, but that doesn't define my overall ability."
Partner forgot to call	"They don't care about me"	Overgeneralization	They didn't call back tonight	They usually do call, and said they were busy	"They missed one call, but they usually show they care."

This structure forces the mind to slow down and examine each layer. At first, it feels mechanical. Over time, it becomes a natural internal dialogue. Someone who once jumped from trigger to rage can eventually pause, catch the distortion, and run through the evidence automatically.

An important nuance here is the **role of physiological arousal**. When anger is peaking, cognitive restructuring is harder to apply. The sympathetic nervous system narrows focus and accelerates thought speed, making balanced reasoning more difficult. That's why timing matters. Practicing restructuring after the fact, once the storm has passed, builds the skill for future episodes. Eventually, you can catch thoughts earlier, before adrenaline hijacks reasoning completely.

Another layer involves **metacognition**, or thinking about your thinking. When you recognize a thought as just a mental event rather than a fact, you gain distance. Saying, "I'm having the thought that he disrespected me," rather than "He disrespected me," subtly changes your relationship to the thought. The first phrasing reminds you it's an interpretation, not an objective truth. That small shift weakens the emotional grip.

Research shows cognitive restructuring significantly reduces **rumination**, which is the repetitive replay of angry events in the mind. Rumination prolongs anger far beyond the original incident, sometimes for hours or days. By dismantling distortions and reframing, restructuring cuts off the fuel supply to rumination. The mind has less material to obsess over because the interpretation has already been neutralized.

Cultural and personal history also shape how restructuring works. Someone raised in an environment where disrespect was a threat to survival may find it harder to let go of personalization distortions. For them, the thought "They're targeting me" feels instinctual. Recognizing that background doesn't excuse unhelpful thinking, but it explains why some distortions grip tighter. Tailoring restructuring to personal triggers makes it more effective.

The practice isn't limited to anger management. Cognitive restructuring is also used in anxiety, depression, and stress reduction. But with anger, the immediacy of distortions makes the technique especially potent. The difference between assuming malice and allowing for uncertainty can mean the difference between escalating into conflict and moving on within minutes.

You can strengthen restructuring with **behavioral experiments**. Instead of only debating thoughts in your head, you test them against reality.

If you believe, "People never listen to me," set up a small experiment: share an opinion in a group and track how many times people respond or engage. Data often contradicts the distortion, and real-world evidence is harder for the brain to dismiss.

It's also worth noting that restructuring works best when paired with **physiological regulation**. Deep breathing, a short walk, or progressive muscle relaxation can lower arousal, making it easier to apply rational analysis. Trying to restructure while your heart rate is at 140 beats per minute is like trying to solve algebra during a fire drill. Calming the body gives the mind space to think clearly.

The effectiveness of restructuring grows with repetition. At first, distorted thoughts feel automatic and convincing. After dozens of practice rounds, they start to feel flimsy. You recognize them the way you recognize optical illusions: they look real, but you know they aren't. That recognition weakens their influence, and anger loses its usual momentum.

Habit Loops and Breaking Anger Cycles

Every habit follows a pattern of **cue, routine, and reward**. Anger often slips into this structure without people noticing. A certain situation acts as the cue, such as being interrupted or feeling disrespected.

The routine becomes the automatic reaction, which may be yelling, withdrawing, or making a cutting remark. The reward is the temporary sense of release or control that follows, even though it damages relationships or leaves regret. Recognizing anger as a habit loop shows why it repeats: the brain conserves energy by running familiar scripts rather than pausing to evaluate.

Habits don't break simply by noticing them. They need to be replaced with new routines that give the brain a different reward. If someone usually slams doors when upset, switching to a brisk walk offers the body the same physical discharge but without the destruction. The key is linking the same cue to a healthier routine while still creating a reward. Over time, the brain rewires to prefer the new pathway because it sees the consistent pattern of benefit.

The **time frame of habit change** often surprises people. Studies on habit formation suggest that the average person needs about 66 days of repetition before a new habit feels automatic. Some people adapt faster in as little as 21 days, while others take over 200 days, depending on the complexity of the behavior.

This means that anger patterns don't vanish after a week of effort. The brain's reliance on old shortcuts means slip-ups will happen. Treating those slips as part of the timeline, not as failure, keeps the process steady.

Short-term improvements often mislead people into thinking change is permanent. For instance, someone may go two weeks without blowing up and then snap unexpectedly. That single incident convinces them that they are "back at square one." In truth, the new routine is still consolidating, and the old habit is still lingering in memory circuits. The nervous system defaults to what feels familiar under pressure. Recognizing that progress builds in layers prevents discouragement.

Patterns of anger often embed themselves over years. A child who learns to lash out at siblings may carry that same strategy into adulthood, refined but unchanged at its core. Breaking such a long-standing pattern requires patience equal to the years of reinforcement behind it. Just as a well-trodden path in the woods takes time to grow over, neural pathways take time to lose dominance. The alternative pathway must be walked again and again until it becomes the new route the brain expects.

To track the process, it helps to map out cues, routines, and rewards. Someone might realize that being criticized at work sparks an immediate defensive routine, such as arguing with colleagues. The reward is avoiding shame. By deliberately substituting the routine with taking three deep breaths and asking for clarification, the person gains a new reward: composure and clarity. Writing this cycle down daily shows patterns more clearly than memory alone, and over weeks, the new pattern solidifies.

A table makes this visible:

Cue	Old Routine	Old Reward	New Routine	New Reward
Interrupted in conversation	Raise voice, dominate talk	Sense of control	Pause, listen, and respond calmly	Respect from others, real influence
Criticism from supervisor	Argue or shut down	Avoidance of shame	Ask clarifying questions	Better understanding, less conflict
Traffic jam	Yelling at drivers	Temporary release	Play calming music, deep breathing	Reduced stress, calmer mood

| Feeling ignored by partner | Silent treatment | Passive control | State needs directly | Connection, resolution |

This chart shows why substitution is more effective than suppression. Suppressing anger without a replacement routine creates a vacuum, and the old habit fills it again.

An overlooked aspect is **emotional rehearsal**. Before entering predictable situations, mentally practicing the new routine helps strengthen it. For example, picturing yourself staying calm in traffic primes the brain to follow through when the cue arrives. Sports psychologists use similar mental practice to reinforce motor memory, and the same principle applies to emotional habits. The brain rehearses the routine until it feels less foreign.

Stress amplifies old habits. When someone is sleep-deprived, hungry, or under pressure, the brain tends to lean on default pathways. That's why early in habit change, people notice they slip more during stressful weeks. Building supportive routines around sleep, nutrition, and recovery makes it easier to sustain change. The habit loop doesn't exist in isolation; it's influenced by overall resilience.

Breaking cycles also means noticing **secondary gains** of anger. Some people use outbursts to avoid deeper feelings like fear or sadness. Others use it to gain compliance from those around them.

Unless those hidden rewards are identified, the cycle persists. If anger brings temporary relief from vulnerability, a healthier alternative must address that vulnerability directly, not just suppress the surface reaction.

The concept of **keystone habits** applies here. A keystone habit is a change that triggers improvement in other areas. For anger management, exercise often functions as a keystone habit. Regular physical activity regulates stress hormones, reduces baseline tension, and makes it easier to pause before reacting. The habit of moving the body cascades into better emotional control across situations. Identifying one or two keystone replacements accelerates the broader rewiring.

Environment shapes habit loops as well. Someone trying to stop yelling might still succeed at home but fail in traffic. That's because cues differ across settings. Adapting routines to each environment, rather than expecting a single universal strategy, produces better results.

For example, using calming music works in traffic, but counting to five before responding may be more effective in arguments. Treating each context as a separate loop respects how cues vary.

Technology can be both a hindrance and a helper. Instant messaging, for example, allows quick venting that reinforces anger. But apps that track mood, remind you to breathe, or log daily reflections provide accountability. People who monitor their routines with technology often stick with change longer because the feedback reinforces progress.

Breaking cycles requires experimentation. Not every replacement routine will succeed. One person may find deep breathing useless but respond well to walking away. Another may find journaling essential while a friend thinks it's tedious. Flexibility matters because the brain accepts new routines more easily when they feel natural. The habit loop isn't broken by force; it's redirected by consistency and adaptability.

The **timeline of progress** must always be emphasized. Neuroscience shows that early wins in habit change often rely on willpower. Later stability comes from rewired neural pathways. This is why the first month feels draining: the brain hasn't yet automated the new behavior. By the third month, routines feel smoother because the basal ganglia begin to encode them as default. A year later, many people barely remember the old reaction unless reminded.

What sustains motivation through the long middle stretch is tracking evidence of progress. Keeping a journal where incidents are rated on intensity or duration shows measurable improvement. Someone who once screamed for ten minutes may note they now calm down in three. These incremental changes, while small, prove that rewiring is occurring. Without documentation, progress can feel invisible, and discouragement sets in.

Breaking anger cycles isn't about eliminating anger altogether. It's about shifting automatic responses so that anger no longer controls behavior. When new habits replace destructive routines, anger still arises but follows a different path. That's why patience with the timeline matters so much. Expecting instant change ignores how the brain is wired. Respecting the process of cue, routine, and reward allows real, lasting transformation.

Exposure and Response Prevention for Triggers

When anger feels uncontrollable, it's often tied to specific **triggers** that activate old emotional pathways almost instantly. These triggers can be words, tones of voice, or particular situations that carry heavy meaning from past experiences. Exposure and Response Prevention (ERP), a method originally used for anxiety and obsessive-compulsive disorder, adapts well to anger management. It works by gradually exposing a person to anger triggers while preventing the automatic reaction that usually follows. Over time, the nervous system learns that the trigger doesn't require the old destructive routine, and the cycle weakens.

The first step is identifying the **triggers** with as much detail as possible. Someone may think, "I get angry when people disrespect me," but that needs precision. Does it mean being interrupted, receiving criticism, or not getting a reply to a text? The more specific the trigger, the easier it is to design controlled exposures. Without clarity, the brain only lumps everything into "disrespect," making it harder to dismantle the pattern. Once the triggers are mapped out, they can be ranked from least to most provoking. This hierarchy becomes the roadmap for exposure.

ERP begins with **controlled exposure** to mild triggers. If raised voices are a strong anger cue, a person might start by listening to recordings of arguments at low volume. Instead of reacting, they practice breathing steadily or repeating calming phrases. The goal isn't to suppress anger but to teach the body that the trigger can exist without leading to an outburst. Repeated practice builds tolerance. Over time, the nervous system doesn't spike as sharply when hearing raised voices, and the person feels less enslaved to that cue.

As exposures move up the hierarchy, the process gets closer to real-world scenarios. Someone who struggles with criticism might start by writing out fake criticisms and reading them aloud. Later, a friend or therapist delivers mild critical statements while the person practices staying calm.

Eventually, they can handle real feedback at work without spiraling. Each step rewires the brain's response, showing that criticism doesn't have to lead to defensive anger.

A common misconception is that exposure means enduring overwhelming situations all at once. In truth, **gradual exposure** is the key. Throwing someone into their most explosive trigger without preparation usually backfires, reinforcing the old pattern. Instead, ERP carefully builds tolerance, similar to how allergy shots expose people to tiny doses of an allergen until their immune system adapts. The nervous system works the same way with emotional triggers.

Response prevention is the other half of the method. Exposure alone doesn't break the cycle unless the old reaction is blocked. If someone hears criticism and immediately shouts, the old pathway is reinforced. But if they prevent the shout by using replacement routines, the brain learns a new association. This requires practice before exposure. Tools like deep breathing, grounding techniques, or rehearsed calming statements act as anchors. With them in place, exposure creates new wiring instead of reinforcing the old one.

The repetition of ERP is what makes it effective. One exposure session doesn't change much, but dozens across weeks begin to show results. Each time the person resists their old response, the brain records a new memory: "This trigger isn't dangerous." Gradually, the intensity of the anger spike lessens, and triggers lose their power. What once felt intolerable becomes manageable. This shift is measurable, and people often keep logs to track their progress.

Here's an example table showing how ERP could be structured for anger triggers:

Trigger	Old Response	New Exposure Practice	Prevented Reaction	Outcome Over Time
Being interrupted in conversation	Raise voice, dominate	Practice interruptions in staged dialogues	Stay calm, finish when possible	Lower reactivity, more patience
Receiving mild criticism	Argue or deflect	Read written criticisms aloud	Deep breathing, ask clarifying Qs	Better tolerance for feedback
Waiting in long lines	Mutter, sigh, glare	Stand in lines deliberately during errands	Slow breathing, neutral posture	Reduced agitation, calmer presence

Partner ignoring messages for hours	Accusations, sulking	Delay reading phone notifications	Journal feelings before reacting	Increased patience, less escalation
Traffic jams	Yelling at drivers	Listen to recordings of honking and congestion	Play music, focus on rhythm	More relaxed driving experience

Each row shows how a specific trigger can be deconstructed, tested in safe contexts, and paired with a new routine. Over time, the nervous system no longer views the trigger as a threat requiring anger.

A deeper principle behind ERP is **habituation**. When the body repeatedly experiences a trigger without the old response, the emotional spike naturally diminishes. Think of how someone who moves near a train track stops noticing the noise after a while. The brain learns to stop wasting energy on what isn't dangerous. With anger, the same process occurs. Once the old habit is prevented long enough, the trigger feels neutral.

Another key mechanism is **extinction learning**. Old associations between triggers and anger don't disappear; they weaken when new associations are built. This explains why under stress, old patterns sometimes reappear.

A person who has practiced ERP for months may still snap after a bad day. This isn't failure but a reminder that extinction is fragile. Continued exposure and prevention strengthen the new pathways until they dominate.

ERP also highlights the role of **anticipatory anxiety**. Sometimes the fear of being triggered creates more tension than the trigger itself. People might avoid family gatherings because they anticipate being provoked. Exposure breaks this avoidance by showing the brain that anticipation is worse than reality. As tolerance grows, the fear of triggers shrinks, making life less restricted.

The **time frame** for ERP to work varies. Some people notice improvement within a few weeks, while others need months of consistent practice. The number of repetitions matters more than the calendar. A person who practices daily exposures progresses faster than someone who practices occasionally. The brain values frequency over intensity when rewiring emotional responses. This is why short, regular exposures are more effective than rare, dramatic ones.

ERP can be emotionally taxing, so self-care is critical. After exposure sessions, people often feel drained, similar to how a workout leaves muscles sore. Reflection, journaling, and relaxation practices help consolidate learning.

Without recovery, the brain can associate ERP with exhaustion, making it harder to continue. Balancing effort with rest ensures sustainability.

Social support strengthens ERP. Friends, partners, or therapists can create controlled exposures and provide feedback. Having someone present reduces the risk of slipping into old reactions unnoticed. Support also offers encouragement when progress feels slow. Many people underestimate how motivating it is to share victories, like calmly handling a situation that used to spark an outburst.

ERP also connects with the idea of **self-efficacy**. Each successful exposure builds confidence: "I handled that trigger without losing control." Over time, this belief spreads beyond specific triggers into a broader sense of mastery. People start trusting themselves not only with known triggers but with unexpected ones. The growing confidence itself reduces anger, since much of it stems from feeling powerless.

There are challenges. Some triggers are tied to deep wounds or trauma, making exposure delicate. In those cases, working with a trained therapist ensures safety. Jumping into high-intensity triggers without guidance risks reinforcing pain rather than healing it. Patience and pacing become crucial here. ERP isn't about toughness but about steady, repeated teaching of the nervous system.

It's also worth noting that ERP is not suppression. Suppression pushes anger down, often making it resurface later with more intensity. ERP allows anger to arise naturally but channels it into new responses. This distinction matters. Suppression feels like holding a lid on boiling water, while ERP feels like gradually turning down the heat so the water stops boiling.

ERP also reshapes relationships. Someone who once exploded at minor slights now responds with calm, altering how others interact with them. Partners, coworkers, and friends learn that they don't need to walk on eggshells. This feedback loop reinforces the person's new identity as someone steady rather than volatile. Change becomes visible not only internally but socially.

The long-term success of ERP depends on maintenance. Even after progress, periodic exposures help keep triggers from regaining strength. Just as muscles weaken without exercise, emotional tolerance fades if never tested. People who integrate small exposures into daily life (like standing in long lines without distraction) maintain their resilience. ERP is less a one-time treatment than a lifelong skill of retraining the nervous system.

In summary, Exposure and Response Prevention takes anger triggers that once felt unbearable and gradually strips them of power. By pairing controlled exposure with deliberate prevention of the old reaction, the brain learns new patterns. Habituation, extinction learning, and self-efficacy all play a role in this rewiring. The process takes consistent practice, often over weeks or months, but its results endure far longer than quick fixes. Anger becomes less a controlling force and more an emotion that can be managed with choice.

Using Problem-Solving Frameworks Instead of Venting

Anger is often described as energy without a clear outlet. When people vent, they release that energy in bursts of words or actions that feel satisfying in the moment but rarely change the situation. Complaining can feel like a short-term release valve, yet the problem itself stays the same, waiting to trigger anger again. By contrast, **problem-solving frameworks** provide a structured way to transform raw emotion into tangible action. They redirect the energy of anger away from spirals of blame and into processes that identify causes, generate solutions, and reduce the chance of repeat frustrations.

Why Venting Feels Good but Fails

When someone vents, they believe they are relieving pressure, and on a biological level, they often are. Speaking loudly, pacing, or letting frustrations pour out releases adrenaline and cortisol. The nervous system interprets this activity as a discharge, which is why it feels satisfying at first. Yet venting usually reinforces the anger script. The more someone rants about how unfair or intolerable something is, the more they rehearse the very thought patterns that keep them angry.

Research shows that constant venting can actually escalate aggression. Instead of calming the system, the act of going over grievances deepens the sense of being wronged. Complaining also places control outside the self: the world is at fault, other people are incompetent, the system is broken. If the problem is always external and unchangeable, then the only option is to complain again tomorrow when the same issue arises.

Problem-solving frameworks flip that cycle. They acknowledge the anger but ask a different question: **What can I do about it?** This question shifts attention from the uncontrollable to the controllable. It moves anger away from being a storm that sweeps through someone's life toward being fuel for constructive action.

The First Step: Defining the Problem Clearly

Anger often grows because problems are vaguely defined. A person may say, "My boss disrespects me," but what does that mean in practice? Is it being interrupted in meetings, receiving critical emails late at night, or not being acknowledged for work? Each version of "disrespect" calls for a different solution. Without precision, any attempt to solve the problem becomes misdirected, like trying to hit a target that hasn't been drawn.

Frameworks such as **problem statements** help. A problem statement describes the situation in neutral, observable terms. Instead of "My coworkers never listen," the statement could be "During team meetings, my suggestions are often overlooked without discussion." This reframing strips away the heat of interpretation and lays out something concrete that can be addressed.

Once the problem is stated clearly, the brain is less likely to spiral into self-righteous anger. Clarity itself often reduces frustration because it provides a foothold for action. The vagueness of "They never listen" fuels helplessness, while the concreteness of "My suggestions are not discussed" makes solutions feel possible.

Framework One: Root Cause Analysis

One of the simplest and most effective frameworks is **Root Cause Analysis**. Instead of reacting to the surface-level frustration, it digs into why the frustration keeps happening. A common method is the "Five Whys." The process involves asking "Why?" repeatedly until the deeper issue emerges.

Take the example of someone getting angry every morning at traffic. The surface complaint is obvious: "The traffic is terrible." But asking "Why?" reveals layers:

1. Why is traffic stressful? Because it makes me late to work.
2. Why am I late? Because I leave the house at 8:00 when traffic is at its worst.
3. Why do I leave at 8:00? Because I stay up too late and sleep in.
4. Why do I stay up too late? Because I scroll on my phone at night.
5. Why do I scroll? Because it's my only downtime.

The root problem isn't the traffic. It's how the person structures their evenings. Complaining about cars on the road will never fix that, but changing evening habits might. Following the chain down to the root, the person has actionable options that venting alone would never uncover.

This process is powerful because anger tends to focus attention outward. Root Cause Analysis brings attention back inward, where real leverage exists. Instead of railing against the unchangeable, it highlights patterns that can be adjusted.

Framework Two: Brainstorming and Divergent Thinking

Once the problem is defined and its roots identified, the next step is **generating solutions**. Anger narrows the mind. When people are upset, they fixate on one or two obvious responses, often extremes like confrontation or avoidance. Problem-solving frameworks encourage **divergent thinking**, the process of generating many possible options before selecting one.

Brainstorming works best when judgment is suspended at the start. The goal isn't to evaluate ideas right away but to produce as many as possible, even ones that seem unrealistic. Quantity breeds creativity.

For example, someone frustrated with how long household chores take might list options such as hiring help, reorganizing the schedule, buying better tools, teaching children to assist, or even turning chores into a timed challenge game. Some ideas may be impractical, but the process opens new possibilities that anger alone would obscure.

Only after ideas are collected should evaluation begin. Each option can be assessed based on feasibility, cost, time, and potential impact. What matters here is that the angry energy has been transformed into structured exploration. The act of brainstorming shifts the mind from dwelling on problems to seeking opportunities.

Framework Three: Decision Matrices

When multiple solutions are available, anger can still interfere by pulling attention toward whichever feels emotionally satisfying in the moment.

For example, when upset at a coworker, confronting them harshly may feel most appealing, but it might not solve the problem. To avoid impulsive choices, structured tools like a **decision matrix** provide clarity.

A decision matrix involves listing possible solutions, then scoring them against chosen criteria. For workplace conflicts, criteria might include effectiveness, likelihood of cooperation, and long-term relationship impact. The solutions are then compared not by emotional weight but by reasoned analysis. This doesn't eliminate emotion, but it integrates it with logic, so that the chosen action aligns with long-term goals rather than short-term gratification.

Let's look at an example:

Possible Action	Effectiveness (1–5)	Likelihood of Cooperation (1–5)	Long-Term Relationship Impact (1–5)	Total Score
Confront harshly in the moment	2	1	1	4
Ignore the issue completely	1	3	2	6
Address calmly in private	5	4	5	14
Send a direct but neutral message	4	3	4	11
Escalate to manager immediately	3	2	2	7

Framework Four: Implementation and Feedback Loops

Problem-solving doesn't end when a solution is chosen. Implementation requires monitoring and adjustment. Anger often makes people impatient, expecting instant results. Frameworks remind us that solutions require feedback loops. If a new communication strategy at work reduces misunderstandings by half, that's progress even if it hasn't eliminated every frustration. Adjustments can refine the approach further.

This phase emphasizes **progress over perfection**. Complaining seeks immediate validation, but problem-solving recognizes that change unfolds over time. Recording progress helps. By keeping notes on how a solution affects daily life, the improvement becomes visible, reducing the urge to slip back into venting.

Emotional Regulation Within Problem-Solving

Frameworks succeed only if emotions are regulated enough to allow rational thought. A furious mind cannot generate solutions effectively. That's why the first step before engaging in problem-solving is often **downshifting arousal**. Techniques such as deep breathing, short walks, or even brief distractions can lower intensity so the brain can think clearly.

It's important to note that this isn't suppression. Emotions are acknowledged but not allowed to dictate the process. Anger becomes data: it signals that something feels unjust or frustrating. The framework then uses that data to ask, "What change would reduce this feeling next time?" In this way, anger is converted from destructive energy into a problem-detection system.

The Habit of Solution-Oriented Thinking

Shifting from venting to problem-solving is not automatic. It requires **habit formation**. At first, people may still find themselves complaining, but with practice, they can catch the moment earlier. A useful habit loop looks like this:

1. **Trigger**: Feeling the urge to complain.
2. **Routine**: Instead of venting, pause and ask, "What's the specific problem here?"
3. **Reward**: The sense of progress that comes from finding at least one possible action.

Over weeks of practice, the brain begins to favor the problem-solving path. Research on habit formation suggests that new patterns take several weeks of consistent repetition to feel automatic. During that time, slips into old venting habits should be seen not as failures but as part of the learning curve.

A Comparative Table

To highlight the difference between venting and problem-solving, here's a structured comparison:

Aspect	Venting/Complaining	Problem-Solving Frameworks
Emotional effect	Temporary relief, often increased frustration	Initial regulation followed by reduced long-term anger
Focus	External blame, what others did wrong	Internal leverage, what actions can be taken
Outcome	Situation stays the same, triggers repeat	Solutions implemented, triggers reduced
Cognitive process	Narrow, repetitive thoughts	Broad exploration, structured evaluation

| Long-term result | Dependence on venting for relief | Growing confidence in ability to handle challenges |
| Relationship impact | Others feel drained or defensive | Others see constructive engagement and cooperation |

This table makes clear that while venting looks easier in the moment, frameworks create lasting change and healthier dynamics.

Real-Life Applications

In the workplace, anger often arises from feeling unrecognized. Venting might mean griping with colleagues over lunch, which creates solidarity but changes nothing. A problem-solving framework might involve setting up a meeting with a manager, clearly defining what recognition looks like, and proposing a feedback system. The latter approach requires effort but has the potential to resolve the problem permanently.

In relationships, venting often takes the form of repeated complaints: "You never listen," or "You always ignore me." These statements rarely lead to change. A problem-solving framework reframes the issue into specifics: "When I'm speaking and the television is on, I feel ignored. Could we agree to mute it during important conversations?" The difference is the shift from accusation to actionable request.

Even with personal habits, the distinction is clear. Someone angry at themselves for procrastinating may vent by calling themselves lazy. That internal complaint doesn't produce progress. A problem-solving framework might involve analyzing the root cause of procrastination, breaking tasks into smaller steps, and tracking daily progress. Instead of stewing in anger, they design a system to prevent the trigger.

Building a Solution-Oriented Identity

Over time, repeatedly practicing frameworks changes more than just reactions. It shifts identity. Someone who was once known for fiery complaints may become known for steady problem-solving. This identity shift reinforces the new behavior. People begin to seek their input not because they vent loudly but because they reliably generate solutions. Social feedback strengthens the internal belief: "I'm someone who finds answers, not someone who complains."

This shift in identity can reduce anger overall. Anger thrives in feelings of helplessness and injustice. A solution-oriented person rarely feels helpless because they trust their ability to influence outcomes. They still feel anger, but it becomes a prompt for action rather than an endless loop of venting.

Reinforcement and reward systems for self-control

Self-control isn't about sheer willpower. It's about building systems that make discipline easier to maintain and anger easier to regulate. Reinforcement works because the human brain is designed to repeat behaviors that produce pleasant outcomes. By attaching positive consequences to acts of restraint, you turn self-control into something your nervous system wants to repeat, instead of something it resists. Anger often produces a short burst of satisfaction because venting releases tension quickly.

That's why it can become habitual. Reinforcement and rewards give you a healthier replacement by making calm behavior feel just as rewarding as an outburst.

Think about how dopamine functions in this process. When you anticipate a reward, your brain releases dopamine before the action is even completed. That chemical signal tells your body and mind that it's worth investing energy in repeating the behavior. Anger hijacks this system, rewarding itself with the relief of release. If you're trying to build self-control, you need to rewire this mechanism by teaching your brain that holding back, calming down, or addressing a conflict thoughtfully gives you a better payoff than snapping. The science is clear: rewards don't have to be big to work. They just have to be consistent and linked tightly to the desired behavior.

The kinds of rewards people respond to vary. Some people thrive on tangible rewards like treating themselves to a meal after a week of good self-control, while others find emotional rewards like self-respect and pride more motivating. A mixed approach usually works best. If every small act of restraint is paired with something affirming, your nervous system begins to attach a new association to restraint: calm equals reward, not punishment. It's important to keep in mind that the timing of reinforcement is just as critical as the type of reward. Immediate reinforcement is far more effective than delayed reinforcement when you're trying to build habits related to self-control.

The idea of reinforcement also ties closely to **negative reinforcement**, which isn't punishment but rather the removal of something unpleasant when a behavior occurs. For example, if you take a few deep breaths and calm down instead of lashing out, you might notice tension leaving your body. That physical relief is itself a form of negative reinforcement. You've reduced discomfort by engaging in the calmer behavior. Pairing that with a positive reinforcement, such as a mental note of pride or a physical reward, doubles the likelihood of repeating the behavior in the future.

Building a reward system works better when you map it clearly. People often fail to maintain self-control because their rewards are inconsistent, vague, or too far in the future. That's why creating a structure can make reinforcement practical rather than abstract. For example, you can use a point system where every time you stop yourself from escalating an argument, you give yourself a point. At the end of the week, those points add up to something enjoyable like a break, a small purchase, or even just permission to relax in a way that feels earned. The physical act of recording the success also gives your brain a concrete marker, which itself can be rewarding.

The effectiveness of reinforcement and rewards has been studied across many contexts, from addiction treatment to weight loss. Self-control in anger works under the same principles. If restraint is consistently rewarded, it gradually becomes less effortful and more automatic.

However, reinforcement requires patience. A new behavior takes repetition to settle into long-term memory.

On average, psychologists find that it takes around 66 days for a new habit to become automatic, but the range can vary widely from 18 days to more than 200 depending on complexity and consistency. Self-control in anger tends to fall on the higher side because the impulse to vent feels immediately rewarding. That means your reinforcement schedule needs to be robust enough to compete with the instant payoff of releasing anger.

People sometimes dismiss rewards as childish, but the truth is adults respond to reinforcement in nearly the same way children do. You're not bribing yourself, you're shaping behavior. Think about how workplace bonuses or performance reviews affect adult motivation. The principle is identical: behavior that produces rewards continues, behavior that doesn't fades. By treating your own restraint with the seriousness of a professional goal, you elevate it beyond a casual effort and give it the weight of structured improvement.

When reinforcement is poorly designed, though, it can backfire. If the reward is too indulgent, it might undo progress. For example, if you control your temper during a stressful day but then "reward" yourself by binge drinking, you're reinforcing one positive behavior with a damaging one. That type of mismatched reinforcement makes the entire system unstable. Rewards should always align with the larger goal of building health and control. Ideally, they contribute to well-being, not detract from it.

One way to keep reinforcement aligned with goals is to categorize rewards by type and rotate them. This prevents any single reward from becoming stale and losing impact. Here's a way to visualize the options:

Reward Type	Example	Benefit to Self-Control Practice
Tangible	Buying a small item	Provides external motivation and sense of treat
Experiential	Watching a favorite movie	Builds positive association with calm behavior
Social	Sharing success with a friend	Adds accountability and emotional reinforcement
Intrinsic	Self-praise or journaling success	Strengthens internal motivation and pride
Wellness	Taking a walk or meditating	Reinforces calm through additional relaxation

Notice how each type ties directly into reinforcing calm restraint rather than undermining it. This is essential because rewards can otherwise slip into distractions that don't strengthen the habit of control.

Another important dimension is reinforcement schedules. There are **fixed ratio schedules** where you reward yourself after a set number of successes, and

variable ratio schedules where rewards come unpredictably after different amounts of success. Casinos use variable ratio schedules because they're highly addictive, but in anger management, a balanced combination is usually better.

For instance, you might give yourself a small acknowledgment every single time you practice restraint, but then every fifth or sixth time you provide a larger reward. This layering keeps the reinforcement engaging without it becoming predictable and boring.

Punishment, on the other hand, rarely works for long-term anger management. People sometimes try to punish themselves for outbursts, whether through guilt or actual deprivation, but this often reinforces anger instead of reducing it. Punishment creates stress, which makes anger more likely. Reinforcement flips the equation by attaching calm behavior to pleasure. You don't want self-control to feel like deprivation; you want it to feel like something that enriches you.

The consistency of reinforcement also matters more than intensity. Giving yourself a huge reward once a month is far less effective than small, regular reinforcements daily. Your brain builds habits through repetition, not rare peaks. If you think of reinforcement as fuel, small doses at regular intervals keep the engine running, while occasional large doses might cause surges but no stability. This is why keeping track of every small success is so important. Even if the reward is nothing more than a quick acknowledgment, it's still a reinforcement.

Reinforcement systems can also be extended socially. For instance, you might share progress with a partner, friend, or therapist who acknowledges each instance of restraint. That acknowledgment acts as a reward, especially if you're someone who values external validation.

Humans are inherently social, and approval from others can amplify reinforcement far more than internal rewards alone. The key is to use social reinforcement carefully, making sure it encourages real progress and doesn't slip into showing restraint only for appearance's sake.

Another layer of reinforcement comes from reflection. After you've successfully managed your anger in a tough moment, writing about it in a journal, even for just two minutes, can become a reward. The act of recording the success makes it tangible, which strengthens the memory of control. Over time, reviewing these entries also becomes reinforcing, because you see clear evidence of progress. Reflection, when tied to reinforcement, becomes an ongoing cycle of recognition and reward.

Self-control is rarely built in isolation. Reinforcement connects daily actions to long-term outcomes, making each small success meaningful. Without reinforcement, restraint feels like constant sacrifice. With reinforcement, it feels like progress. The shift is subtle but critical. You're no longer depriving yourself of the release of anger; you're actively choosing something better and teaching your brain to enjoy it. That shift from suppression to reward-based choice is the foundation of making self-control sustainable.

Self-Talk and Thought Substitution

When anger builds, it often starts with the language you use in your own head. Thoughts shape emotions, and emotions shape behavior. If your inner voice is filled with phrases like "This always happens to me" or "I can't stand this," your body reacts as if you're under attack. That response fuels anger, making it harder to calm down.

Self-talk is the practice of deliberately changing the words you tell yourself in order to change how you feel and act. By swapping destructive language for constructive alternatives, you can short-circuit the cycle of escalation and regain control before the outburst takes over.

The brain is wired to respond to repetition. The more you tell yourself something, the more it becomes a default pathway. If you repeatedly say "I'm furious" or "They're disrespecting me," those thoughts strengthen and the emotion grows sharper. On the other hand, if you train yourself to say "I can handle this" or "This will pass," you guide your nervous system toward calmer states.

This process is known as **thought substitution**, which means replacing unhelpful mental statements with ones that are neutral, balanced, or constructive.

One of the biggest challenges is that anger-driven self-talk often feels automatic. It happens so quickly you barely notice the words flashing through your mind. That's why awareness is the first step. By paying attention to the exact phrases that pop up when you're triggered, you gain the power to interrupt them. For example, instead of repeating "I hate this traffic," you can substitute "Traffic is frustrating, but I'll get through it." The new statement doesn't deny reality but reframes it so the anger doesn't spiral.

What makes substitution effective is that the brain responds to the meaning of the words, not just the sound. When you tell yourself "This is unfair," your body interprets it as a threat to your well-being. When you shift to "This isn't ideal, but I can adjust," the threat signal weakens. Over time, consistently substituting angry thoughts with constructive ones builds new neural patterns. It's like carving a fresh path through a forest: the more you walk it, the clearer it becomes, while the old path fades from disuse.

The habit doesn't form overnight. Studies show it takes weeks, sometimes months, of deliberate repetition for new thought habits to take hold. The exact time frame depends on consistency. If you only practice substitution occasionally, your old angry patterns remain strong. If you practice daily, even in small ways, your brain starts to favor the new track. It's helpful to view self-talk as mental exercise. Each substitution is a rep that strengthens your ability to stay in control.

Different people respond to different substitution styles. Some prefer **neutral replacements**, which keep statements factual and simple. Others find **positive affirmations** more effective, focusing on strengths and resilience. For example, one person might change "This is awful" into "This is temporary." Another might change it into "I'm capable of handling this calmly." Both are forms of substitution, but one focuses on grounding, while the other focuses on empowerment.

The practice also benefits from pairing with physical cues. Saying calming words while taking a slow breath reinforces the shift. You're not only replacing language, you're pairing it with a bodily state that matches the message.

Over time, the association grows stronger. You begin to calm down more quickly because your body and mind learn to work together.

Keeping track of substitutions in writing can make the practice more effective. A simple notebook or phone log where you write the angry thought alongside its substitute helps solidify the habit. When you revisit the log later, you also see evidence of progress, which motivates you to continue. Progress tracking can act as a reward system, reminding you that your efforts are paying off in measurable ways.

To illustrate the transformation clearly, it's useful to compare common angry self-talk patterns with constructive substitutes.

Common Angry Self-Talk	Thought Substitution	Effect on Emotion
"This is unbearable."	"This is hard, but I can manage it."	Lowers intensity by affirming ability to cope
"They never respect me."	"I can set boundaries and communicate clearly."	Shifts focus from blame to action
"I always lose control."	"I'm learning new ways to stay calm."	Encourages growth mindset and patience
"Everything's ruined."	"This setback doesn't define the whole day."	Reduces catastrophizing, restores perspective
"I hate dealing with this."	"I don't enjoy this, but I can get through it."	Keeps emotion grounded without denial

The goal isn't to force yourself into fake positivity but to create accurate, balanced statements that prevent escalation. If you try to deny anger with overly cheerful language, your brain resists because it feels false. Substitution works best when the new thought acknowledges the situation while lowering the intensity.

It's also worth noting that **self-talk can be spoken aloud**. Saying your substitution out loud adds weight, making it harder for the angry thought to dominate. Whispering "I'm calm" or "This will pass" gives your nervous system a verbal anchor. Over time, this becomes second nature, and you find yourself instinctively reaching for calmer words instead of harsher ones.

Another layer to this practice is personalization. Everyone has unique triggers, so the most effective substitutions are the ones tailored to your specific thought patterns.

A phrase that soothes one person might not soothe another. The key is experimentation. Try out different replacements until you find ones that genuinely reduce your emotional intensity. Once you find them, repeat them often. Familiarity is what makes them stick.

Anger often convinces you that venting is the only way to feel better, but self-talk provides an alternative form of relief. By redirecting the narrative, you give yourself permission to cool down without denying the frustration. This balance is critical because it prevents suppression, which can build pressure, while also avoiding destructive outbursts. Substitution is not about ignoring your feelings. It's about translating them into language that serves you instead of sabotaging you.

Consistency remains the heart of success. Just as reinforcement systems rely on repeated rewards, self-talk relies on repeated substitutions. At first, you may feel like you're catching yourself too late or struggling to remember the new phrases. With practice, the substitutions come faster.

Eventually, they appear on their own before the angry thought even has time to settle. That's the point where habit has taken root.

The payoff is significant. Strong self-talk not only reduces the frequency of outbursts but also enhances confidence. When you know you can manage your reactions, you feel less controlled by external triggers. You no longer fear situations that once seemed overwhelming because you trust your ability to handle them. This trust builds resilience, which feeds into every other area of life, from relationships to work.

Thought substitution doesn't erase anger, but it reshapes how you experience it. Instead of being a fire that consumes everything, anger becomes a signal you can interpret and redirect. With practice, your words become tools rather than weapons. By guiding your own inner dialogue, you gradually build a mind that works with you instead of against you.

Chapter 7: Long-Term Lifestyle Approaches

The Role of Sleep in Emotional Stability

Sleep and anger have a tighter bond than most people realize. When you think about a night where you barely slept, you can probably recall how everything felt harder the next day. The smallest frustrations turned into irritations. Someone walking slowly in front of you felt like a personal insult, and minor delays caused outsized reactions. This isn't simply a matter of being grumpy. Lack of rest directly alters how the brain manages emotion, and anger is one of the first states to become amplified when sleep falters.

As covered earlier in the book, the **amygdala**, a part of the brain that reacts to perceived threats, becomes more reactive when you haven't had enough sleep. Functional imaging studies show that people who sleep poorly exhibit heightened amygdala activity when exposed to emotionally charged images. That means the brain shifts into a defensive mode more quickly.

At the same time, the **prefrontal cortex**, which normally regulates emotional responses and dampens unnecessary anger, loses efficiency without rest. The combination of an overactive threat detector and an underperforming control system creates a perfect environment for irritability.

A single bad night of sleep already changes your emotional balance. Research shows that after only one night of restricted sleep, participants report higher stress, quicker temper, and more negative moods. Extend this over several nights, and the body begins to interpret the lack of rest as a chronic stressor. Cortisol levels rise, heart rate variability declines, and the nervous system starts operating in a state of constant readiness. That biological stance makes anger harder to control because the body is primed for fight-or-flight.

Sleep also influences **neurotransmitter systems** that regulate emotion. Serotonin, dopamine, and GABA all shift with poor rest. These chemicals usually help maintain calmness, regulate impulses, and support flexible thinking. Without enough sleep, serotonin declines, which has been linked to mood instability and aggression. Dopamine regulation also falters, making rewards less satisfying and frustration tolerance weaker.

The cycle deepens when anger itself disrupts sleep. Many people lie awake replaying arguments or imagining comebacks. This keeps the brain in a high-arousal state, preventing the body from entering deeper stages of rest. Over time, insomnia can form around the habit of ruminating at night, which means poor sleep both triggers anger and is worsened by it. Breaking this loop requires intentional changes.

One of the most effective ways to restore stability is to **set a consistent sleep schedule**. The brain operates on circadian rhythms that regulate hormone release, body temperature, and sleep cycles. Going to bed and waking up at irregular hours confuses those systems, much like jet lag. Aligning sleep with natural rhythms helps the body transition into deeper, restorative stages.

Sleep quality is just as important as sleep length. Even if someone gets eight hours, waking up frequently or struggling to stay in deep sleep undermines the process. **Sleep hygiene** practices, such as keeping the bedroom dark and cool, removing electronic devices, and avoiding caffeine late in the day, directly impact quality. Exposure to bright light in the evening, especially from screens, suppresses melatonin and makes it harder to fall asleep.

The timing of sleep matters too. Studies show that people who consistently delay bedtime until very late experience more emotional instability. Shifting sleep earlier, even by an hour, can improve regulation. Naps can help, but only if used carefully.

Short naps under 30 minutes restore alertness without interfering with nighttime rest. Long or late naps can disrupt circadian cycles and make it harder to fall asleep at the right time.

It's worth emphasizing that restoring sleep isn't just about avoiding tiredness. It directly changes how likely you are to snap at a coworker, yell at a partner, or escalate in traffic. By protecting sleep, you protect your emotional stability.

Here's a clear way to see the relationship between sleep and anger regulation:

Sleep Pattern	Emotional Effect	Anger Response
Consistent 7-9 hours nightly	Balanced neurotransmitters, strong prefrontal control	Irritations are manageable, recovery after conflict is quick
Fragmented sleep with frequent waking	Heightened cortisol, reduced serotonin	Anger flares more easily, harder to calm down
Chronic short sleep under 6 hours	Overactive amygdala, weakened impulse control	Frequent outbursts, misinterpretation of neutral cues as hostile
Irregular sleep schedule	Confused circadian rhythm, low sleep efficiency	Emotional swings, unpredictable bursts of irritation
Rest after anger episode	Reduced physiological arousal, restoration of control	Perspective regained, less rumination

The lesson is simple but not easy: anger becomes harder to manage when sleep suffers, and it becomes easier when sleep is reliable. For people trying to control emotional reactions, sleep is not optional recovery. It's a primary method of regulation.

Think about how long it takes for habits around sleep to shift. Many people assume a few early nights will solve everything. In reality, the body needs several weeks of consistency to reset circadian rhythms and neurochemical balance. If you've been sleeping poorly for years, the adjustment period may take longer, but improvements in mood usually appear within the first two weeks.

It helps to approach sleep improvement the same way you'd approach managing anger. Both require daily attention, not occasional effort. If someone tries to control outbursts but stays up until 2 a.m. scrolling through their phone, they're setting themselves up to fail. A rested brain can resist the pull of anger far more effectively than an exhausted one.

Diet, Caffeine, and Alcohol's Effect on Anger

What you eat and drink has a direct influence on how your body and brain process emotion. Many people look at anger as a purely psychological issue, but the truth is that nutrition, stimulants, and substances can either strengthen or weaken your ability to regulate emotional reactions. Every choice at the table shifts hormones, neurotransmitters, and energy balance in ways that alter your threshold for irritability. When you think about controlling anger, food and drink habits can't be ignored.

The connection between diet and mood starts with **blood sugar stability**. When blood glucose levels fluctuate too sharply, mood instability rises. Eating refined carbohydrates, such as white bread, candy, or soda, causes a quick spike in glucose followed by a sharp crash. That crash triggers adrenaline and cortisol release, which the body interprets as stress.

In that state, patience wears thin and small frustrations spark outsized reactions. Studies have shown that aggressive behavior rises when individuals experience hypoglycemia, even mild cases. Stable blood sugar, on the other hand, supports steadier mood regulation and more controlled reactions to triggers.

Protein intake helps buffer these swings. Foods rich in protein slow down the absorption of glucose, creating a more gradual rise and fall in blood sugar. Beyond that, proteins supply amino acids like tryptophan and tyrosine, which are precursors to **serotonin** and **dopamine**. These neurotransmitters regulate impulse control, decision-making, and reward sensitivity. A diet that skimps on protein often leaves people feeling edgy, restless, and less able to handle irritations.

Fats also influence anger management. Diets high in **omega-3 fatty acids**, found in fish, walnuts, and flaxseeds, correlate with lower aggression and better emotional regulation. These fats help maintain neuronal membrane fluidity, making neurotransmission more efficient.

Low levels of omega-3s have been linked with higher irritability, impulsive behavior, and even violent outbursts. In contrast, diets dominated by trans fats or heavily processed oils may increase inflammation in the brain, which has been tied to mood dysregulation.

Micronutrients matter too. Deficiencies in **magnesium, zinc, and vitamin B6** impair the production and regulation of calming neurotransmitters. For instance, magnesium acts as a natural relaxant of the nervous system, and when intake is low, people experience greater irritability and higher stress responses. Zinc supports dopamine regulation, while B6 helps convert tryptophan into serotonin. Without them, emotional stability weakens.

Caffeine deserves close attention. While moderate caffeine use can improve alertness and focus, excess consumption directly increases **physiological arousal**.

Heart rate rises, adrenaline surges, and the nervous system shifts into a state of readiness. In this heightened condition, anger is harder to resist because the body feels like it's under pressure even when nothing threatening is happening. High caffeine intake also interferes with sleep quality, which compounds irritability the next day.

Tolerance doesn't eliminate the problem. Even people who drink coffee daily still experience elevated cortisol and adrenaline after a strong dose. The difference is that they may not consciously feel the jitters, but their body remains in a more reactive state. This is why caffeine-heavy habits often lead to short tempers in stressful environments. Energy drinks, with their combination of caffeine, sugar, and other stimulants, magnify the issue by delivering a rapid spike followed by a steep crash.

Alcohol shifts the equation in another way. It lowers **inhibitory control** by suppressing prefrontal cortex activity. That means impulses that would normally be filtered get expressed more quickly. People who rarely explode when sober may lash out after drinking, not because the anger suddenly appeared, but because the brakes came off. Alcohol also disrupts serotonin balance, which increases aggression in some individuals. Studies on domestic violence and bar fights consistently show alcohol as a major factor because it reduces restraint.

The problem extends beyond immediate intoxication. Even moderate drinking disrupts sleep cycles, particularly REM sleep, which is critical for emotional regulation. A person may think they slept after drinking, but the brain didn't reach the restorative stages it needed.

The next day, irritability rises, and small problems feel larger. Chronic drinking compounds the effect by altering dopamine and serotonin pathways long term, making emotional regulation consistently more difficult.

Diet also influences gut microbiota, which has a surprisingly large effect on mood. The gut produces a significant portion of the body's serotonin, and the types of bacteria present determine how well this system works. Diets rich in fiber, vegetables, and fermented foods support a more balanced microbiome, which corresponds with lower irritability and more emotional stability. Diets heavy in processed foods, sugar, and alcohol reduce microbial diversity, weakening this stabilizing effect.

A common mistake is to assume that one meal or one drink won't matter. In reality, the nervous system reacts quickly. For example, a single night of drinking can impair next-day anger regulation. A morning with too much caffeine can raise baseline irritability for hours. Eating nothing but refined carbs for lunch can create a mid-afternoon crash where patience evaporates. The body constantly reacts to input, and the margin for emotional stability can be either strengthened or weakened daily.

It's helpful to compare dietary patterns and their impact on anger regulation:

Intake Pattern	Biological Effect	Anger Impact
High refined sugar	Glucose spikes and crashes, cortisol release	Sudden irritability, quick temper
Balanced protein and carbs	Stable blood sugar, serotonin production	More control, steadier mood
Omega-3 rich diet	Reduced inflammation, efficient neurotransmission	Lower aggression, better impulse control
High caffeine	Elevated adrenaline, disrupted sleep	Heightened irritability, impatience
Moderate alcohol	Prefrontal suppression, serotonin disruption	Reduced restraint, quicker outbursts
Chronic alcohol	Altered dopamine systems, poor sleep quality	Consistent irritability, unstable mood
Nutrient deficiencies (magnesium, zinc, B6)	Impaired neurotransmitter synthesis	Greater susceptibility to anger triggers

Managing anger through diet isn't about perfection. It's about reducing the factors that make the nervous system more volatile and increasing the ones that make it more stable. Eating balanced meals that avoid sudden spikes in blood sugar, moderating caffeine, and limiting alcohol intake create a biological foundation where self-control is possible.

One of the most overlooked aspects is timing. Going long stretches without eating can induce hypoglycemia, which reliably increases irritability. For many people, the phrase "hangry" isn't a joke but a genuine reflection of how low blood sugar affects mood. Regular meals or snacks with protein and healthy fats prevent those dips.

Another important point is that dietary changes require time to influence mood consistently. Taking an omega-3 supplement once won't transform emotional stability. It takes weeks of consistent intake for cell membranes to incorporate these fats and improve neurotransmission. Similarly, reducing caffeine may take several weeks before sleep patterns normalize and irritability declines. Nutrition works on both immediate and long-term timelines.

For people actively working on anger management, food and drink become part of the strategy. It's not just about resisting temptation or counting to ten. It's about giving the body fewer reasons to be reactive in the first place. With a stable biological foundation, psychological techniques like deep breathing or reframing thoughts become more effective, because the nervous system isn't primed against them.

Regular Exercise as a Regulator of Emotions

Exercise is often promoted as a way to stay fit, but its influence on emotional balance is just as powerful. When people struggle with anger, frustration, or irritability, they often look for mental strategies alone, yet the body plays an equally important role. Movement changes the brain's chemistry, calms the nervous system, and gives built-up tension a safe release. When you see anger as stored energy that needs an outlet, physical activity becomes not just helpful but essential.

One of the most immediate effects of exercise is the reduction of **stress hormones**. Activities that raise the heart rate, like running or cycling, lower circulating cortisol and adrenaline over time. These are the very hormones that make you feel wired and quick to snap.

By exercising regularly, the baseline levels of these hormones decrease, which lowers the chances that minor frustrations will trigger disproportionate anger. Even short workouts can produce measurable reductions in stress markers, making consistency more important than intensity.

Exercise also stimulates the release of **endorphins**, natural opioids that create a sense of calm and well-being. After a brisk walk, swim, or weightlifting session, people often report that irritations which seemed unbearable before no longer feel significant. This isn't just distraction. Endorphins change how the brain processes discomfort, both physical and emotional. They essentially buffer the perception of stress, leaving you more resilient when conflicts arise.

Beyond endorphins, movement increases **serotonin** and **dopamine**, neurotransmitters tied to impulse control, reward, and motivation. Low serotonin has long been linked to aggression and irritability, while dopamine influences whether you can see long-term benefits over short-term gratification. Exercise provides a natural boost to these systems, improving patience and self-control. The brain also becomes more responsive to these neurotransmitters when exercise is consistent, meaning that mood regulation improves in a lasting way rather than only during the workout itself.

There is also a mechanical element. Anger often carries with it a surge of physical tension: clenched jaws, tight shoulders, faster breathing, and increased heart rate. When the body doesn't use this energy, it lingers and amplifies irritability.

Exercise functions as a **release valve** for this physiological buildup. Muscles relax more easily afterward, the parasympathetic nervous system takes over, and the body learns to return to a calm baseline faster. This conditioning effect teaches the body to downshift more effectively after stress.

Different kinds of exercise bring different benefits.

Aerobic exercise such as running, swimming, or biking improves cardiovascular health and reduces overall arousal levels, making the nervous system less jumpy.

Strength training creates a sense of mastery and control, which can counter feelings of helplessness that often trigger anger.

Mind-body practices like yoga and tai chi combine physical movement with breathing control, reinforcing calm states while still using the body as an outlet. Even something as simple as walking has been shown to regulate mood because it changes both physical state and mental perspective.

It's also important to note that exercise influences **sleep quality**, which is one of the strongest predictors of irritability. People who exercise consistently fall asleep faster, reach deeper stages of sleep, and wake up more refreshed. Poor sleep, in contrast, weakens prefrontal control over emotional responses, making people more prone to snapping at small annoyances. Through better sleep, exercise indirectly improves patience and tolerance.

Consistency is the key. Sporadic workouts give temporary benefits, but the nervous system adapts most effectively to regular patterns. Anger management programs that include structured physical activity show significantly better outcomes than those relying on cognitive strategies alone. A routine of three to five exercise sessions per week creates stability in mood, energy, and self-control.

There is also a social dimension. Group exercise, whether it's team sports, classes, or even casual jogging groups, provides opportunities for **social connection**.

Anger often thrives in isolation, while shared activity reduces stress and increases feelings of belonging. Being part of a group also provides accountability, which increases the likelihood of maintaining the exercise habit, reinforcing its emotional benefits.

People sometimes worry that intense exercise could make them angrier, especially competitive sports. The research shows the opposite when activity is structured and voluntary. The competition may trigger bursts of adrenaline, but the physical release, endorphin boost, and sense of mastery override any temporary spikes. What matters most is intention. Exercise done with the goal of self-regulation promotes emotional stability, while activity done in an already hostile state, such as picking fights in sports settings, can reinforce aggression.

The cumulative effect of exercise on emotions can be seen across multiple dimensions:

Mechanism	Impact on Emotions	Long-Term Effect
Lower cortisol and adrenaline	Reduced baseline stress	Less reactive to triggers
Endorphin release	Increased calm and resilience	Frustrations feel less overwhelming
Boost in serotonin and dopamine	Improved impulse control and patience	Stronger self-regulation habits
Muscle relaxation	Release of physical tension	Faster return to calm baseline
Improved sleep quality	Better prefrontal control	Reduced irritability
Social engagement in group activity	Reduced isolation, more belonging	Lower likelihood of anger outbursts

Exercise also builds a sense of **agency**. People who struggle with anger often feel at the mercy of their emotions, but building strength, endurance, or flexibility gives a tangible reminder that they can take control of their state. Progress in exercise mirrors progress in emotional regulation, reinforcing the idea that change is possible through steady effort.

The habit component deserves attention. Just as diet takes time to show consistent benefits, exercise must be woven into lifestyle. Starting small prevents burnout. Even ten minutes of daily movement creates a foundation.

Over time, the body begins to expect and crave the outlet, making anger management easier because the system has a built-in regulation practice. People who miss their workouts often notice they feel edgier, which shows how integrated exercise becomes in emotional balance.

The most practical takeaway is that exercise doesn't need to be extreme to help regulate anger. What matters is regularity, variety, and choosing activities that feel enjoyable enough to repeat. This combination supports both the biology and psychology of self-control. It turns the body from a container of tension into a mechanism for release and resilience.

Time Management and Reducing Daily Stress

Anger rarely appears in a vacuum. For most people, it grows out of the grind of daily obligations, tight schedules, and the sense that there's never enough time. Poor time management increases background stress, which primes the body and mind to snap at the smallest irritation. When every hour feels crammed, even a minor delay in traffic or an unexpected request can trigger rage that feels disproportionate. By improving **time management**, you lower the base level of stress, which makes anger less likely to erupt.

One of the key links between poor time management and anger is **decision fatigue**. Every day requires choices, from responding to emails to deciding what task to prioritize. Without structure, the brain becomes overloaded, which depletes self-control. This depletion makes it harder to regulate emotional reactions.

Creating a predictable schedule reduces unnecessary decisions, leaving more mental energy to deal with challenges calmly. For instance, planning your day the night before eliminates the stress of waking up and scrambling to figure out what to do first.

Time stress also shortens patience. When you believe you're late, or when your list of tasks keeps growing, the brain interprets interruptions as threats to your goals. That perception amplifies irritation. People who build **time buffers** into their schedules experience less anger because they aren't forced to react as if every minute is an emergency. A ten-minute cushion before meetings or leaving early for appointments often makes the difference between calm and hostility.

The physiological side is also clear. Stress hormones rise in response to perceived overload. When schedules are unrealistic, the body reacts as if under attack: heart rate climbs, breathing becomes shallow, and the nervous system shifts into a high-alert state. This arousal mirrors the state seen during anger. By reducing overload through better planning, you prevent the body from spending the entire day close to its boiling point.

Prioritization is one of the most effective ways to reduce daily stress. Not all tasks carry equal importance, but when everything feels urgent, the nervous system never relaxes. Identifying what truly matters and letting go of lesser items reduces the sense of drowning. Many people use variations of the Eisenhower Matrix, which divides tasks into urgent/important, important/not urgent, urgent/not important, and neither. Even without a formal system, the act of labeling priorities makes daily life feel more under control.

Interruptions are another source of daily frustration. Every distraction, whether it's a phone notification or a coworker dropping by, forces the brain to switch focus.

Each switch consumes time and energy, which builds stress and shortens temper. Strategies like silencing non-essential notifications, setting aside blocks for deep work, or scheduling specific times to check messages all prevent anger from snowballing. The fewer unexpected pulls on attention, the less edgy you feel.

A table can show how different time-management practices directly reduce anger triggers:

Time Management Practice	Stress/Anger Trigger Reduced	Long-Term Benefit
Planning the night before	Morning decision fatigue	More calm energy at start of day
Building time buffers	Feeling rushed or trapped	Increased patience and flexibility
Prioritization	Overload and overwhelm	Greater control and focus
Limiting interruptions	Attention switching fatigue	Steadier mood throughout day
Delegating or outsourcing	Carrying all burdens yourself	Reduced resentment
Setting realistic goals	Chronic failure to "catch up"	Less frustration and guilt

Delegation is worth highlighting. Many people cling to every responsibility, either from perfectionism or distrust, but this overload breeds resentment. Anger often hides behind the thought "why am I the only one doing this?" By sharing responsibilities at work or home, you lighten the load and reduce hidden sources of hostility. Even small shifts, like asking a partner to handle one household chore consistently, can prevent simmering frustration.

Breaks are another overlooked factor. When you work without rest, stress accumulates. Short breaks let the nervous system reset. This doesn't always mean leaving your desk for an hour. Even five minutes of stretching or walking helps the body release tension. Skipping breaks is one of the fastest paths to irritability because the brain loses the capacity to regulate emotions effectively.

Time management also influences **sleep quality**, which directly impacts anger control. Overpacked schedules push people to stay up late or cut into rest, creating a cycle of fatigue and irritability. Proper planning protects bedtime.

When tasks are done earlier or spaced more realistically, sleep stops being a casualty of poor organization. Since lack of sleep lowers impulse control, this connection between scheduling and rest is critical for emotional stability.

The mental framing of tasks matters too. When schedules are vague, everything feels unfinished, which feeds agitation. Writing tasks down creates **external memory**, freeing mental space and reducing rumination. The act of crossing items off also provides a sense of completion, which reinforces calm. Without this, people carry the weight of invisible "open loops" in their minds, making them irritable without knowing why.

Technology can help but also hurt. Calendar apps, reminders, and task managers reduce cognitive load, but overreliance on constant alerts can increase stress. The healthiest use of technology is to automate structure (like recurring reminders for bills or appointments) while minimizing intrusive notifications. This balance keeps life organized without feeling harassed by devices.

An often overlooked aspect of time management is **alignment with personal values**. Anger isn't just triggered by busyness, but by spending time on things that feel meaningless while neglecting what matters most. Scheduling time for exercise, family, or personal projects prevents resentment from growing. People who constantly sacrifice meaningful activities for urgent but unimportant demands often explode in anger because they feel robbed of autonomy.

Finally, reducing daily stress involves acceptance that not everything can be done. Many angry outbursts stem from unrealistic expectations of control. By managing time well, you gain clarity on what's possible, which reduces the anger that comes from chasing the impossible. Ironically, saying no to certain demands is one of the strongest ways to preserve both time and calmness.

Building Supportive Relationships

Anger is often shaped by the environment a person lives in. If someone is surrounded by hostility, criticism, or emotional neglect, their tolerance for frustration drops. By contrast, **supportive relationships** create buffers that reduce anger before it even rises. They act as stabilizers, giving people a sense of safety and belonging that lowers stress. Support is not only about comfort but also about accountability, since people who feel connected are less likely to lash out impulsively.

A good relationship creates a feedback system. When someone reacts harshly, supportive friends or partners provide honest but nonjudgmental reflections. This stops anger from spiraling unchecked. For example, if a coworker notices you're stressed and reminds you to take a step back, that small nudge prevents escalation. Without such feedback, anger builds silently until it bursts.

Isolation intensifies anger. People who lack trusted connections often ruminate more, replaying insults or frustrations in their minds. With no outlet for perspective, those thoughts grow heavier. Talking to someone who listens cuts this loop short. It shifts the brain away from internal rumination toward external processing, which reduces emotional charge. Even short conversations where someone simply acknowledges frustration can prevent hours of simmering resentment.

Supportive relationships also shape **physiological responses**. Studies show that physical presence of trusted people lowers cortisol, slows heart rate, and dampens adrenaline spikes. These changes matter because anger is not only a mental reaction but a bodily state.

When your body feels calmer around someone, angry impulses lose intensity. This is why people often feel less reactive when they vent to a trusted friend compared to yelling alone in a room.

Trust is the foundation of all supportive bonds. Without trust, communication becomes guarded, and honesty vanishes. Anger thrives in environments where people feel misunderstood or judged. Building trust requires consistent behavior: keeping commitments, listening carefully, and showing empathy. Over time, this consistency builds emotional security. Once secure, people are less defensive, which means anger has fewer openings to erupt.

Different types of relationships provide distinct forms of support. Family offers history and unconditional bonds, but sometimes carries old conflicts. Friends often provide shared perspective and humor, which relieves tension. Colleagues bring practical understanding of work-related pressures. Even pets create calming effects through companionship. Relying on a mix of these relationships creates resilience.

One useful way to view support systems is by examining their functions rather than their labels:

Relationship Function	Example	Effect on Anger
Emotional support	A friend who listens without judgment	Reduces rumination and tension
Practical support	A colleague who helps with workload	Prevents overload that fuels irritability
Honest feedback	A partner pointing out rising stress	Interrupts escalation before outburst
Shared activity	Exercising with a sibling	Provides healthy outlet for stress
Physical presence	Sitting quietly with someone you trust	Calms physiological arousal

Conflict inside relationships is inevitable, but how it is handled determines whether anger grows or shrinks. Supportive people know how to argue without humiliating or threatening. They use **assertive communication**, where feelings are expressed directly but respectfully. This reduces defensive reactions. By contrast, relationships that rely on blame or contempt keep anger alive long after the argument ends.

Another important feature of supportive networks is reciprocity. When help flows only one way, resentment builds. People feel drained or taken for granted, which eventually sparks anger.

Balanced relationships, where both sides give and receive, maintain stability. This reciprocity can be simple, like alternating who checks in or who helps with errands. What matters is that both parties feel valued.

Support systems are also protective against anger in stressful transitions. Major life changes, such as job loss or illness, strain emotional resources. Without connection, anger can dominate. But when people lean on supportive relationships during these times, they're reminded they aren't facing challenges alone. That reminder shifts perspective, lowering the sense of unfairness that often fuels rage.

The quality of conversations within relationships matters more than the quantity. Short but genuine interactions are more calming than long but distracted ones. Listening fully without multitasking shows care, which directly reduces the feeling of being dismissed. Anger thrives when people feel unheard. By practicing attentive listening, relationships cut anger at its roots.

Boundaries are another part of maintaining supportive ties. Not every relationship should provide unlimited access. If someone crosses lines repeatedly, anger builds.

Setting clear boundaries about what is acceptable creates respect. Boundaries prevent resentment, which otherwise festers and leads to explosive anger later. Respectful relationships respect time, privacy, and individuality.

Supportive groups can extend beyond personal circles. Community involvement, clubs, or spiritual groups provide broader networks that reinforce belonging. These environments reduce loneliness and offer structured outlets for stress. When individuals face anger-inducing situations, these wider networks can step in with advice, distraction, or shared activity that dilutes intensity.

It's also important to note that not all relationships are supportive. Some are toxic, filled with manipulation, criticism, or constant negativity. These connections amplify anger instead of reducing it. Recognizing this distinction is essential. If someone consistently makes you more irritable, that relationship may need distance or boundaries. A smaller but healthier network is far better for anger management than a large but draining one.

Supportive relationships also help with **perspective shifting**. When angry, people often exaggerate the seriousness of an event. A trusted person can reframe it, showing that the situation may not be as catastrophic as it feels. This reframing reduces the urge to lash out. Over time, consistent exposure to balanced perspectives trains the brain to adopt less reactive interpretations even when alone.

Technology complicates modern relationships. Digital communication allows constant contact, but it also creates superficial interactions. A quick "like" on a post doesn't soothe anger the way a real conversation does. While online networks can supplement, they rarely replace the calming power of face-to-face or voice-to-voice connections. Prioritizing direct contact strengthens the emotional stability needed to regulate anger.

Children raised in supportive environments learn emotional regulation more effectively. Parents who model calm communication and mutual respect teach kids to handle anger without aggression. This shows how relationships aren't only buffers for current stress but also shape lifelong patterns of emotional response. Adults who lacked such models may need to intentionally seek new environments that teach and reinforce healthier behaviors.

Support networks must be nurtured actively. People often assume relationships sustain themselves, but neglect weakens them. Regular check-ins, appreciation, and shared experiences keep bonds strong. This maintenance ensures the support is available when anger-inducing situations arise. Just as muscles strengthen with exercise, relationships deepen with use.

Preventing Burnout and Overload

Burnout develops when daily demands outweigh the resources a person has to cope. It is not simply about being tired but about feeling emotionally drained, detached, and ineffective. **Overload** builds slowly, often disguised as productivity, until the body and mind begin to resist even small tasks. Preventing this state requires a mix of awareness, balance, and consistent self-management before the breaking point arrives.

The first step is recognizing early signs. People often wait until exhaustion forces them to stop, but small clues appear much earlier. Increased irritability, difficulty concentrating, sleep problems, or a sense of cynicism about work are signals that stress has moved beyond normal limits. Paying attention to these signs allows someone to intervene before damage deepens.

Time boundaries are critical. Many people slip into overload because they blur the line between work and rest. Emails at midnight or weekend obligations slowly erode recovery. Preventing burnout requires setting clear limits and protecting rest as seriously as any other commitment. Those who schedule downtime without guilt often recover faster and sustain performance longer.

Recovery also comes from variety. The brain and body need shifts between effort and relaxation. Constant focus on one kind of task strains limited systems. Mixing physical activity, social connection, and quiet rest prevents monotony and renews energy. Even short breaks scattered through the day serve as resets that lower the risk of chronic fatigue.

Prioritization reduces overload by making choices about what truly matters. Not every request deserves immediate attention. People who filter tasks through questions like "Is this essential?" or "Does this align with my goals?" avoid drowning in obligations. Without such filtering, days fill with low-value activities that consume energy but offer little reward.

Supportive environments are another safeguard. When workloads are shared fairly and communication is open, stress disperses. By contrast, toxic or competitive settings push individuals to carry more than they can manage. Building networks of cooperation protects against the loneliness that often fuels burnout.

Physical care ties directly into emotional endurance. **Sleep, nutrition, and exercise** form the foundation for resilience. A well-rested brain processes stress more calmly, while poor sleep magnifies irritability. Balanced meals stabilize energy, preventing spikes and crashes that make pressure feel heavier. Regular movement flushes stress hormones and restores a sense of control. These routines are often neglected during overload, but they're exactly what allow people to handle challenges.

Cognitive reframing helps prevent emotional exhaustion. When individuals view every obstacle as personal failure, stress becomes unbearable. By seeing setbacks as temporary or as chances to learn, they lighten the mental load. This shift doesn't remove challenges but reduces their toxic weight. Optimistic perspectives act like buffers, softening impact and preserving motivation.

Technology contributes both solutions and risks. Productivity apps can organize tasks, but constant alerts keep the brain in a state of vigilance. Learning to use technology intentionally rather than reactively is key. Turning off notifications during focused work or designated rest protects attention and reduces overload.

An important tool is **energy mapping**. Everyone has times of day when focus peaks and times when it drops. Aligning demanding work with natural highs and leaving routine tasks for slower periods preserves strength. Ignoring these rhythms forces the brain to push against its own biology, which accelerates fatigue.

The long-term prevention of burnout often rests on aligning work with personal values. People who see meaning in what they do experience less exhaustion, even under heavy pressure. When values and actions diverge, stress increases. Regular reflection on whether tasks align with deeper goals ensures effort feels worthwhile rather than draining.

Preventive Factor	Description	Effect on Burnout
Early warning signs	Irritability, cynicism, poor focus	Allows intervention before collapse
Time boundaries	Limiting work hours and protecting rest	Preserves recovery cycles
Physical care	Sleep, nutrition, exercise	Builds resilience to stress
Cognitive reframing	Viewing setbacks as temporary	Reduces emotional exhaustion
Energy mapping	Matching tasks to natural rhythms	Maximizes efficiency and lowers fatigue
Value alignment	Ensuring tasks match personal meaning	Sustains motivation under pressure

Preventing overload is not about cutting off every form of stress, because stress by itself isn't always harmful. Stress can act as a driver, sharpening focus, forcing adaptation, and encouraging people to grow. Athletes, students, and professionals alike experience that edge where pressure fuels performance. The real problem starts when the pendulum swings too far in one direction, where the demands never let up and the body or mind isn't given space to reset. Growth depends on cycles, not constant strain, and ignoring the recovery phase makes even manageable challenges feel unbearable.

When recovery is sidelined, the nervous system remains on high alert. Sleep becomes shallow, patience runs thin, and simple irritations trigger outsized reactions. That constant activation drains energy reserves and erodes motivation.

Over time, what once felt stimulating shifts into exhaustion. The solution isn't to remove challenges entirely but to integrate **rest, boundaries, support, and physical care** so the system can recharge. Rest includes real downtime without multitasking, boundaries mean knowing when to stop saying yes, support comes from leaning on trusted people, and physical care requires sleep, nutrition, and movement. These pieces don't just add comfort, they act as safeguards against the creeping accumulation of stress.

By weaving these elements into daily life, challenges no longer pile on top of each other without relief. Instead, they're met with a body and mind that can absorb strain and then reset. That rhythm turns stress into a catalyst rather than a weight. Burnout doesn't have to be an inevitable crash; it becomes something that can be anticipated and prevented. With consistent recovery, overload shifts from an approaching threat to a manageable risk, and resilience comes from the balance between effort and renewal.

Chapter 8: Special Contexts and Situations

Anger in the Workplace

Workplaces are often designed around deadlines, performance reviews, and hierarchical structures, which means tension isn't rare. Anger in this setting usually comes from three clusters: **perceived unfairness, communication breakdowns, and workload imbalance**. Each has a unique effect on behavior, and if unmanaged, the fallout spreads far beyond the original source of frustration.

Perceived unfairness is one of the strongest triggers. When employees believe promotions, assignments, or recognition are distributed unevenly, anger surfaces quickly. This isn't just about money or titles; fairness taps into basic human psychology. Studies show that workers who feel treated unjustly are more likely to disengage, make errors, or sabotage colleagues. That reaction isn't always conscious, but it signals how potent anger can be when linked to equity.

Communication breakdowns trigger another layer of workplace hostility. A poorly worded email, lack of feedback, or misinterpreted tone can spark conflict that spirals. Anger thrives in ambiguity.

Without clear information, people fill the gaps with assumptions, often negative ones. One misunderstanding between a manager and employee can quickly harden into resentment that colors every future exchange.

Workload imbalance is harder to quantify, but equally corrosive. If one person consistently carries more weight than others, anger builds. Over time, the imbalance becomes personal, directed not only at colleagues but also at leadership for allowing the situation to persist. Once anger takes root in this way, productivity declines and turnover risk rises.

Short bursts of irritation aren't always destructive. Research suggests that mild, well-directed anger can flag inefficiencies and spur innovation. The key lies in **channeling anger into structured communication** instead of letting it fester or explode. Workplaces that allow open but respectful expression of frustration often use anger as an early warning system rather than treating it as purely destructive.

Uncontrolled anger, though, leaves a trail. Verbal outbursts damage reputations, often more than the issue that caused them. Colleagues remember who raised their voice, not the substance of the complaint. Anger that turns personal creates long shadows; one harsh meeting exchange can sour trust for years. This damage isn't limited to peer-to-peer interactions but extends to clients, customers, and external partners, which can directly affect business outcomes.

Managers face unique challenges. Their anger carries extra weight because of power dynamics. A sharp comment from a peer may sting, but the same words from a boss can devastate morale. Employees often interpret managerial anger as a judgment of personal worth rather than a reaction to a specific situation. That's why leaders must be especially deliberate in how they handle irritations.

Different job roles also experience anger differently. High-pressure environments like emergency medicine, finance, or law enforce constant vigilance and speed. Mistakes can be costly or dangerous, so tempers often flare more easily. In contrast, creative industries rely on collaboration and feedback loops. Anger in those settings often stems from perceived criticism or the rejection of ideas. The context shapes the way anger emerges and how it should be managed.

Coping strategies must match the setting. Employees at all levels benefit from **de-escalation techniques**, which range from short breathing exercises to structured pause routines before responding. Simple policies such as a five-minute "cooling off" walk before meetings can prevent rash decisions. Structured conflict resolution processes, such as mediation, formalize this by creating safe environments for expression without escalation.

Technology has altered workplace anger too. Digital communication lacks nonverbal cues, which increases misinterpretation. A terse Slack message might be efficiency to one person but hostility to another. Anger driven by digital tone misfires is now common, and companies are slowly teaching staff to add clarity through context, punctuation, or even intentional use of emojis to soften ambiguous remarks.

There's also the silent form of anger at work: **passive aggression**. Instead of yelling, people delay tasks, give minimal effort, or subtly resist instructions. This behavior can be harder to detect but often more damaging, since it corrodes trust over time. Understanding that passive aggression is often unspoken anger can help managers address the root issue rather than just the symptom.

Organizations that want to mitigate workplace anger invest in **emotional intelligence training**. The idea isn't to eliminate frustration, which isn't realistic, but to increase awareness of how anger surfaces and spreads. People with higher emotional intelligence can catch the physiological signs of anger early, like a quickened heartbeat or tension in the jaw, and use this awareness to step back before reacting.

Source of Workplace Anger	Typical Expression	Productive Redirection
Perceived unfairness	Complaints, disengagement, turnover	Transparent decision-making, equity reviews
Communication breakdowns	Misinterpretation, heated exchanges	Clear guidelines for messaging, feedback culture
Workload imbalance	Resentment, withdrawal, reduced performance	Regular workload audits, resource reallocation
Managerial outbursts	Morale decline, fear, disengagement	Leadership training, structured check-ins

| Digital tone misfires | Misunderstanding, unnecessary tension | Context-rich communication, clarity norms |
| Passive aggression | Missed deadlines, quiet resistance | Direct but respectful dialogue, mediation |

The legal and organizational risks tied to anger at work can't be ignored. Harassment claims often stem from unchecked angry outbursts. Even when no lawsuit follows, reputational damage from public incidents can linger for years. Anger management training is increasingly included in corporate wellness programs not as an afterthought, but as a safeguard for both productivity and liability.

It's worth noting that not all workplaces treat anger equally. In some cultures, showing irritation is read as commitment to excellence, while in others it's seen as unprofessional and damaging.

For global teams, this cultural variability complicates things further. A behavior tolerated in one office might cause serious rifts in another. Training in cross-cultural communication reduces friction and clarifies norms before misunderstandings trigger conflict.

The physiological side of workplace anger is often overlooked. Stress hormones like cortisol and adrenaline spike during angry episodes, which impair complex decision-making. When leaders make high-stakes calls in an angry state, accuracy and judgment decline. This has concrete costs, especially in industries where decisions involve safety or large sums of money. Encouraging leaders to delay final calls until anger subsides improves both outcomes and credibility.

Some workplaces implement peer accountability systems to curb anger escalation. By allowing employees to privately point out when colleagues are slipping into hostile communication, anger is interrupted early. This approach requires trust, but when successful, it lowers the need for top-down intervention and normalizes self-regulation as a collective responsibility.

The future of workplace anger management is moving toward proactive design. Open floor plans, once thought to encourage collaboration, actually increased irritability in many offices by raising noise and lowering privacy. Now, companies experiment with flexible workspaces and hybrid models that reduce triggers. Less physical crowding often translates into fewer anger incidents.

At its core, managing anger in the workplace comes down to whether it's recognized as information or as an uncontrollable threat. When treated as a signal of unmet needs, miscommunication, or inequity, anger directs improvement. When ignored or punished, it mutates into chronic conflict or silent disengagement. The difference isn't whether anger exists but how systematically it's addressed.

Anger In Romantic Relationships

When anger enters a romantic relationship it can turn ordinary disagreements into destructive battles. Couples often underestimate how quickly irritation builds into resentment, especially when daily stress piles on top of long-standing patterns. Romantic bonds carry emotional weight that magnifies conflict. A cutting remark from a partner feels heavier than the same words from a stranger because attachment magnifies sensitivity. Learning to recognize anger in its earliest form, before it escalates, protects the relationship from cycles that chip away at trust.

In romantic partnerships **anger often surfaces when expectations clash with reality**. One partner might believe household responsibilities should be evenly split while the other unconsciously expects traditional divisions. The result is frustration when assumptions go unspoken. Anger here isn't about dirty dishes or unpaid bills, it's about feeling unseen or unsupported. To untangle these tensions, partners need to articulate specific expectations rather than assume mutual understanding.

Anger in relationships is also tied to **communication styles**. Some individuals argue loudly, others withdraw into silence. A couple where one partner pushes for immediate discussion while the other retreats to cool down creates a mismatch that amplifies tension. Neither approach is wrong in isolation, but together they can feed conflict. Awareness of these tendencies allows couples to time conversations more effectively. For example, setting an agreement to pause arguments for thirty minutes gives the withdrawing partner space without leaving the other feeling abandoned.

Power dynamics influence how anger unfolds. If one partner consistently dominates decisions, the other may carry unspoken resentment. That resentment eventually bursts out in ways that appear irrational or overly harsh. Anger in this sense functions as a signal that equilibrium is off balance.

Addressing power distribution requires both partners to examine how decisions are made, who controls resources, and whether each voice carries equal weight. Couples often benefit from documenting decision-making patterns to see whether hidden hierarchies exist.

Emotional regulation skills directly impact how couples handle disputes. A person with higher **self-control thresholds** can absorb minor provocations without reacting, while someone with a shorter threshold responds with sharp outbursts. Romantic partners need to understand each other's thresholds because mismatches can create cycles of blame. If one partner explodes while the other remains calm, the calmer partner may start feeling superior, which builds contempt. If both partners have short thresholds, volatility becomes the norm.

Trust sits at the center of romantic anger. When trust feels secure, anger can be expressed without destabilizing the relationship. But when trust has been weakened through betrayal, dishonesty, or neglect, anger grows sharper and harder to resolve. For this reason, couples often struggle more with conflict after breaches of trust, even if the issue at hand seems minor. A forgotten chore sparks disproportionate anger because it echoes deeper fears of unreliability. Repairing trust requires consistent follow-through, not just apologies.

Patterns also develop across time. Some couples establish routines where one person criticizes and the other defends. Over months, criticism breeds defensiveness, which then invites further criticism. These cycles reinforce anger until ordinary interactions feel hostile. Breaking such a cycle requires an intentional shift. Rather than criticizing, partners can learn to make **specific requests**. Instead of saying, "You never help around the house," the request becomes, "Could you take the trash out tonight since I'm working late?" Requests invite cooperation, while criticism ignites anger.

Physiological responses matter too. Romantic anger activates increased heart rate, rapid breathing, and muscle tension. Couples rarely recognize that once their heart rate crosses a certain threshold, rational conversation becomes impossible. Research suggests that when the heart rate climbs above 100 beats per minute during conflict, the brain shifts into survival mode. At that point, logical problem-solving shuts down. Couples who track these signs can pause and return to the discussion when the body calms, preventing escalation.

Certain triggers appear consistently in romantic anger. Money disputes are among the most common. Spending habits often reflect deeper values about security, freedom, or status. When one partner spends freely and the other saves diligently, anger isn't just about money, it's about clashing values.

Intimacy also creates conflict. If one partner feels rejected sexually, anger emerges from perceived rejection of the self, not just the act. Family involvement is another common trigger, particularly disagreements about in-laws or parenting. Each of these triggers requires a tailored approach rather than generic conflict advice.

Technology has introduced new dimensions to anger in relationships. Smartphones make it easier to track or question a partner's actions. Delayed responses to texts can create suspicion. Excessive screen time can make a partner feel ignored. These situations spark anger not because of the devices themselves but because attention is a currency in relationships.

Couples often need to set **technology boundaries** to protect their connection. For example, agreeing to keep phones away during meals reinforces presence and minimizes avoidable conflict.

Gender socialization shapes anger expression in couples as well. Men often learn to externalize anger through raised voices or physical postures, while women may internalize it and express irritation indirectly. These socialized differences can create misinterpretations. A woman's silent withdrawal may not mean disinterest but rather anger expressed through withholding. A man's raised voice may not signal danger but frustration shaped by early conditioning. Recognizing these patterns allows couples to decode anger more accurately.

Therapists often guide couples to map conflict patterns through structured exercises. One common exercise involves each partner writing down the sequence of events during their last major argument. Comparing timelines reveals where escalation occurs. For example, Partner A might recall feeling dismissed when Partner B checked a phone during conversation. Partner B might recall frustration at being interrupted repeatedly. Mapping the sequence exposes misunderstandings that fuel anger.

Anger management strategies within relationships often combine individual regulation with joint practices. Individually, deep breathing, grounding techniques, or short walks reduce physiological arousal. Jointly, couples can use agreed-upon signals to pause arguments when they escalate. A pre-agreed phrase like "time out" creates structure that feels safe for both partners. Without such agreements, one partner's withdrawal can be misread as avoidance rather than de-escalation.

Anger in romantic relationships also links with attachment styles.

Anxious attachment often leads to clingy behavior during arguments, while **avoidant attachment** encourages withdrawal.

These opposing tendencies amplify anger when paired. An anxious partner escalates to get reassurance, while an avoidant partner shuts down to protect independence. Couples with these dynamics need to learn language that communicates reassurance without smothering, and space without abandonment. Secure attachment, in contrast, allows anger to be expressed but also repaired more easily.

Conflict frequency can also depend on relationship stage. Early relationships often involve less anger because novelty masks irritation. As routines form, conflict increases. Couples living together face more frequent opportunities for small irritations to pile up.

Long-term relationships, particularly marriages, sometimes cycle through stages where anger spikes and then stabilizes as couples adjust expectations. Recognizing these natural phases prevents couples from overreacting to temporary spikes in conflict.

Romantic anger can be productive when directed into **problem-solving conversations**. If one partner expresses frustration about unequal chores and the other responds with openness, the anger functions as a motivator for change. When anger highlights unmet needs, it can strengthen the relationship if addressed constructively. Avoidance, on the other hand, corrodes intimacy because problems remain unresolved. The goal isn't to eliminate anger but to channel it into resolution.

The presence of children complicates anger expression between partners. Arguments in front of children increase stress for the family and influence how kids learn to manage their own emotions. Couples often underestimate how much children absorb, even at young ages. Managing romantic anger in ways that minimize exposure benefits not just the couple but the household environment. Some parents use structured check-ins after children sleep to handle disagreements privately.

Data from long-term relationship research shows that couples who maintain high **positive-to-negative interaction ratios** experience more stability. The often-cited guideline is five positive interactions for every negative one during conflict discussions.

Positive interactions include humor, empathy, or acknowledgment of the other's perspective. When negative interactions outweigh positives, anger becomes corrosive. Couples who actively track this balance increase their odds of long-term stability.

Outlining typical sources of anger in relationships along with constructive alternatives:

Common Trigger	Anger Response	Constructive Alternative
Unequal chores	Criticism or sarcasm	Specific request with timeframe
Money disputes	Accusations of irresponsibility	Shared budget meeting
Technology use	Silent resentment	Agreed tech-free time
Sexual rejection	Harsh withdrawal or blame	Honest discussion of needs
Family conflicts	Shouting or avoidance	Setting clear boundaries jointly
Perceived disrespect	Raised voices	Stating impact calmly

Long-term couples sometimes require professional intervention when anger becomes entrenched. Therapy provides structured environments where each partner speaks without interruption. Mediators or therapists can identify repeating cycles and teach techniques to interrupt them. Couples may resist therapy due to stigma, but research consistently shows its effectiveness in reducing destructive anger patterns.

At the same time, self-education through relationship books or structured workshops builds awareness. Couples who commit to regular check-ins, whether weekly or monthly, stay more aware of simmering tensions. These check-ins don't need to be long; even fifteen minutes of uninterrupted conversation can reset emotional balance before anger erupts. Consistency, not length, drives effectiveness.

Anger in romantic relationships has no single solution because each couple carries unique histories, temperaments, and triggers. What's consistent is that unmanaged anger corrodes trust, intimacy, and respect. Addressing anger means attending to physiological responses, communication styles, attachment patterns, and trust repair. Couples who view anger not as an enemy but as a signal to adjust expectations build resilience in the face of inevitable conflict.

Parenting And Anger Management At Home

Parenting is one of the most emotionally demanding roles a person can take on, and anger often slips into the family environment when stress, exhaustion, and unmet expectations collide. Unlike other areas of life, parenting doesn't offer regular breaks or easy escapes. Children test limits, routines break down, and parents juggle work responsibilities alongside household needs. In such a high-pressure context, it's not surprising that anger flares. The challenge lies in managing it so that it teaches rather than harms, and in creating a home environment where discipline and affection exist together rather than in opposition.

At its core, **anger in parenting often reflects deeper needs**. A parent who yells when a child refuses to clean their room may not be angry about the mess itself but about feeling disrespected or ignored. Similarly, a parent who lashes out when a toddler throws food may actually be struggling with fatigue and overwhelm. Recognizing what sits beneath anger helps parents respond more thoughtfully. By naming the true need (whether for rest, respect, or support) parents can shift from explosive reactions to clearer communication.

Children themselves are emotional mirrors. When a child senses anger in a parent, they often respond with fear, resistance, or anger of their own. This creates a feedback loop that escalates conflict. The parent's raised voice provokes a child's defiance, which fuels even more parental frustration. Understanding this cycle allows families to intervene early. A parent who pauses to regulate their breathing after a child's misbehavior interrupts the loop before it intensifies.

The developmental stage of the child shapes how anger should be managed. With toddlers, anger often arises over safety issues. A child running into the street naturally triggers fear that quickly converts into yelling. With adolescents, anger frequently centers on boundaries, privacy, or independence. A teenager who stays out past curfew may provoke parental rage because the behavior challenges authority and ignites worry. Knowing that anger at different stages reflects different concerns helps parents tailor their responses.

Parental modeling plays a profound role in how children learn to regulate their own anger. If a child grows up hearing constant shouting, they internalize shouting as a legitimate way to express frustration. If a parent handles irritation by calmly stating their feelings and setting limits, the child sees emotional regulation in practice. This modeling shapes long-term emotional intelligence. Even a single instance of self-control during a heated moment demonstrates to children that anger doesn't need to overpower behavior.

Stress outside the home spills into parenting. A parent who feels undervalued at work may snap at their children over trivial matters. The anger isn't about the spilled milk but about a buildup of stress that found its release at home.

This phenomenon, known as **displaced anger**, is common and dangerous in families. Children misinterpret it as their fault, leading to guilt or anxiety. Parents benefit from separating workplace frustration from home life by building rituals that help them decompress before engaging with their kids. A short walk, deep breathing, or simply changing clothes upon arriving home can create a psychological reset.

Family routines often influence how much anger surfaces. In homes with irregular schedules, sleep deprivation, skipped meals, or constant rushing contribute to heightened irritability.

Predictable routines reduce stress for both parents and children. When everyone knows when meals, homework, and bedtime occur, there are fewer opportunities for conflict. Anger thrives in chaos but weakens in structured environments.

Conflict between parents also affects children's experience of anger at home. If children witness parents arguing frequently, they may become anxious or act out to distract attention from the conflict. In other cases, they may imitate the same argumentative styles in their own interactions. Couples who establish rules about how to argue in front of children reduce the negative impact. Some disagreements can be modeled constructively in front of children (showing how compromise works) but intense shouting or name-calling damages their sense of security.

Parents must also recognize **triggers unique to their own temperament**. Some parents lose patience when children whine, others when rules are broken, and others when order is disrupted. Identifying these triggers helps prevent overreactions.

Writing down which behaviors consistently spark the strongest emotional reactions allows parents to anticipate and prepare for them. For example, if whining provokes disproportionate anger, a parent can practice responses in advance, such as calmly repeating the rule or offering a choice, instead of reacting with shouting.

Discipline strategies strongly affect anger levels at home. Harsh punishments like spanking or repeated yelling increase anger on both sides. They may achieve short-term compliance but at the cost of long-term resentment.

On the other hand, consistent and fair consequences teach responsibility without escalating conflict. Parents who explain the reason behind rules reduce the likelihood of anger because children understand rather than simply obey. For example, saying, "You can't ride your bike without a helmet because it protects your brain," frames discipline as protection rather than control.

A significant factor in parental anger management is the balance between **self-care and caregiving**. Parents who neglect their own needs (skipping meals, losing sleep, or giving up personal time) find themselves with shorter fuses. Self-care isn't indulgence in this context, it's maintenance.

Parents who prioritize even small rituals like reading, exercising, or spending time with friends sustain emotional reserves that prevent anger from dominating family life. When children see parents balancing responsibility with self-nurturing, they also learn healthy boundaries.

Family culture around emotions matters. In some households, anger is openly expressed, while in others it's suppressed. Both extremes create problems. Suppression teaches children to fear anger and avoid conflict entirely, while excessive expression normalizes volatility. A balanced culture acknowledges anger as natural but insists it be managed constructively. Families that normalize talking about feelings give children vocabulary to express frustration without lashing out physically or verbally.

Technology has created new arenas for anger between parents and children. Arguments about screen time, online safety, or social media use now dominate many households. Parents may feel disrespected when children sneak devices into their rooms at night, while children may feel unfairly controlled when rules seem too strict. Negotiating these issues requires transparency and flexibility. Instead of sudden bans, parents who involve children in creating screen time agreements reduce anger because the rules feel collaborative rather than imposed.

Sibling dynamics also generate parental anger. When children fight constantly, parents may explode from sheer exhaustion. Yet these conflicts offer learning opportunities. By guiding siblings to resolve disputes fairly, parents shift the burden away from anger and toward skill-building. For instance, teaching children to take turns expressing their perspective without interruption models conflict resolution. Parents must resist the urge to immediately take sides, which only intensifies anger among siblings and frustration for the parent.

Cultural background shapes how families approach anger. In some cultures, obedience is emphasized, and parental authority is rarely questioned. In others, open negotiation between parents and children is encouraged.

These cultural frameworks influence how anger is expressed and perceived. Parents benefit from reflecting on their own upbringing and asking whether their anger responses reflect values they want to continue or patterns they wish to change.

The role of extended family further complicates anger management. Grandparents, uncles, or in-laws may interfere in discipline, creating tension. When a parent feels undermined by a relative, they may displace frustration onto the child. Setting clear boundaries with extended family members preserves consistency and reduces unnecessary anger in the household.

Below are common parenting situations that spark anger and suggests healthier approaches:

Parenting Situation	Typical Anger Response	Healthier Approach
Toddler throws food	Yelling or scolding	Calmly remove plate and explain consequence
Teen breaks curfew	Heated lecture	Planned conversation next day about trust
Child refuses chores	Nagging escalation	Offer clear choice with consequence
Sibling fighting	Shouting at both	Guide them through conflict resolution steps
Excessive screen time	Sudden device removal	Collaborative rule-setting on usage
Spilled drink or mess	Irritated yelling	Involve child in cleanup calmly

Parenting anger also intersects with mental health. Parents experiencing depression or anxiety often find their patience diminished. Anger in these cases may be more about internal struggles than children's behavior. Seeking support through therapy or support groups reduces stigma and builds healthier coping strategies. Children benefit when parents model seeking help rather than pretending to manage everything alone.

Economic stress magnifies anger within families. Financial insecurity leads to heightened tension over bills, groceries, or rent. Children often sense this stress and misinterpret irritability as rejection. Families under financial strain may benefit from community resources or budgeting strategies that reduce constant pressure. Even small financial wins create a sense of stability that lowers anger.

Co-parenting arrangements after divorce create unique challenges. Differences in parenting styles between households often spark anger. A child allowed to stay up late at one parent's home may resist bedtime at the other's, leading to conflict. Clear communication between co-parents, even if limited to structured emails or apps, reduces these battles. Presenting a united front prevents children from exploiting differences and reduces anger in each home.

Long-term patterns of anger at home leave deep marks. Children raised in volatile households may develop anxiety or anger problems of their own. The cycle can repeat unless interrupted by intentional change. Families that acknowledge the impact of anger and commit to new strategies demonstrate resilience. Apologies from parents carry particular weight. When a parent admits, "I lost my temper earlier and I'm sorry," children learn that mistakes can be repaired and that relationships can recover.

Parenting and anger management at home isn't about eliminating frustration but about guiding it toward constructive outcomes. Anger signals that values are being challenged, needs are unmet, or limits are unclear. When parents treat anger as information rather than as a weapon, they create homes where children learn resilience, respect, and empathy. A family that can navigate anger with clarity and compassion builds a foundation strong enough to endure stress without fracturing.

Road Rage and Public Encounters

Anger in public spaces often feels sharper than anger at home because strangers lack the patience and forgiveness that family members might show. On the road, at a store, or in a crowded public setting, tensions rise quickly, and the anonymity of the environment can fuel hostility. Road rage is the clearest example, where ordinary frustrations like traffic jams or lane changes escalate into aggressive driving, shouting, or even physical confrontations. Understanding why these encounters feel so volatile and how to manage them is essential for personal safety and peace of mind.

At the root of **road rage** is the human brain's tendency to personalize impersonal events. When another driver cuts into your lane without signaling, the act itself may be nothing more than carelessness, but the mind often interprets it as deliberate disrespect. Drivers feel wronged, as if their safety or dignity has been attacked. This perception of insult fuels anger, and because cars create a sense of distance, people often express aggression more openly than they would face-to-face. The steel and glass barrier emboldens drivers who might otherwise remain polite.

Stress and fatigue amplify these reactions. A person driving home after a difficult day at work has fewer emotional reserves. Minor frustrations like red lights, honking, or someone driving too slowly can trigger outsized reactions. In this way, road rage is less about the specific traffic event and more about the driver's overall stress load. Recognizing this connection helps reframe encounters: the irritation isn't entirely about the traffic, it's about accumulated pressure.

Public encounters outside of cars follow a similar pattern. Crowds, long lines, or noise overload test patience. People feel disrespected when someone cuts in line, when a cashier seems dismissive, or when a stranger behaves rudely. Because public spaces involve shared resources and limited personal space, small conflicts can flare into large ones. A person who shouts in a grocery store isn't just angry about waiting; they're angry about feeling powerless in a space where they expect fairness and order.

Social psychology explains part of the problem through the concept of **deindividuation**, where anonymity reduces self-awareness and self-control. Drivers don't see one another as full people with families and emotions; they see obstacles or threats. Similarly, in a crowded store, strangers become faceless competitors for space or service. This loss of empathy fuels harsher reactions. Restoring perspective (reminding yourself that the other driver might be late for work, or the shopper might be stressed about caring for a child) reduces the intensity of anger.

Some individuals enter public spaces already primed for conflict. They see the world as hostile and expect others to cross them.

For these people, even neutral interactions can trigger defensive aggression. In road rage, this shows up as tailgating, honking aggressively, or chasing another car. In public, it appears as glaring, snapping at strangers, or demanding special treatment. Recognizing this type of person and refusing to escalate is crucial for safety. Engaging only prolongs and intensifies the conflict.

The consequences of letting anger run unchecked in public can be severe. On the road, aggressive driving leads to accidents, injuries, or even fatalities. Confrontations at stoplights sometimes escalate into physical violence. In stores or public areas, arguments can draw in bystanders or lead to security intervention. What begins as irritation over a parking space or a slow-moving line can end in police involvement. The stakes are higher in public because the environment magnifies visibility and consequences.

Managing road rage begins with **anticipating triggers**. Heavy traffic, aggressive drivers, or delays are inevitable. If drivers expect these frustrations, they're less likely to react explosively. Practical strategies include leaving earlier to allow time for delays, listening to calming music or audiobooks, and keeping a steady breathing rhythm. When another driver behaves aggressively, resisting the urge to retaliate is key. Slowing down or changing lanes de-escalates tension, even if pride feels wounded in the moment.

Public encounters require a different but related mindset. The goal is to separate inconvenience from insult. If someone cuts in line, responding calmly or addressing the issue with the staff avoids direct confrontation. If a stranger is rude, walking away protects dignity without escalating conflict. Some people fear that not confronting rudeness makes them weak, but in reality, **self-control in public is strength**. It signals mastery over emotion and preserves safety.

A useful tool in both road and public settings is **reframing the situation**. Instead of viewing another driver's reckless move as an attack, consider that they might be inexperienced, distracted, or dealing with an emergency. Instead of interpreting a stranger's sharp tone as hostility, consider that they might be overwhelmed. This reframing doesn't excuse bad behavior but shifts the focus away from personal insult and toward empathy or neutrality.

Another important principle is **detachment from control**. Public spaces are unpredictable by nature. Drivers can't control traffic lights or the behavior of others, and shoppers can't control how quickly a cashier works.

Accepting this lack of control reduces frustration. People who expect perfection in public environments set themselves up for constant anger, while those who accept imperfections navigate more calmly.

Technology adds new dimensions to public anger. Recording devices and viral videos mean that any outburst can become public within minutes. A moment of rage in traffic or in a store can spread online, damaging reputations and careers. This risk provides another reason to exercise restraint. What feels justified in the heat of the moment may look unreasonable to thousands of strangers later.

Road rage and public anger are also shaped by cultural factors. In some cities, aggressive driving is normalized, and horns blare constantly. In others, politeness dominates, and such behavior is shocking. Understanding the norms of the environment helps set realistic expectations. Travelers often experience anger when adjusting to different public cultures, but awareness reduces unnecessary frustration.

Long-term solutions involve building resilience. Regular stress management practices such as exercise, meditation, or journaling expand emotional capacity. People with healthier stress outlets are less likely to explode on the road or in public. Therapy or anger management courses provide tools for those who find these encounters consistently overwhelming.

Ultimately, road rage and public anger highlight the challenge of living in a shared world. Strangers will make mistakes, inconvenience will happen, and tempers will flare. The choice lies in whether to feed the fire or let it cool. People who master their anger in public preserve safety, dignity, and peace, turning encounters that could have ended in conflict into opportunities to practice patience.

Cultural Differences in Anger Expression

Anger exists in every society, but how it is expressed, interpreted, and managed varies greatly across cultures. What counts as a normal outburst in one country may be viewed as disrespectful or even dangerous in another. Some cultures encourage open confrontation, while others expect emotional restraint in the name of harmony. These differences shape not only personal interactions but also workplace dynamics, family relationships, and even international politics. Understanding cultural patterns of anger expression allows people to navigate cross-cultural situations with awareness and reduces the risk of misinterpretation.

In **individualistic cultures** like the United States or many parts of Western Europe, anger is often seen as a natural and acceptable way to assert one's rights. Expressing displeasure directly is framed as honesty, even if the tone is sharp. For example, Americans may raise their voice during disagreements without assuming the relationship is permanently damaged. The underlying cultural value is autonomy: each person has a right to their opinion and to defend it. In these settings, suppressing anger is sometimes viewed as weakness, a failure to stand up for oneself.

By contrast, **collectivist cultures**, such as Japan, China, Vietnam, or Korea, emphasize group harmony. Open displays of anger are often discouraged because they disrupt social balance. A Japanese employee who feels insulted by a manager might remain outwardly calm, offering only subtle signs of frustration, because maintaining harmony is valued above individual expression. Instead of shouting or confronting, individuals might use silence, avoidance, or indirect communication to convey displeasure. Here, emotional restraint demonstrates maturity and respect.

Religious and philosophical traditions also influence anger expression. In many Buddhist cultures, such as in Thailand, anger is considered a loss of face and a barrier to spiritual growth. Openly expressing rage not only damages relationships but also harms the individual's inner peace.

In contrast, in cultures influenced by Mediterranean traditions, such as Greece or Italy, showing anger can be a legitimate and even expected response to injustice. Loud debates in public may be interpreted as passionate engagement rather than personal hostility.

Gender expectations further complicate cultural differences. In Middle Eastern contexts, men may be expected to display anger to demonstrate strength, while women are discouraged from open expression. In some Scandinavian cultures, gender differences in anger expression are narrower, as emotional restraint applies to both men and women equally. These norms reflect broader cultural values about masculinity, femininity, and social order.

To see how cultural norms operate in practice, it helps to compare specific regions.

Region/Culture	Typical Anger Expression	Social Meaning	Common Management Strategy
United States	Direct confrontation, raised voice	Assertiveness, standing up for self	Problem-solving, apology, or avoidance afterward
Japan	Suppression, subtle nonverbal cues	Maturity, self-control	Silence, indirect communication, later discussion in private
Mediterranean (Italy, Greece)	Loud speech, expressive gestures	Passion, authenticity	Open argument, followed by quick reconciliation
Middle East	Male-dominant displays, strong tone	Strength, authority	Verbal expression, mediated resolution
Northern Europe (Sweden, Norway)	Reserved, calm tone	Emotional balance, respect	Rational discussion, delayed expression
Latin America	Expressive but relational	Connection, sincerity	Family or group mediation, reconciliation rituals

This comparison illustrates that anger is never just an emotion; it is also a **cultural signal**. A raised voice in Italy may say, "I care about this issue," while the same volume in Sweden may say, "I've lost control." Misunderstandings arise when people interpret these signals through their own cultural lens.

Immigration and globalization increase the chances of such clashes. A Japanese employee working in a U.S. company may seem disengaged when they withhold anger, but in their cultural frame, they are showing professionalism. An American manager in China may think employees are too passive for not confronting issues directly, while employees view the manager as rude or aggressive. Without awareness of cultural context, people misjudge one another's intentions.

Cultural differences also extend to **timing and intensity** of anger expression. In some African cultures, anger may be delayed and addressed in communal gatherings rather than immediately in private. The belief is that strong emotions require collective processing.

In contrast, in many Western settings, people are encouraged to "clear the air" quickly so that lingering tension does not build. One culture views delay as patience, while another sees it as avoidance.

Another dimension is **face-saving**. In East Asian contexts, maintaining face is critical, and expressing anger in front of others risks shaming both parties. This is why conflict resolution often happens through intermediaries or after cooling-off periods. In Arab cultures, preserving honor may mean expressing anger strongly in public to avoid appearing weak. Thus, what is face-saving in one context is face-losing in another.

Children learn cultural anger norms early. In the United States, parents often tell children, "Use your words, not your fists," encouraging verbal expression. In Japan, parents may tell children to endure teasing without reacting, teaching endurance and self-control. By adolescence, these lessons solidify into adult patterns. This early training explains why cross-cultural encounters can feel so jarring: each person assumes their way of handling anger is common sense, when in fact it is culturally constructed.

Even within a single culture, **regional and class differences** shape anger expression. In Southern Italy, animated arguments on the street are common and not necessarily hostile, while in Northern Italy, restraint is more typical. In the United States, working-class contexts may accept louder and more physical anger, while middle-class professional contexts demand calm, reasoned tones. Culture, then, is not a monolith but a layered influence that interacts with socioeconomic factors.

Media representations further reinforce these norms. American films often portray heroes expressing anger directly at injustice, reinforcing the cultural value of confrontation. Japanese media, on the other hand, often depict heroes enduring hardship silently until a breakthrough moment, reinforcing patience and discipline. Viewers internalize these scripts and carry them into real interactions.

Cultural neuroscience research shows that even **physiological responses** to anger differ by culture. Studies reveal that people from collectivist cultures may experience lower blood pressure increases during conflict, suggesting that emotional regulation is internalized at a biological level. In contrast, individuals from individualistic cultures may show stronger physiological arousal, reflecting more frequent external expression. Culture not only shapes outward behavior but also the body's reaction to anger itself.

Global businesses must manage these differences carefully. Multinational teams often face conflict not from the content of disagreements but from how anger is expressed. A German employee's blunt criticism may feel aggressive to a Chinese colleague, while the Chinese colleague's silence may feel evasive to the German. Companies increasingly provide cross-cultural training to teach employees how to interpret anger cues and respond in culturally sensitive ways.

Law and justice systems also reflect cultural views of anger. In the United States, expressions of anger in court are often tolerated as passion, while in Japan, a defendant who shows anger may be seen as unrepentant and receive harsher judgment. In some African tribal courts, anger expression is part of reconciliation rituals, viewed as cleansing rather than disruptive. These differences demonstrate how deeply cultural views of anger penetrate institutions.

Sports and competition provide another window (which we'll look at more below). In Latin American soccer, visible displays of anger at referees are common and often tolerated, while in Scandinavian sports, such behavior may lead to quick penalties. These cultural rules shape how athletes train and how fans interpret behavior. What seems like misconduct in one league may be celebrated as passion in another.

Migration adds a final layer of complexity. Immigrants often face pressure to adapt their anger expression to the host culture, while also maintaining their original cultural norms at home.

This creates internal tension. A child raised in a collectivist household may learn to suppress anger at home but express it openly at school, navigating two sets of rules. Over time, hybrid styles of anger management emerge, blending elements of both cultures.

Cultural differences in anger expression remind us that no style is inherently right or wrong. Each has strengths and weaknesses. Direct cultures may resolve conflict faster but risk rupturing relationships. Indirect cultures preserve harmony but may leave problems unresolved. Passionate cultures show engagement but can escalate quickly, while restrained cultures avoid escalation but may bottle resentment. The challenge lies in adapting expression to context, recognizing when to shift styles, and avoiding the assumption that one's own cultural script is universal.

Anger in Competitive Sports and Performance Settings

Few environments bring out intense emotions more than sports and high-level performance. The competitive atmosphere, the pressure to succeed, the scrutiny of fans, and the expectations from coaches or teammates all create fertile ground for anger.

Whether it comes from a questionable referee call, a taunt from an opponent, or frustration with one's own mistakes, anger in sports is both common and complex. Some athletes channel it into focused energy, while others lose control and harm their performance or reputation. Exploring anger in competitive settings reveals not just how emotions influence performance but also how individuals and teams manage one of the most volatile forces in sport.

At its root, **anger in competition arises from blocked goals**. Sports revolve around scoring, winning, or outperforming others, and anything that threatens progress toward those goals can spark frustration. A runner boxed in during a race, a basketball player called for a foul they didn't commit, or a gymnast penalized harshly by judges can all feel that surge of unfairness. Unlike casual settings, competition amplifies these triggers because so much is at stake.

Not all anger is destructive. Psychologists distinguish between **instrumental anger** and **hostile anger**. Instrumental anger is controlled and directed toward improving performance.

For example, a sprinter who feels cheated by a false start may use that emotion to explode out of the blocks with greater determination in the restart. Hostile anger, however, is uncontrolled and reactive, leading to technical errors, fouls, or disqualification. An athlete who throws a tantrum after a bad call may lose focus entirely, letting their emotions dictate their play.

Sports history is filled with examples of both. Michael Jordan often admitted to inventing slights from opponents or coaches to fuel his competitiveness. This use of anger as fuel helped him raise his intensity without losing discipline. By contrast, tennis star John McEnroe's infamous outbursts against officials in the 1980s often cost him points and occasionally matches. The same emotion, handled differently, can either sharpen or sabotage performance.

The context of the sport matters.

Contact sports like football, rugby, or hockey naturally involve aggression, and players often walk a fine line between productive anger and dangerous hostility. In such sports, anger can increase physical intensity, but if unchecked, it leads to penalties or fights that hurt the team.

In **precision-based sports** like golf, archery, or gymnastics, anger tends to be more harmful, since the fine motor control required is disrupted by heightened arousal. A golfer who slams a club after a bad shot may find it even harder to sink the next putt.

To illustrate how anger plays out differently across performance domains, consider the following table.

Sport/ Performance Domain	Typical Anger Triggers	Potential Positive Effects	Common Negative Outcomes
Basketball	Referee calls, trash talk, missed shots	Increased energy, aggressive defense	Fouls, technical penalties, poor shot selection
Soccer	Rough tackles, crowd pressure, referee bias	Stronger physical effort, rallying teammates	Red cards, reckless challenges, team disadvantage

Tennis	Opponent antics, self-criticism, disputed calls	Motivation to fight back, sharper focus	Loss of rhythm, unforced errors, emotional collapse
Gymnastics	Judge scoring, performance errors	Drive for perfect execution	Overthinking, tension, stiff movements
Track and Field	False starts, lane interference	Faster starts, heightened competitiveness	Disqualification, wasted energy
Performing Arts (music, acting)	Stage errors, equipment failure, audience reaction	Intense emotional expression, authentic performance	Broken concentration, mistakes, visible frustration

This comparison shows that anger is not just about temperament but also about context. What helps in one sport may destroy performance in another.

Research in **sports psychology** shows that anger is closely tied to arousal levels. According to the **inverted-U theory of performance**, athletes perform best at moderate arousal.

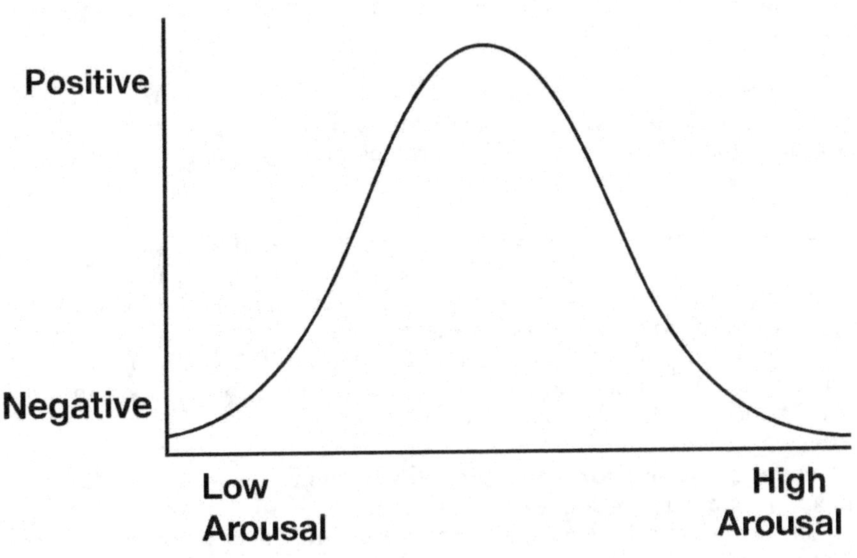

The **audience factor** adds another layer. Athletes often feel provoked not only by opponents but also by fans. Booing, heckling, or chants can push competitors toward anger. Some athletes thrive on it, using negative energy from the crowd to fuel their determination. Others become rattled, allowing external hostility to break their concentration. The same is true in performing arts, where a disruptive audience member may inspire some actors to channel the emotion into their role while leaving others shaken.

Coaches and leadership styles also shape how anger emerges. A coach who yells aggressively at players may inadvertently stoke hostile anger, while a coach who teaches athletes to frame anger as energy can help channel it productively.

Many elite teams now hire sports psychologists to train athletes in emotion regulation. Breathing exercises, reframing thoughts, and pre-performance routines are taught to transform anger into focus rather than chaos.

Too little energy leads to sluggishness, while too much arousal creates mistakes. Anger spikes arousal, which can either push an athlete into the optimal zone or overshoot it into loss of control. Experienced athletes learn how to balance on this curve, using anger to stay sharp but not letting it overwhelm them.

Cultural differences also influence how athletes express anger in competition. In American sports, outward displays like yelling or chest-thumping are often celebrated as passion. In Japanese martial arts, however, such behavior is discouraged, as discipline and composure are prized. These differences affect how referees, fans, and teammates interpret anger across contexts.

Team dynamics magnify anger's effects. One player's outburst can inspire teammates to rally or can demoralize them if it spirals into hostility. A captain who channels anger into leadership, urging teammates to fight harder, transforms emotion into cohesion.

By contrast, a player who berates teammates in frustration can fracture unity. Teams often develop unwritten rules about anger expression, deciding whether it is acceptable to argue with referees, show frustration publicly, or settle conflicts privately.

Beyond performance outcomes, anger in sports raises **ethical and safety concerns**. Physical fights in hockey, violent fouls in soccer, or retaliatory hits in football can lead to serious injuries. Leagues impose fines and suspensions to discourage uncontrolled anger, yet fans sometimes glorify such behavior. The line between entertainment and danger is constantly negotiated. Athletes themselves must weigh the short-term emotional satisfaction of venting anger against the long-term consequences for health, reputation, and career.

Training in **anger regulation** has become central in modern sports psychology. Techniques include visualization, where athletes imagine frustrating scenarios and rehearse calm responses; cue words, where a single phrase like "focus" is repeated to redirect attention; and mindfulness, which helps athletes observe anger without acting on it. These skills are not about eliminating anger but about harnessing it. Coaches often remind athletes that emotion is a tool: powerful when managed, destructive when neglected.

Performance arts, though different from sports, reveal similar patterns. A musician who becomes angry after a missed note may lose flow and stumble through the rest of the piece. Yet some performers use anger to intensify their delivery, adding raw emotion to their work. Actors sometimes channel personal anger into scenes, producing authentic portrayals that captivate audiences. As in sports, the key is control: anger expressed through craft, not anger that takes over.

The **media spotlight** amplifies anger in competitive settings. Every outburst from a famous athlete is replayed, dissected, and judged. A single angry gesture can overshadow years of achievement. Serena Williams's heated arguments with tennis officials, for example, sparked debates about gender, race, and fairness, showing how anger in sports carries social and cultural weight far beyond the game itself. The way anger is received often depends not just on the behavior but also on public perception and cultural context.

Finally, anger in competition highlights the human side of athletes and performers. They are not machines but people under extraordinary pressure. Anger shows their vulnerability and desire to excel.

When managed skillfully, it sharpens focus and drives achievement. When mismanaged, it exposes fragility and undermines goals. The difference lies not in avoiding anger but in learning to understand it, control it, and, when possible, transform it into fuel for excellence.

In competitive sports and performance settings, anger is inevitable. It arises from blocked goals, unfair treatment, mistakes, and external provocation. Its impact depends on whether it is harnessed or allowed to run wild. At its best, anger is a motivator that drives athletes and performers to push beyond limits. At its worst, it is a saboteur that unravels discipline and damages careers. The challenge is not to eliminate anger but to master it, turning a volatile emotion into a source of strength rather than weakness.

Chapter 9: Professional Help and Advanced Strategies

When to Seek Therapy

People often wait too long before considering professional help for anger. They tell themselves the problem is temporary, that they just need to relax, or that they can manage on their own.

Yet anger that keeps disrupting relationships, sleep, health, or work usually won't fade without structured guidance. Therapy becomes necessary when the frequency, intensity, or consequences of anger exceed what simple self-management techniques can handle.

A useful starting point is to examine **patterns of escalation**. If arguments with partners, family, or colleagues often spiral into shouting, insults, or slammed doors, the threshold for professional help may already be crossed. Even when physical aggression isn't present, repeated emotional volatility can create lasting damage to trust. A partner might stop confiding, a child may become anxious around conflict, or coworkers could avoid collaboration. When anger consistently blocks connection and communication, therapy offers structured ways to break the cycle.

Another indicator is **physical strain**. Uncontrolled anger activates the sympathetic nervous system, raising blood pressure, accelerating heart rate, and spiking stress hormones like cortisol.

Over time, this reactivity contributes to hypertension, headaches, sleep problems, and even increased risk of cardiovascular events. Someone who notices their body reacting strongly to minor frustrations, such as traffic delays or small mistakes at work, may be caught in a loop of hyperarousal. Therapy gives people methods to calm physiological responses before they turn into chronic health conditions.

There's also the question of **legal and occupational risk**. If outbursts threaten someone's job security, custody arrangements, or even freedom under the law, professional help is urgent. Many court-mandated anger management programs exist because unresolved rage has led to violence, harassment, or reckless acts. Waiting until the consequences reach this stage narrows options for recovery. Voluntarily seeking therapy before external pressure forces the issue gives a person far greater control over the process.

Some individuals find anger masking other emotions they don't want to feel. A person might shout rather than admit fear, criticize others to avoid acknowledging insecurity, or argue instead of confronting grief. In these cases, anger acts as a shield. Therapy helps uncover the **secondary emotions** beneath the anger and addresses them more directly. Without that uncovering, anger remains the default outlet.

Children raised in environments where anger dominated often bring those patterns into adulthood. If yelling, intimidation, or emotional withdrawal were normalized, they may have few examples of healthier conflict management. Therapy provides new models and teaches alternative ways of responding. Breaking generational cycles requires deliberate intervention, and professionals can guide that shift more effectively than trial and error.

People sometimes resist therapy because they equate it with weakness. Yet learning how to control anger requires **skills training**, no different from learning a language or sport. Techniques like cognitive restructuring, stress inoculation, or relaxation training are teachable, but without a skilled guide it's difficult to master them consistently. Seeking therapy signals readiness to develop those skills, not failure.

Practical signs for considering therapy can be organized as follows:

Indicator	What It Looks Like	Why Therapy Helps
Frequent conflict in relationships	Arguments escalate quickly, reconciliation takes long	Therapy teaches de-escalation and communication skills
Physical health effects	High blood pressure, headaches, sleep disruption	Techniques reduce physiological arousal and restore balance
Legal or job risks	Threats of firing, court involvement, strained professional reputation	Professional guidance prevents further consequences
Masking deeper emotions	Anger appears instead of sadness, fear, or insecurity	Therapy identifies and works with underlying emotions
Childhood exposure to anger	Habitual shouting, avoidance, or intimidation carried into adulthood	Professional models introduce alternative responses
Failure of self-help strategies	Breathing, exercise, or journaling aren't enough	Structured therapy provides advanced tools and accountability

The table highlights how therapy isn't just for crisis moments. It's a proactive investment when earlier strategies don't provide relief.

One of the clearest signs that therapy is overdue is the **loss of control**. If someone feels themselves boiling over, saying things they later regret, or even experiencing blackouts during rages, the risk is too high to manage alone. Losing control damages trust and safety in relationships, and professional intervention gives immediate containment strategies.

It's also important to recognize that the **impact on others** may be larger than the person's own perception. A parent may think they only yelled once in a while, but a child could interpret each outburst as unpredictable and frightening. A manager may believe their sharp tone is just directness, but employees may describe it as hostile. Therapy can incorporate feedback from others, providing perspective that's difficult to see from within the anger.

Some people fear therapy will force them to suppress anger completely. In practice, therapists encourage **healthy expression**. The goal isn't erasing anger but guiding it into forms that protect dignity, boundaries, and problem-solving. A skilled therapist differentiates between assertive expression and destructive venting, showing clients that anger can motivate change without damaging relationships.

Finally, therapy becomes necessary when anger starts to reshape identity. If someone begins to see themselves primarily as an "angry person," or others consistently label them that way, the emotion has taken on a defining role. Identity-based anger feels harder to separate from the self, but therapy helps rebuild alternative narratives. People discover they can be assertive, passionate, or protective without being consumed by fury.

Cognitive-Behavioral Therapy (CBT) for Anger

Cognitive-behavioral therapy (CBT) has become the most widely researched and applied method for addressing anger. Unlike approaches that only explore the past or focus solely on relaxation, CBT targets the thought patterns and behavioral choices that directly fuel outbursts. Its central idea is that emotions like anger don't arise in a vacuum. They are triggered and intensified by how people interpret situations. By challenging distorted interpretations and practicing new responses, individuals learn to prevent escalation before it begins.

At the heart of CBT lies the **cognitive model**: event, thought, emotion, behavior.

For example, imagine being cut off in traffic. The event is neutral until interpreted. A thought such as "That driver disrespected me" will lead to frustration and possibly shouting or tailgating. A different thought like "Maybe they didn't see me" might produce irritation but not rage. Therapy trains people to catch these automatic interpretations and question whether they're accurate or helpful. This isn't about denying frustration, but about preventing unnecessary escalation.

One of the earliest steps in CBT for anger is **self-monitoring**. Clients are encouraged to keep records of triggers, thoughts, emotional intensity, and responses. A diary might reveal that anger spikes most often when someone feels ignored, when deadlines approach, or when certain family members make critical remarks. Without this documentation, people usually underestimate the frequency of their anger or misidentify triggers. Once patterns are clear, therapy can target the most common and disruptive scenarios.

Therapists then guide clients through **cognitive restructuring**. This process involves evaluating the accuracy and usefulness of recurring thoughts. A belief such as "People should never make mistakes" will guarantee frequent frustration, since mistakes are inevitable. In CBT, this thought would be challenged: is it realistic, is it fair, does it help the person function? Over time, rigid expectations are replaced with more flexible ones like "Mistakes happen, but I can respond without exploding." Each shift reduces the emotional fuel that keeps anger burning.

CBT also emphasizes the **connection between body and mind**. Anger has unmistakable physiological signs: muscle tension, clenched jaw, rising heart rate, shallow breathing. Learning to identify these early cues allows intervention before behavior escalates. Therapists often teach **relaxation strategies** such as progressive muscle relaxation, paced breathing, or guided imagery. These don't eliminate the trigger, but they bring the nervous system back to baseline so rational choices remain possible.

Another central component is **behavioral rehearsal**. Clients practice alternative responses in role-play settings, preparing them for real-world encounters. If someone often yells when criticized, therapy may involve practicing assertive statements that communicate frustration without hostility. Rehearsal builds confidence and creates memory templates the brain can call on when stress is high. This step matters because anger tends to shut down creativity, leaving people locked into old patterns unless they've rehearsed alternatives.

CBT also incorporates **problem-solving training**. Many people default to venting or withdrawal because they lack structured strategies to handle conflict. Problem-solving in CBT means breaking issues into smaller parts, brainstorming multiple solutions, weighing pros and cons, and testing the best option. This approach shifts energy from raw emotional reaction to constructive action. Instead of yelling about household chores, someone might brainstorm schedules, negotiate with family members, and experiment with reminders until a workable system emerges.

Some therapists add **exposure techniques** when avoidance feeds anger. For instance, a person who avoids conversations with authority figures may build resentment that bursts out unexpectedly. Gradual exposure helps them face situations calmly, reducing the buildup that leads to explosions. While exposure is more commonly used for anxiety, in anger work it teaches tolerance for frustration and reduces hypersensitivity to perceived threats.

The benefits of CBT extend beyond anger episodes themselves. Research shows CBT reduces **hostile attribution bias**, the tendency to assume others act with negative intent. Someone who used to see every interruption as disrespectful begins to recognize that many interactions are neutral. This shift dramatically lowers the number of daily anger triggers.

Practical sessions often combine several methods. A therapist may begin with reviewing a client's diary, then guide them through cognitive restructuring of a specific thought, and end with behavioral rehearsal of a calmer response. Homework consolidates the learning, ensuring that strategies don't remain theoretical. Over weeks and months, these repeated cycles build lasting skills.

CBT's structured nature makes it adaptable to many settings. Anger management classes, probation programs, and workplace interventions often use CBT protocols.

The method's step-by-step format means progress can be tracked, making it easier to measure improvement. For clients, this concreteness can feel more motivating than abstract discussions of emotion.

Still, CBT has limitations. Some clients resist because they see their anger as justified. If someone insists "My boss really is an idiot, so my anger is reasonable," challenging thoughts may feel invalidating. In such cases, therapists must carefully balance empathy with cognitive restructuring, ensuring the client feels heard while still questioning whether explosive responses serve them. Others struggle with homework, either because of time constraints or resistance to self-examination. Without practice outside sessions, progress slows.

CBT can also be complemented by other approaches when necessary. People with trauma histories may need trauma-focused therapy alongside anger work, since triggers may connect to unresolved past events. Clients with severe physiological reactivity may benefit from biofeedback to support relaxation training. The adaptability of CBT allows it to integrate with these adjunct methods without losing its core principles.

The specific skills emphasized in CBT for anger can be grouped as follows:

Skill Area	Examples	Purpose
Self-Monitoring	Anger diaries, rating scales, identifying triggers	Increases awareness of patterns and escalation
Cognitive Restructuring	Challenging rigid beliefs, reframing assumptions	Reduces intensity of anger by altering interpretations
Relaxation Training	Breathing techniques, progressive muscle relaxation, imagery	Lowers physiological arousal to keep control
Behavioral Rehearsal	Role-playing responses, practicing assertiveness	Builds confidence and alternatives to aggression
Problem-Solving	Defining issues, generating solutions, testing outcomes	Shifts energy toward constructive action
Exposure	Facing frustrating situations gradually	Reduces avoidance and lowers hypersensitivity

The table shows how CBT isn't a single intervention but a suite of interconnected skills. Each addresses a different component of the anger cycle.

The effectiveness of CBT for anger is supported by decades of research. Controlled studies have shown significant reductions in aggressive behavior, improved relationships, and lower physiological stress markers in participants who completed CBT programs. Meta-analyses consistently rank CBT among the most effective interventions for anger in both clinical and non-clinical populations.

CBT also offers long-term benefits because it teaches **self-sufficiency**. Once clients internalize the skills, they can apply them to new challenges without constant professional input. This contrasts with approaches that rely heavily on the therapist's presence. People who complete CBT often describe a sense of having a "toolbox" they can carry into any situation.

Interestingly, CBT's impact isn't limited to the individual. When one person in a family learns to regulate anger differently, the relational climate shifts. Arguments de-escalate faster, children feel safer, and workplace teams operate with less tension. The ripple effects highlight how anger management through CBT improves entire systems, not just individuals.

Some programs have adapted CBT into digital platforms, allowing self-guided modules for those unable to attend in-person sessions. While therapist guidance remains more effective, digital CBT expands access to people in remote locations or with limited schedules. These programs often include video demonstrations, interactive exercises, and automatic tracking, mirroring traditional CBT components.

In practice, CBT works best when clients approach it with commitment. The therapy isn't quick or effortless. It requires repeated practice, openness to challenging one's own assumptions, and patience as new habits form. Yet the structured nature ensures that every effort produces measurable progress, giving clients tangible motivation to continue.

Anger Management Groups and Workshops

Anger management groups and workshops offer structured environments where individuals learn and practice strategies alongside others facing similar challenges. Unlike one-on-one therapy, these settings emphasize **shared experience** and **peer accountability**, which can reduce feelings of isolation. Participants often find relief in hearing others describe familiar triggers and struggles, realizing their own difficulties are neither unique nor shameful.

Workshops typically follow a **curriculum-based model**. Sessions may cover topics like recognizing early signs of anger, challenging unhelpful thoughts, and rehearsing healthier responses. Facilitators often use role-play, guided discussion, and practical exercises. Because groups meet regularly, there's a built-in rhythm that reinforces practice and encourages consistent reflection. Participants track their progress across weeks, creating momentum that's harder to sustain alone.

One strength of group settings is the **diversity of perspectives**. While a single therapist may guide techniques, hearing multiple people explain how they've applied the same tool offers richer learning. For example, someone may describe using deep breathing at work, while another explains how assertive communication transformed family disputes. This variety helps participants see the broad applicability of skills.

Workshops also foster **accountability**. Knowing that others will ask about progress often motivates individuals to complete homework assignments and apply techniques between sessions. Peer encouragement creates a sense of responsibility that differs from professional oversight. Many report that they stick with behavior changes longer because of this community aspect.

Some programs are designed for specific populations such as adolescents, couples, or employees referred by workplaces. Others operate within probation systems as part of court mandates. While voluntary groups often emphasize personal growth, mandated ones may stress compliance and measurable outcomes. Both share the goal of reducing destructive patterns and equipping participants with lasting tools.

The following table highlights typical components of anger management groups and workshops:

Component	Description	Benefit
Group Discussion	Sharing experiences and triggers	Normalizes struggles and builds community
Skill Training	Teaching relaxation, reframing, and communication techniques	Provides concrete strategies for control
Role-Play	Practicing scenarios in a safe environment	Builds confidence in real-world application
Homework Assignments	Tracking triggers and practicing new responses	Reinforces learning between sessions
Peer Feedback	Constructive input from fellow participants	Encourages accountability and new insights

Despite their advantages, group settings aren't always ideal for everyone. Some may feel too self-conscious to share openly, while others may require more individualized attention to address complex issues. Still, many benefit from the structured and interactive environment, especially when combined with personal therapy.

Ultimately, anger management groups and workshops provide a **practical bridge** between theory and daily life. They transform abstract skills into lived practice, supported by community, structure, and ongoing feedback. For many, these group experiences spark not just improved control of anger but also stronger relationships and renewed confidence in handling stress.

Role of Medication in Anger Control

Medication isn't usually the first recommendation for managing anger, but it can help in situations where the intensity of emotional reactions connects to underlying psychiatric or neurological conditions. **Anger itself isn't a diagnosis**, but it often surfaces as a symptom in disorders like bipolar disorder, borderline personality disorder, ADHD, intermittent explosive disorder, or certain mood and anxiety conditions. In these cases, targeting the broader condition with medication may indirectly reduce anger outbursts.

Mood stabilizers are sometimes prescribed when anger relates to rapid mood shifts or emotional volatility. Drugs like lithium or anticonvulsants such as valproate can reduce impulsivity and temper swings. People with bipolar disorder often describe not only relief from extreme highs and lows but also fewer sudden bursts of irritability or rage. By flattening the peaks of mood dysregulation, stabilizers reduce the risk that anger escalates into destructive behavior.

Antidepressants can also affect anger, particularly selective serotonin reuptake inhibitors (SSRIs). Research has shown that SSRIs reduce aggression and irritability in some individuals by increasing serotonin availability in the brain. This doesn't eliminate normal frustration, but it can reduce the intensity of emotional spikes. Someone who previously snapped at minor provocations may find themselves pausing long enough to choose a more measured response. For those with comorbid depression and anger issues, antidepressants often address both sets of symptoms simultaneously.

Antipsychotic medications are sometimes used in cases of severe aggression, especially when tied to psychotic disorders or extreme behavioral dysregulation. Atypical antipsychotics like risperidone or olanzapine may be prescribed short-term to stabilize behavior. They can dampen the neurological pathways that drive explosive reactions, making them more manageable. However, side effects such as weight gain, sedation, and metabolic changes make them less appealing for long-term use unless clearly necessary.

Stimulants, commonly prescribed for ADHD, can also reduce anger indirectly. Many individuals with ADHD struggle with poor impulse control, which makes them prone to lashing out before considering consequences.

By improving attention and impulse regulation, stimulants help them pause and redirect their responses. Parents often notice that children on ADHD medication not only focus better but also argue less aggressively or recover from frustration more quickly.

Anti-anxiety medications can help in cases where chronic tension or hyperarousal feeds irritability. Benzodiazepines calm the nervous system quickly, though they're rarely recommended long-term due to dependence risk. Non-addictive alternatives like buspirone or certain antihypertensives (such as propranolol) may also reduce physiological arousal tied to anger. By lowering the heart rate and calming the body, these medications give individuals more space to use behavioral strategies effectively.

It's important to note that medication alone rarely resolves anger problems. It can reduce the intensity of emotional surges but doesn't automatically teach healthier communication, problem-solving, or coping skills. That's why psychiatrists often combine prescriptions with **psychotherapy or structured anger management programs**. Medication buys time and stability so that other interventions can take root.

Not every case benefits from pharmacological support. Some individuals experience minimal improvement, while others deal with side effects that outweigh benefits. Careful monitoring and ongoing adjustment are essential. Doctors usually start with low doses and gradually increase, tracking whether anger frequency or intensity actually declines. This trial-and-error process helps balance effectiveness with tolerability.

For people whose anger puts them at risk of harming relationships, careers, or safety, medication can be part of a comprehensive strategy. By altering neurochemical imbalances that amplify irritability, drugs create a more stable baseline. This stability allows other anger management techniques to work more effectively, reducing the cycle of repeated outbursts and regret.

Biofeedback and Neurofeedback Approaches

Biofeedback and neurofeedback use technology to make unconscious processes visible so a person can learn to regulate them. Instead of guessing what the body or brain is doing during moments of stress, these systems provide **real-time data** that guide practice and self-control. For anger management, the benefit is straightforward: when people see how their physiology reacts to frustration, they can intervene earlier and practice responses that quiet the reaction before it escalates.

Traditional **biofeedback** focuses on physical signals like heart rate, skin temperature, breathing rate, and muscle tension. Sensors attached to the body track these signals and display them on a monitor.

For example, someone may see their heart rate spike when recalling a conflict or when asked to imagine a stressful scenario. Instead of being unaware of this change until they already feel overwhelmed, the person sees it instantly and begins practicing breathing techniques, relaxation strategies, or visualization exercises while the monitor shows whether those efforts are effective. Over time, the body learns to adopt calmer patterns more automatically.

Neurofeedback, sometimes called EEG biofeedback, works in a similar way but focuses on the brain's electrical activity. Electrodes placed on the scalp measure brainwave patterns, which shift during different emotional states. Certain frequencies, like excessive beta activity, can signal tension or agitation, while stronger alpha rhythms may reflect relaxation. When a person tries to calm themselves and the brainwaves shift in the desired direction, the feedback device provides a reward signal, often in the form of a tone or a visual change on the screen. By repeating these exercises, people learn to stabilize brain patterns linked with reduced irritability and better emotional control.

The training requires consistency. A single session won't change much, but repeated practice rewires habits. People who undergo structured neurofeedback training over weeks or months often report they can recover from irritation faster or resist urges to lash out.

What makes this different from standard relaxation techniques is the **objective feedback** that confirms progress. Without the technology, someone may believe they're calming down when their body is still in a heightened state. With the sensors, there's no guesswork.

Clinicians sometimes use a combination of biofeedback and traditional anger management strategies. A person might practice progressive muscle relaxation while connected to sensors that show whether muscle tension is actually decreasing. This prevents people from going through the motions without real effect. Others may combine cognitive-behavioral therapy with biofeedback, using the technology to reinforce the mental skills learned in therapy.

The range of tools is broad, from clinical-grade equipment used in psychology offices to consumer devices marketed for stress reduction. Professional systems measure multiple physiological markers at once and allow tailored protocols. Portable devices, often wristbands or headbands, usually track fewer signals but can still be useful for at-home practice. Some smartphone apps pair with sensors to guide breathing or provide alerts when stress levels rise.

The evidence base for these methods has grown over the last two decades. Biofeedback has strong support in reducing physiological arousal, including lowering heart rate variability and blood pressure, both of which correlate with emotional regulation. Neurofeedback studies have shown promise in treating disorders that involve aggression and poor impulse control, such as ADHD and certain mood disorders. The research isn't uniform, but enough results suggest that **self-regulation of physiological and brain activity** can reduce the intensity of anger responses.

One practical advantage is that the skills generalize. A person doesn't need to be hooked up to equipment at all times. After training, the body learns new regulation patterns that carry into daily life. A man who once clenched his jaw unconsciously during conflict may notice the tension earlier and release it without needing sensors.

A teenager who once erupted during arguments may find themselves naturally taking slower breaths before speaking. These changes reflect learning at the nervous system level.

The main drawback is accessibility. Professional biofeedback and neurofeedback require trained clinicians and equipment, which can be costly. Insurance coverage varies, and the time commitment for repeated sessions can be significant. Consumer devices lower the entry barrier but often provide less precise data. People need to balance their goals with available resources.

Below are examples of different signals targeted by biofeedback and neurofeedback, with their relevance to anger regulation.

Signal Tracked	What It Measures	Connection to Anger	Training Goal
Heart Rate Variability	Balance between sympathetic and parasympathetic nervous systems	Spikes during stress or irritation	Increase variability to promote calm recovery
Skin Conductance	Sweating response from sympathetic arousal	Rises with agitation or hostility	Learn to reduce spikes during triggering events
Muscle Tension (EMG)	Electrical activity in specific muscles	Jaw clenching or tight shoulders during frustration	Release tension and maintain relaxed baseline
EEG Brainwaves	Electrical activity patterns across brain regions	Excess fast-wave activity linked to agitation	Strengthen calm, focused rhythms
Breathing Rate	Number and depth of breaths per minute	Rapid shallow breathing fuels escalation	Train slow, even breathing

What makes this approach engaging is the element of practice and reward. People often feel more motivated when they can literally see progress on a screen. The direct feedback makes self-regulation more tangible, transforming abstract advice like "relax" into a skill that can be measured. The process resembles training a muscle, where repeated sessions create long-term change in capacity.

For anger management, this means people don't just suppress reactions temporarily, they learn to alter the **physiological foundation of anger**. By making the nervous system more flexible and responsive, biofeedback and neurofeedback provide a path to deeper control that complements therapy, lifestyle changes, and, when necessary, medication.

Digital Methods and Apps for Tracking Progress

Technology has expanded the range of options for anger management. While traditional therapy and structured programs remain the foundation for many people, **digital tools** now provide additional ways to track progress, reinforce practice, and deliver feedback outside clinical settings. These tools don't replace therapy, but they extend it, giving users constant access to monitoring and self-regulation strategies.

Smartphone apps designed for anger management typically combine three features: **tracking**, **guidance**, and **reminders**. Tracking involves recording triggers, emotional intensity, and responses. Some apps ask users to rate their anger on a scale of 1 to 10 several times a day, while others prompt entries after conflicts. This consistent record-keeping creates a personal dataset that reveals patterns. For example, someone may discover their irritability peaks at the end of workdays or after specific interactions. Having this knowledge turns vague feelings into identifiable trends that can be addressed directly.

Guidance is the second function. Apps often include built-in exercises like breathing timers, visualization practices, or short audio lessons on cognitive restructuring. These tools provide immediate strategies during moments of rising anger. A person can open the app, follow a guided breathing exercise for two minutes, and calm their physiology before responding. Because phones are always within reach, this guidance becomes more practical than relying on memory alone.

Reminders act as the third feature. Notifications prompt users to pause, reflect, or complete short exercises. For people trying to change long-standing habits, these cues help maintain consistency. An app may send a message at lunchtime reminding someone to check in on their mood or to take three slow breaths. Over time, the reminders condition regular practice, which gradually builds automatic self-regulation.

Beyond apps, **wearable technology** adds another layer. Devices like smartwatches or specialized stress bands track heart rate, skin conductance, or activity levels in real time. Because anger often produces measurable physiological changes before conscious awareness, these wearables can act as early warning systems. A sudden spike in heart rate variability, for instance, may trigger a vibration or notification. That signal encourages the wearer to pause and regulate before escalation.

These tools also create records that can be shared with therapists. Instead of relying only on memory during therapy sessions, a client might bring weeks of data showing when anger spikes occurred, how long they lasted, and what interventions worked. This **objective information** helps therapists refine treatment strategies and hold clients accountable for practice between sessions.

The variety of apps reflects different approaches. Some focus on **cognitive-behavioral strategies**, offering structured journals and thought-challenging prompts. Others prioritize **mindfulness**, guiding meditation practices and monitoring consistency. There are also **biofeedback-linked apps**, which pair with sensors to show live data about heart rate or breathing. Each category appeals to different needs.

Accessibility stands out as one of the biggest strengths. Not everyone has access to therapy due to cost, location, or scheduling barriers. Digital tools lower the entry threshold. Many are free or inexpensive, and they can be used anytime. This means a teenager in a rural area without specialized anger programs can still use a well-designed app to practice calming skills daily. For those already in therapy, the tools make homework more engaging and structured.

Still, there are limitations. Apps depend on **self-reporting**, which can be inconsistent. Wearables provide more objective data, but they require proper calibration and interpretation. Another issue is overreliance.

Some people may depend on the technology rather than developing internal awareness. The goal isn't to outsource regulation to a device but to use it as a training partner until the skills become self-sustaining.

Privacy is also a concern. Emotional and physiological data are sensitive, and not all apps have strong protections. Users need to review privacy policies before storing personal information. Professional-grade apps used in clinical settings often have better safeguards, but consumer products vary widely.

Despite these challenges, digital tools remain promising because they **blend immediacy with accountability**. Anger erupts in everyday life, not just in therapy offices. Having a resource in your pocket or on your wrist ensures strategies are available in the moment. This makes practice more realistic and anchored to real triggers rather than artificial exercises.

The best results often come when digital tools integrate with other methods. A person may attend therapy sessions weekly, practice skills with feedback from a smartwatch during the week, and record their progress in an app that summarizes trends for the next appointment. This **multilayered approach** leverages human support and technology to reinforce each other.

Some platforms now use **artificial intelligence** to personalize recommendations. By analyzing user data, the system might predict which times of day anger episodes are most likely and suggest preventive exercises. Over time, these predictive models can become more accurate, making interventions feel timely rather than reactive.

Schools and workplaces have also begun experimenting with digital anger management programs. A student might log their emotional responses during the day as part of a mental health curriculum, while employees may use corporate wellness apps that encourage breaks and mindfulness during high-stress tasks. These contexts normalize the idea of tracking emotions and create collective support for regulation skills.

The integration of biofeedback into mobile platforms continues to grow. Some apps now allow people to place a finger on the phone camera to measure heart rate and receive instant feedback. Others pair with chest straps or wrist sensors, showing live graphs of breathing patterns. The more feedback aligns with the body's signals, the faster the user learns to intervene at the right moment.

Consistency remains the deciding factor. Even the most advanced app is ineffective if it isn't used regularly. That's why the best designs focus on **simplicity and habit-building**, making it easy to log moods in a few seconds or complete a short calming exercise without disruption.

People who commit to steady use often find that their awareness of anger shifts. Instead of being surprised by sudden outbursts, they recognize the early steps and feel prepared to manage them.

Digital tools, then, are not stand-alone cures. They're training companions that make anger management more practical in the messy reality of daily life. By turning abstract advice into visible metrics and by offering immediate guidance, they give people a way to practice regulation at the exact times they need it most.

Appendix: Historical Timeline and Key Terms

Timeline of Anger Management Research and Approaches

The history of anger management reflects humanity's ongoing struggle to understand and regulate one of its most volatile emotions. Across cultures and centuries, thinkers, healers, philosophers, and scientists have offered explanations and strategies for controlling anger, each shaped by the values and knowledge of their time.

In **ancient Mesopotamia**, anger was viewed through a religious lens. Clay tablets and early mythological stories describe wrath as a force given by the gods, often leading to destruction or divine punishment. People believed ritual offerings and prayers were the best ways to calm anger, both in themselves and in deities who showed rage.

In **ancient Egypt**, medical papyri reveal attempts to connect emotional disturbances with physical imbalances. Egyptian physicians believed anger could disrupt the heart and circulation of vital energy. Remedies often included herbs, rest, and ritual purification. Control of anger was linked to maintaining harmony with *ma'at*, the principle of cosmic balance.

The **Hebrew Bible** provides some of the earliest moral discussions of anger. While acknowledging it as a natural human feeling, scripture warned against wrath leading to sin. Proverbs, Psalms, and later rabbinic commentaries advised patience, forgiveness, and faith as counterbalances. Religious teachings became an early form of anger guidance by encouraging restraint.

In **ancient Greece**, anger became the subject of systematic philosophical reflection. Homer's *Iliad* famously opens with "the wrath of Achilles," showing anger as a force shaping human destiny. Later philosophers explored how to live with this powerful emotion. Hippocrates framed anger as a bodily imbalance within the humoral system, specifically tied to yellow bile. Treatments included diet, bloodletting, and lifestyle adjustments to restore equilibrium.

Plato saw anger as part of the tripartite soul, connected to the spirited element that gave courage but needed reason to govern it. **Aristotle**, in *Nicomachean Ethics*, treated anger as morally neutral. For him, virtue lay in expressing anger in the right amount, toward the right people, at the right time. His call for moderation influenced later ethical traditions.

In **ancient India**, early Hindu texts such as the *Mahabharata* and teachings in Buddhism emphasized anger as a destructive emotion that fueled suffering and karma. Buddhism, in particular, treated anger as one of the three poisons of the mind, alongside greed and ignorance. Techniques like meditation, mindfulness, and compassion were prescribed as antidotes. These practices foreshadowed modern mindfulness-based anger interventions.

In **ancient China**, Confucianism and Daoism provided contrasting perspectives. Confucian scholars urged self-discipline and social harmony, warning that anger disrupted family and political order. Daoist teachings instead encouraged flowing with emotions without clinging to them, suggesting breathing and meditative exercises to maintain balance. Both traditions recognized anger's destabilizing potential but offered different routes to manage it. In practice, these approaches shaped not only personal conduct but also governance, as leaders were expected to embody calm restraint or natural ease in their rule. The dual influence of Confucian and Daoist views continues to inform modern Chinese perspectives on emotional regulation.

Moving into the **Roman period**, Stoicism advanced structured methods for controlling anger. Philosophers like Seneca wrote entire treatises on the subject. His *De Ira* (On Anger) argued that anger was irrational and harmful, both to the individual and society. Stoics advocated cognitive reframing, self-control, and avoidance of emotional extremes, anticipating aspects of modern cognitive behavioral therapy. These teachings influenced Roman law, military discipline, and civic life, where measured conduct was prized over impulsive reaction. The Stoic legacy left a deep mark on Western thought, shaping later Christian, Enlightenment, and even contemporary therapeutic approaches to anger.

During the **early Christian era**, Church fathers like Augustine framed anger as a moral failing but also recognized righteous anger as possible if directed toward injustice. Christian monastic traditions emphasized patience, humility, and prayer as defenses against wrath. Anger was classified as one of the seven deadly sins, embedding the idea of moral regulation deeply into Western culture.

In the **Islamic Golden Age**, scholars like Al-Ghazali expanded on Aristotle's ideas, emphasizing moderation and moral responsibility in handling anger. Islamic medical scholars also linked anger to humoral imbalances, prescribing dietary and lifestyle remedies alongside spiritual guidance from the Qur'an and Hadith.

Through the **medieval period in Europe**, anger management was tied to religious morality and medical theory. Physicians continued to rely on humoral explanations, while religious leaders preached against wrath as a sin. Chivalric codes also sought to channel anger into controlled martial valor rather than reckless violence.

The **Renaissance** revived classical approaches, bringing Aristotle and Stoicism back into focus. Humanist scholars encouraged education in rhetoric and self-discipline as a means to regulate passions. Art and literature of the time portrayed anger both as destructive and as a dramatic force in human affairs.

In the **seventeenth century**, early modern philosophy began treating emotions as psychological phenomena rather than purely moral or medical issues. Descartes analyzed anger as a passion caused by bodily spirits, while Spinoza argued that understanding emotions could increase freedom and self-control. The scientific revolution shifted explanations of anger from theology to natural processes.

The **eighteenth century Enlightenment** expanded interest in emotions as part of moral philosophy and emerging psychology. David Hume and Adam Smith analyzed anger in terms of social interaction and moral sentiment. Smith in *The Theory of Moral Sentiments* described resentment and anger as natural reactions to injustice, but warned that reason and sympathy should moderate them.

By the **nineteenth century**, psychology and psychiatry began formalizing the study of anger. With the rise of psychiatry, anger was increasingly framed as a symptom of mental illness in some contexts. Sigmund Freud interpreted anger through psychoanalysis as displaced aggression and repressed drives. Catharsis became a debated idea, with Freud suggesting that repressed anger could cause neurosis but uncontrolled expression could be dangerous.

In the **early twentieth century**, behaviorism shifted focus to observable actions. Anger was studied as a conditioned response to stimuli, and therapies emphasized behavior modification. Techniques such as relaxation training and systematic desensitization began to appear as ways of altering angry reactions.

By the **mid-twentieth century**, humanistic psychology and stress research contributed new perspectives. Carl Rogers and others highlighted empathy, self-awareness, and communication as vital in managing emotions. The growth of occupational stress studies also linked anger to health outcomes like hypertension and heart disease, making it a public health concern.

The **1960s and 1970s** saw major developments in cognitive psychology. Albert Ellis introduced Rational Emotive Behavior Therapy (REBT), teaching clients to challenge irrational beliefs fueling anger. Aaron Beck's cognitive therapy also emphasized identifying and restructuring distorted thoughts.

These methods built the foundation for **cognitive behavioral therapy (CBT)**, which remains central to anger management today.

During the **1980s**, structured anger management programs emerged in correctional facilities and clinical settings. These programs combined relaxation techniques, cognitive restructuring, and social skills training. Research began testing the effectiveness of different interventions, making anger management a recognized therapeutic field.

The **1990s** introduced broader approaches, integrating multicultural perspectives and expanding to schools, workplaces, and community programs. Emotional intelligence, popularized by Daniel Goleman, highlighted self-awareness and regulation as keys to success. Anger management became part of leadership and organizational training.

The **early twenty-first century** brought advances in neuroscience that deepened understanding of anger's biological roots. Brain imaging identified the amygdala and prefrontal cortex as central in anger responses, with regulation involving executive control. This knowledge informed therapies that blend mindfulness, biofeedback, and cognitive training.

The **2010s** saw digital innovation. Smartphone apps began offering anger tracking, guided breathing, and reminders. Wearable devices monitored physiological markers like heart rate, providing real-time feedback. These tools democratized access to anger management resources, allowing people to practice skills outside therapy offices.

Today, anger management reflects a **pluralistic landscape**. Cognitive behavioral approaches remain dominant, but mindfulness-based programs, acceptance and commitment therapy, and compassion-focused interventions add variety. Neuroscience continues to refine understanding of brain circuits, while public health initiatives stress anger regulation as part of wellness. Courts often mandate anger management programs, and schools integrate social-emotional learning to teach children early strategies. Technology continues evolving, with artificial intelligence beginning to predict triggers and recommend personalized exercises.

The path from ritual offerings in Mesopotamia to AI-driven interventions today reveals a consistent theme: anger has always demanded attention, and every era has sought ways to tame it. What differs is the framework: religious, medical, philosophical, psychological, or technological. Together, these layers show that anger management isn't a new invention but a continuous adaptation of human knowledge to one of the most enduring challenges of emotional life.

Glossary of key terms and definitions

- **Acceptance and Commitment Therapy (ACT)** – A therapeutic approach that teaches acceptance of emotions, including anger, while committing to values-based actions.
- **Adrenaline** – A hormone released during anger or stress that increases heart rate, energy, and physical readiness.
- **Aggression** – Behavior intended to harm another person physically or psychologically, often linked with anger but not identical to it.
- **Amygdala** – A brain structure central to processing anger, fear, and other strong emotions.
- **Anger Management** – Strategies and techniques used to recognize, regulate, and express anger in healthy ways.
- **Assertiveness** – Communicating needs and feelings firmly but respectfully without aggression.
- **Biofeedback** – A technique that uses monitoring devices to help individuals control physiological responses linked to anger.
- **Cognitive Behavioral Therapy (CBT)** – A therapy model that focuses on changing thought patterns that fuel anger and negative emotions.
- **Catharsis** – The idea that venting anger provides relief, though research shows it often increases hostility.
- **Chronic Anger** – Long-lasting patterns of anger that disrupt relationships, health, or daily life.
- **Conflict Resolution** – Processes and skills used to resolve disagreements without escalation to anger or violence.
- **Coping Mechanisms** – Mental and behavioral strategies people use to manage anger and stress.
- **Cortisol** – A stress hormone that interacts with adrenaline in anger responses and impacts long-term health.

- **Defensiveness** – Protective reactions to perceived threats, often escalating anger in conflicts.
- **Dialectical Behavior Therapy (DBT)** – A therapy combining CBT with mindfulness, often used to treat anger in borderline personality disorder.
- **Displacement** – Redirecting anger from its true source to a safer target.
- **Emotional Intelligence (EI)** – The ability to recognize, regulate, and use emotions constructively, including anger.
- **Empathy** – Understanding another's perspective, often reducing anger by fostering compassion.
- **Explosive Anger** – Sudden, intense outbursts of rage that can lead to harm.
- **Fight-or-Flight Response** – The body's automatic reaction to threat, fueling physical readiness during anger.
- **Frustration** – A common trigger of anger, arising when goals or desires are blocked.
- **Hostility** – A persistent attitude of resentment or ill will that often underlies anger.
- **Humor** – A coping strategy that defuses anger through perspective and lightheartedness.
- **Impulse Control** – The ability to stop oneself from acting aggressively when angry.
- **Intermittent Explosive Disorder (IED)** – A psychiatric diagnosis involving recurrent, disproportionate anger outbursts.
- **Irritability** – A heightened sensitivity to triggers that makes anger more likely.
- **Jealousy** – An emotion that often fuels anger in relationships or social competition.
- **Limbic System** – Brain structures, including the amygdala, that process emotions such as anger.
- **Low Frustration Tolerance** – Difficulty handling obstacles without becoming angry quickly.
- **Maladaptive Coping** – Ineffective strategies, like substance abuse or aggression, that worsen anger problems.
- **Meditation** – A practice of focused awareness that reduces reactivity and calms anger.
- **Mindfulness** – Nonjudgmental awareness of the present moment, useful for defusing anger.
- **Modeling** – Learning anger responses by observing others, often in childhood.
- **Mood Disorders** – Conditions like depression or bipolar disorder where anger is a common symptom.
- **Neurotransmitters** – Brain chemicals such as serotonin and dopamine that influence anger regulation.
- **Nonviolent Communication (NVC)** – A method of expressing feelings and needs without blame or hostility.
- **Oppositional Defiant Disorder (ODD)** – A childhood condition marked by defiant, angry, and argumentative behavior.
- **Outburst** – A sudden expression of anger, often loud or aggressive.
- **Overgeneralization** – A cognitive distortion where anger is triggered by broad, exaggerated conclusions.
- **Passive Aggression** – Indirect expressions of anger, such as sarcasm, procrastination, or subtle resistance.
- **Patience** – The ability to tolerate frustration without becoming angry.
- **Perceived Injustice** – A strong trigger for anger when people feel wronged or treated unfairly.

- **Philosophy of Stoicism** – An ancient system that teaches self-control and rational detachment from anger.
- **Physiological Arousal** – Bodily changes like increased heart rate and muscle tension during anger.
- **Positive Reappraisal** – Reframing an anger-provoking situation in a more constructive way.
- **Projection** – Attributing one's own anger or hostility to others.
- **Provocation** – An act or event that triggers anger.
- **Psychophysiology** – The scientific study of how emotions like anger affect the body.
- **Rage** – Extreme, uncontrollable anger often accompanied by aggression.
- **Relaxation Training** – Techniques like deep breathing and muscle relaxation to reduce anger arousal.
- **Repression** – Unconsciously blocking angry feelings from awareness.
- **Resentment** – Lingering anger about past events or perceived mistreatment.
- **Retaliation** – Anger-driven behavior aimed at punishing someone who caused harm.
- **Rumination** – Repeatedly dwelling on anger-provoking events or thoughts.
- **Self-Awareness** – Conscious recognition of one's own emotions, a foundation for anger control.
- **Self-Regulation** – The ability to monitor and adjust emotional reactions like anger.
- **Serotonin** – A neurotransmitter that helps regulate mood and reduces anger.
- **Social Learning Theory** – The idea that anger and aggression are learned through observation and reinforcement.
- **Stress Inoculation Training (SIT)** – A method teaching coping skills to handle stress and anger more effectively.
- **Suppression** – Consciously trying to hold back anger, often leading to long-term tension.
- **Tantrum** – An outburst of anger, usually involving yelling, crying, or physical agitation, common in children.
- **Temper** – A person's baseline tendency toward anger, ranging from mild to volatile.
- **Therapeutic Alliance** – The relationship between therapist and client that supports anger management progress.
- **Time-Out** – A temporary withdrawal from an anger-triggering situation to cool down.
- **Tolerance** – The capacity to accept discomfort without responding angrily.
- **Trauma** – Past emotional injury that can heighten anger reactivity.
- **Trigger** – A stimulus that provokes an anger response.
- **Unhealthy Venting** – Expressing anger aggressively or destructively instead of constructively.
- **Ventilation Hypothesis** – The outdated belief that "blowing off steam" reduces anger.
- **Verbal Aggression** – The use of hostile or insulting words as an expression of anger.
- **Violence** – Physical aggression that escalates beyond verbal or emotional anger.
- **Anger Awareness Training** – A therapeutic program teaching recognition of early anger signs.
- **Anger Rumination Scale** – A psychological tool measuring how much someone dwells on anger.

- **Behavioral Activation** – Using positive actions to counteract anger and depression.
- **Cognitive Distortions** – Biased ways of thinking, like "always" or "never" statements, that fuel anger.
- **De-escalation** – Actions that reduce the intensity of an anger episode.
- **Emotional Regulation** – Strategies used to influence when and how anger is experienced and expressed.
- **Hostile Attribution Bias** – The tendency to interpret others' actions as intentionally hostile.
- **Impulse** – A sudden urge to act on anger without reflection.
- **Jeering Effect** – The escalation of anger in group settings when hostility is socially reinforced.
- **Locus of Control** – A belief about whether one can control outcomes, affecting anger regulation.
- **Mood Stabilizers** – Medications that help regulate intense anger or irritability.
- **Neuromodulation** – Brain stimulation techniques being researched to reduce pathological anger.
- **Occupational Stress** – Work-related pressures that often trigger anger.
- **Oxytocin** – A hormone linked to bonding that may reduce aggression and anger.
- **Paranoia** – Excessive mistrust of others, often fueling anger responses.
- **Physical Aggression** – Using physical force in response to anger.
- **Problem-Solving Training** – Teaching constructive methods to handle anger-provoking situations.
- **Psychodynamic Therapy** – A therapeutic approach that explores unconscious roots of anger.
- **Reappraisal** – Cognitive reframing of a situation to reduce anger.
- **Relaxation Response** – The body's state of calm that counters the fight-or-flight system.
- **Self-Talk** – Internal dialogue that influences anger intensity.
- **Sympathetic Nervous System** – The system that activates during anger, preparing the body for action.
- **Therapeutic Journaling** – Writing exercises to process anger and gain insight.
- **Uncontrolled Aggression** – Anger-driven behavior that lacks restraint and causes harm.
- **Withdrawal** – Avoiding social interaction as an unhealthy way of handling anger.
- **Yoga** – A practice combining physical postures, breathing, and meditation that reduces anger reactivity.

Conclusion

Anger is one of the most familiar emotions in daily life, yet it's also one of the hardest to navigate. By now you've seen that anger isn't random, and it isn't always harmful. It's a signal, a form of energy, and a reaction that evolved to protect. What matters most is how it's managed. When left unchecked, anger damages health, weakens trust, and blocks opportunities. When understood and directed, it can bring clarity, strength, and even fairness.

This book began with the foundations: why anger exists, how it appears in different forms, and the myths that keep people from handling it wisely. You learned about the biology that fuels the surge of adrenaline and the brain systems that sometimes seem to overrule calm thinking. From there, the focus turned to triggers and warning signs, because awareness is the starting line. Once you can see anger rising, you can do something about it.

The middle chapters introduced strategies that work in real time. Breathing, relaxation, reframing, and short pauses are not abstract ideas but techniques backed by science. You saw how communication changes outcomes, how assertiveness builds respect, and how different cognitive strategies help rewire patterns that fuel repeated outbursts. Each method showed that anger management isn't about suppression but about redirection and balance.

Broader lifestyle choices also matter. Sleep, nutrition, exercise, and supportive relationships are not side issues. They set the baseline for emotional regulation. When those areas are neglected, anger finds more cracks to slip through.

When they're strengthened, tolerance increases and resilience grows. Contexts like work, relationships, parenting, and cultural differences revealed that anger takes many shapes, but the principles of awareness and regulation remain the same.

For some, self-guided techniques will be enough. For others, professional help, therapy, or advanced strategies may be needed. What matters is recognizing when anger feels bigger than your own capacity and reaching out for support. Doing so is not weakness but responsibility.

As you close this book, remember that progress with anger isn't about perfection. Everyone will feel it again, and everyone will have moments when it's expressed poorly. What changes over time is the speed of recognition and the quality of response. Even small improvements, such as taking one breath before reacting, using one clear sentence instead of shouting, choosing to walk away instead of escalating, add up.

Anger will always be part of life. The choice is whether it controls you or whether you learn to guide it. With patience, practice, and self-awareness, anger can shift from being a destructive force to being a signal you know how to answer. That shift makes daily life calmer, relationships stronger, and choices clearer. And that's the real purpose of anger management: not erasing the emotion but learning to live with it in a way that builds rather than breaks.

References & Recommended Readings

References

1.   American Psychiatric Association. (2022). *Diagnostic and statistical manual of mental disorders* (5th ed., text rev.).

2.   Averill, J. R. (1982). *Anger and aggression: An essay on emotion.* Springer-Verlag.

3.   Averill, J. R. (1983). Studies on anger and aggression: Implications for theories of emotion. *American Psychologist, 38*(11), 1145–1160. https://doi.org/10.1037/0003-066X.38.11.1145

4.   Beck, A. T. (1999). *Prisoners of hate: The cognitive basis of anger, hostility, and violence.* HarperCollins.

5.   Beck, R., & Fernandez, E. (1998). Cognitive-behavioral therapy in the treatment of anger: A meta-analysis. *Cognitive Therapy and Research, 22*(1), 63–74. https://doi.org/10.1023/A:1018763902991

6.   Berkowitz, L. (1990). On the formation and regulation of anger and aggression: A cognitive-neoassociationistic analysis. *American Psychologist, 45*(4), 494–503. https://doi.org/10.1037/0003-066X.45.4.494

7.   Berkowitz, L., & Harmon-Jones, E. (2004). Toward an understanding of the determinants of anger. *Emotion, 4*(2), 107–130. https://doi.org/10.1037/1528-3542.4.2.107

8.   Blake, E., & Hamrin, V. (2007). The role of the nurse in anger management. *Journal of Child and Adolescent Psychiatric Nursing, 20*(4), 217–224. https://doi.org/10.1111/j.1744-6171.2007.00109.x

9.   Buss, A. H., & Perry, M. (1992). The Aggression Questionnaire. *Journal of Personality and Social Psychology, 63*(3), 452–459. https://doi.org/10.1037/0022-3514.63.3.452

10.   Deffenbacher, J. L. (1992). Trait anger: Theory, findings, and implications. In C. D. Spielberger & J. N. Butcher (Eds.), *Advances in personality assessment* (Vol. 9, pp. 177–201). Lawrence Erlbaum Associates, Inc.

11.   Deffenbacher, J. L. (2011). Anger regulation: A cornerstone of treatment. *Cognitive and Behavioral Practice, 18*(2), 235–244. https://doi.org/10.1016/j.cbpra.2010.04.001

12.   Deffenbacher, J. L., & McKay, M. (2000). *Overcoming situational anger and anxiety.* New Harbinger Publications.

13.   Deffenbacher, J. L., Oetting, E. R., & DiGuiseppe, R. (2002). Principles of empirically supported treatments applied to anger management. *The Counseling Psychologist, 30*(2), 262–280. https://doi.org/10.1177/0011000002030002006

14. Deffenbacher, J. L., Oetting, E. R., Thwaites, G. A., Lynch, R. S., Baker, D. A., Stark, R. S., Thacker, S., & Eiswerth-Cox, L. (1996). State-Trait Anger Theory and the utility of the State-Trait Anger Expression Inventory. *Journal of Counseling Psychology, 43*(2), 131–148. https://doi.org/10.1037/0022-0167.43.2.131

15. Deffenbacher, J. L., Story, D. A., Stark, R. S., Oetting, E. R., & Hogg, J. A. (1990). The Anger Expression Scale for children and adolescents. *Journal of Personality Assessment, 55*(3-4), 406-417. https://doi.org/10.1080/00223891.1990.9674092

16. DiGiuseppe, R., & Tafrate, R. C. (2003). Anger treatment for adults: A meta-analytic review. *Clinical Psychology: Science and Practice, 10*(1), 70–84. https://doi.org/10.1093/clipsy.10.1.70

17. Edmondson, C. B., & Conger, J. C. (1996). A review of treatment efficacy for individuals with anger problems: Conceptual, assessment, and methodological issues. *Clinical Psychology Review, 16*(3), 251–275. https://doi.org/10.1016/0272-7358(96)00004-9

18. Ellis, A. (2001). *Overcoming destructive beliefs, feelings, and behaviors: New directions for rational emotive behavior therapy*. Prometheus Books.

19. Feindler, E. L. (2006). Anger-related disorders. In J. C. Thomas & D. L. Segal (Eds.), *Comprehensive handbook of personality and psychopathology, Vol. 1: Personality and everyday functioning* (pp. 384–405). John Wiley & Sons Inc.

20. Feindler, E. L., & Ecton, R. B. (1986). *Adolescent anger control: Cognitive-behavioral techniques*. Pergamon Press.

21. Fives, C. J., Kong, G., Fuller, J. R., & DiGiuseppe, R. (2011). Anger, aggression, and irrational beliefs in adolescents. *Cognitive Therapy and Research, 35*(3), 199–208. https://doi.org/10.1007/s10608-010-9303-6

22. Forgays, D. G., Forgays, D. K., & Spielberger, C. D. (1997). Factor structure of the State-Trait Anger Expression Inventory. *Journal of Personality Assessment, 69*(3), 497–507. https://doi.org/10.1207/s15327752jpa6903_4

23. Gentry, W. D. (2007). *Anger management for dummies*. Wiley Publishing.

24. Howells, K. (2004). Anger and its links to violence. *Journal of Forensic Psychiatry & Psychology, 15*(3), 375–380. https://doi.org/10.1080/1478994041000171221l

25. Kassinove, H., & Sukhodolsky, D. G. (1995). Anger disorders: Basic science and practice issues. In H. Kassinove (Ed.), *Anger disorders: Definition, diagnosis, and treatment* (pp. 1–26). Taylor & Francis.

26. Kassinove, H., & Tafrate, R. C. (2002). *Anger management: The complete treatment guidebook for practitioners*. Impact Publishers.

27. Lee, A. H., & DiGiuseppe, R. (2018). Anger and aggression treatments: A review of meta-analyses. *Current Opinion in Psychology, 19*, 65–74. https://doi.org/10.1016/j.copsyc.2017.04.004

28. Linehan, M. M. (1993). *Cognitive-behavioral treatment of borderline personality disorder*. Guilford Press.

29. Lochman, J. E., & Wells, K. C. (2002). The Coping Power program at the middle-school transition: Universal and indicated prevention effects. *Psychology of Addictive Behaviors, 16*(4, Suppl), S40–S54. https://doi.org/10.1037/0893-164X.16.4S.S40

30. Meichenbaum, D. (1985). *Stress inoculation training*. Pergamon Press.

31. Millon, T., Millon, C. M., Meagher, S., Grossman, S., & Ramnath, R. (2004). *Personality disorders in modern life* (2nd ed.). John Wiley & Sons.

32. Novaco, R. W. (1975). *Anger control: The development and evaluation of an experimental treatment*. Lexington Books.

33. Novaco, R. W. (1976). Treatment of chronic anger through cognitive and relaxation controls. *Journal of Consulting and Clinical Psychology, 44*(4), 681. https://doi.org/10.1037/0022-006X.44.4.681

34. Novaco, R. W. (2011). Anger dysregulation: A clinical case formulation model. *Canadian Psychology/Psychologie Canadienne, 52*(3), 159–171. https://doi.org/10.1037/a0024132

35. Novaco, R. W. (2016). Anger. In G. Fink (Ed.), *Stress: Concepts, cognition, emotion, and behavior: Handbook of stress series* (Vol. 1, pp. 285–292). Academic Press. https://doi.org/10.1016/B978-0-12-800951-2.00036-2

36. Saini, M. (2009). A meta-analysis of the effect of anger management treatment on aggression by sample type. *Aggression and Violent Behavior, 14*(4), 213–224. https://doi.org/10.1016/j.avb.2009.03.003

37. Spielberger, C. D. (1999). *State-Trait Anger Expression Inventory-2 (STAXI-2) professional manual*. Psychological Assessment Resources.

38. Sukhodolsky, D. G., Kassinove, H., & Gorman, B. S. (2004). Cognitive-behavioral therapy for anger in children and adolescents: A meta-analysis. *Aggression and Violent Behavior, 9*(3), 247–269. https://doi.org/10.1016/j.avb.2003.08.005

39. Tavris, C. (1989). *Anger: The misunderstood emotion* (Rev. ed.). Simon & Schuster.

Recommended Readings

1. Eifert, G. H., McKay, M., & Forsyth, J. P. (2006). *ACT on life not on anger: The new acceptance and commitment therapy guide to problem anger*. New Harbinger Publications.

   ∘ This workbook applies Acceptance and Commitment Therapy (ACT) principles, focusing on mindfulness and values-based living as a way to manage difficult emotions like anger.

2. Ellis, A. (2000). *How to control your anger before it controls you*. Citadel Press.

- ○ Written by the founder of Rational Emotive Behavior Therapy (REBT), this classic self-help book provides practical strategies for identifying and challenging the irrational beliefs that fuel anger.

3. Harris, R. (2008). *The happiness trap: How to stop struggling and start living: A guide to ACT*. Trumpeter.

   - ○ While not exclusively about anger, this book offers a very accessible introduction to ACT, a powerful therapeutic model for handling all painful thoughts and feelings, including anger.

4. Kassinove, H., & Tafrate, R. C. (2019). *The practitioner's guide to anger management: Customizable and reproducible worksheets, exercises, and tools*. Impact Publishers.

   - ○ A companion to their professional guidebook, this resource is filled with practical handouts and exercises that are excellent for both therapists and individuals working on anger issues.

5. McKay, M., & Rogers, P. D. (2000). *The anger control workbook*. New Harbinger Publications.

   - ○ This workbook provides a step-by-step guide to understanding the roots of anger and developing more effective coping strategies using cognitive-behavioral techniques.

6. Potter-Efron, R. (2005). *Letting go of anger: The eleven most common anger styles and what to do about them*. New Harbinger Publications.

   - ○ This book helps readers identify their specific anger "style" (e.g., explosive, passive-aggressive) and provides tailored advice for managing it effectively.

7. Stosny, S. (2007). *How to improve your marriage without talking about it: Finding love beyond words*. Morgan Road Books.

   - ○ This book is particularly useful for understanding and managing anger within intimate relationships. It focuses on building compassion and connection rather than getting stuck in cycles of blame.

8. Williams, R., & Williams, V. (1993). *Anger kills: Seventeen strategies for controlling the hostility that can harm your health*. Times Books/Random House.

   - ○ Written by a cardiologist and a historian, this book connects chronic anger and hostility to negative health outcomes and offers practical strategies for reducing them.